# CURRENT ISSUES IN TEACHER EDUCATION

## ABOUT THE EDITORS

**Cynthia A. Lassonde** is Assistant Professor in the department of Elementary Education and Reading at the State University of New York College at Oneonta. After a twenty-year career of teaching at the elementary level, she now teaches undergraduate and graduate courses in literacy. She is the co-editor with Susan Israel of *Teachers Taking Action: A Comprehensive Guide to Teacher Research* (IRA, 2008) and *The Ethical Educator: Integrating Ethics within the Context of Teaching and Teacher Research* (Peter Lang, 2008). Her role as editor of the New York Association of Colleges for Teacher Education's journal *Excelsior: Leadership in Teaching and Learning* fuels her interest in and concerns about the current issues in teacher education.

**Robert J. Michael** is Dean of the School of Education, State University of New York at New Paltz. He has been a professor in the special education program in the department of Educational Studies at the college. Currently, he serves as President of the New York Association of Colleges for Teacher Education.

**Jerusalem Rivera-Wilson** is Senior Faculty Associate and Director of Clinical Training and Field Experiences in the department of Educational Theory and Practice at the University at Albany, State University of New York. She teaches graduate courses in Assessment and Secondary Education. Jerry is the current President of the New York State Association of Teacher Educators.

# CURRENT ISSUES IN TEACHER EDUCATION

## History, Perspectives, and Implications

*Edited by*

**CYNTHIA A. LASSONDE, Ph.D.**

*State University of New York College at Oneonta*

**ROBERT J. MICHAEL, Ph.D.**

*State University of New York at New Paltz*

**JERUSALEM RIVERA-WILSON, Ph.D.**

*University at Albany, SUNY*

*With a Foreword by*

**Kenneth M. Zeichner, Ph.D.**

**CHARLES C THOMAS · PUBLISHER, LTD.**
*Springfield · Illinois · U.S.A.*

*Published and Distributed Throughout the World by*

CHARLES C THOMAS • PUBLISHER, LTD.
2600 South First Street
Springfield, Illinois 62704

© 2008 by CHARLES C THOMAS • PUBLISHER, LTD.

ISBN 978-0-398-07806-5 (hard)
ISBN 978-0-398-07807-2 (paper)

Library of Congress Catalog Card Number: 2008004195

*With* THOMAS BOOKS *careful attention is given to all details of manufacturing
and design. It is the Publisher's desire to present books that are satisfactory as to their
physical qualities and artistic possibilities and appropriate for their particular use.*
THOMAS BOOKS *will be true to those laws of quality that assure a good name
and good will.*

*Printed in the United States of America
LAH-R-3*

**Library of Congress Cataloging-in-Publication Data**

Current issues in teacher education : history, perspectives, and implications /
by Cynthia A. Lassonde, Robert J. Michael, Jerusalem Rivera-Wilson [editors]
; with a foreword by Kenneth M. Zeichner.
    p. cm.
  ISBN 978-0-398-07806-5 (hard) -- ISBN 978-0-398-07807-2 (pbk.)
 1. Teachers--Training of--United States. I. Lassonde, Cynthia A.  II. Michael,
Robert J.  III. Rivera-Wilson, Jerusalem.  IV. Title.

LB1715.C85 2008
370.71'173--dc22

                                                                    2008004195

# CONTRIBUTORS

**Dale G. Andersen** is Emeritus Dean of Education at the University of Nevada, Las Vegas. He also served as Dean of Education at Washington State University and the University of the Pacific during his career. As a Past President of American Association of Colleges for Teacher Education (AACTE) and the Land Grant Dean's Association and as a member of the Board of Examiners of the National Council for Accreditation of Teacher Education (NCATE) for twenty years, he has been an active, intimate, participant in and observer of teacher education in the United States for over forty years. He also currently serves as a member of the Council for International Recognition in Teacher Education (IRTE).

**Heidi Andrade** is Assistant Professor in Educational Psychology and Methodology at the University at Albany–SUNY. Her research and teaching focus on the relationships between classroom assessment and learning, with an emphasis on student self-assessment.

**Hansel Burley** is Associate Professor of Educational Psychology at Texas Tech University. He teaches graduate courses in educational statistics and cultural foundations of education. He is also principal investigator on two grant projects: The first is Jumpstart Lubbock, an early literacy program, and the other is a research project examining higher education remedial programs.

**Jerrell C. Cassady** is Associate Professor of Psychology in the Department of Educational Psychology at Ball State University. His research interests center on providing optimal learning experiences in educational settings, including specific focus on teacher preparation, enhancing early literacy, combating test anxiety, and implementing effective technologies in education. He serves as evaluator for several federally funded programs directly affiliated with school improvement. In addition, Doctor Cassady is co-editor of *The Teacher Educator* and on the editorial review boards for *Journal of Educational Psychology*, *Journal of Literacy Research*, and *Journal for the Education of the Gifted.*

**Finney Cherian** is Assistant Professor in the Faculty of Education at the University of Windsor, Ontario, Canada. He teaches undergraduate and graduate courses in critical literacy and the sociocultural aspects of education. Doctor Cherian's research interests are in the area of preservice teacher education, critical literacy, cultural studies, and healthy organizations.

**Barbara Fink Chorzempa** is Assistant Professor in the Elementary Education Department at the State University of New York at New Paltz. She teaches undergraduate and graduate courses in literacy and special education. She has taught one of the undergraduate language arts methods courses onsite in a local elementary school to begin the process of developing a PDS partnership.

**Lisa Dieker** is Associate Professor and Lockheed Martin Eminent Scholar at the University of Central Florida. Her primary area of research focuses on collaboration between general and special education at the secondary level with a specific interest in the unique opportunities that exist in urban schools in the areas of mathematics and science. She also has a passion for how technology and specifically virtual classrooms can be used to impact teacher preparation. She has published numerous articles focused on interdisciplinary collaboration, serves on numerous editorial boards and leadership roles and is the co-editor for the *Journal of International Special Needs Education* (JISNE) and *Focus on Exceptional Children.*

**Annette D. Digby** is the 2009–2010 President of the Association of Teacher Educators, and currently serves as Vice President for Academic Affairs and Provost at Lincoln University in Missouri. Prior to assuming her current position, Doctor Digby served as Dean of the Division of Education and Professor in the Department of Middle and High School Education at Lehman College/CUNY. After teaching middle and high school English for twelve years in Mississippi and upon completion of a Doctor of Education degree at the University of Alabama, she began her career in higher education at the University of Arkansas in 1989. During her tenure at Arkansas, she served as Assistant Dean for Professional Education and Associate Dean for Undergraduate Studies and Student Services in the College of Education and Health Professions. Doctor Digby has published articles and edited books on middle-level education, effective teaching and learning strategies, school/university partnerships, and national certification. In addition to numerous other state and national committees, Doctor Digby is President-Elect-Elect and member of the Executive Board of the Association of Teacher Educators. She also serves on the Board of Examiners (BOE) for the National Council for the Accreditation of Teacher Education (NCATE) and as chair for BOE teams.

**Carol Merz Frankel** is Professor Emerita at the University of Puget Sound. She taught in public schools in California and Washington and served in a number of administrative positions before moving to Puget Sound as dean of the School of Education in 1987. She received her BA and MA from Stanford University and her ED.D. from Washington State University. She has published in the areas of politics of education and teacher education. She has had leadership positions at the state and national level in school reform and teacher education. After eighteen years as dean she retired in 2005. She has continued her work with school foundations and international teacher education. Most recently she has led exchanges between the University of Puget Sound and Naruto University of Teacher Education in Japan. In 2008, she will teach teacher education courses in Japan for students from developing countries.

**Jacqueline R. Garvey** has served as the Executive Director of The Indiana Partnerships Center, Parent Information and Resource Center (PIRC) for the state of Indiana. Her professional experiences include twenty years of developing and implementing school/community partnerships through school-based leadership programs. As Director of the Indiana PIRC, she created the Indiana Academy for Parent Leadership, which has now trained hundreds of parents and educators in over sixty-five counties in Indiana.

**Allen D. Glenn** is a Professor of Curriculum and Instruction and former Dean of the College of Education at the University of Washington. His texts and publications focus on social studies, educational technology, and teacher education. He was a recipient of the American Association of Colleges for Teacher Education (AACTE) Edward L. Pomeroy Award for Outstanding Contributions to Teacher Education and served as the AACTE president from 1997–1998.

**Anne T. Henderson** has been a consultant on education policy since 1977 and is widely recognized as a foremost expert in parent engagement and family involvement. She is the author of numerous foundational publications, such as *Beyond the Bake Sale: An Educator's Guide for Working with Parents*, and *A New Generation of Evidence: The Family is Critical to Student Achievement*, plus the series of research syntheses *A New Wave of Evidence*, published by the Southwest Educational Development Laboratory. She is a founder of the National Coalition for Parent Involvement in Education and has affiliations with the Institute for Education and Social Policy at New York University, and the National Center for Family and Community Connections with Schools.

**David Imig** is Professor of Practice in the College of Education at the University of Maryland, College Park where he heads the Teacher Education and Professional Development Unit and serves as Associate Chair for Curriculum and Instruction. Imig also directs the Carnegie Foundation for the Advancement of Teaching Project on the Education Doctorate, a consortium of twenty-four colleges and universities invested in transforming their professional practice doctorate. In addition, he serves as director of a University of Maryland outreach ED.D. program for association and organization mid-level professionals in Washington, DC. Prior to coming to College Park, Imig was president and chief executive officer of the American Association of Colleges for Teacher Education (AACTE) for twenty-five years, a membership organization of some 750 colleges and universities that is based in Washington, DC. He holds the title of President Emeritus from AACTE. He has served on numerous boards and study groups and consulted on teacher education and public policy with colleges and universities in the United States and abroad. He currently serves as chair of the board for the National Society for the Study of Education.

**Aaron D. Isabelle** is Assistant Professor in the Elementary Education Department at the State University of New York at New Paltz. He teaches undergraduate and graduate courses in science education and is active in teacher professional development. His research interests include history-of-science-inspired stories, preservice teacher alternate conceptions, and inquiry-based strategies for improving science teaching.

**Molly M. Jameson** is a doctoral candidate in Educational Psychology at Ball State University. Her primary research interests include mathematics anxiety in children and statistics anxiety in adults, contextual factors that contribute to anxiety, and the effects of anxiety on academic performance. She serves on the editorial review board of *The Teacher Educator*, as well as a guest reviewer for *Teaching Children Mathematics*.

**Randall Lahann** is a doctoral student in Curriculum and Instruction at the Lynch School of Education at Boston College. His research interests include teacher education for social justice and alternate-route teacher preparation programs.

**Judson Laughter** is a doctoral student in the Department of Teaching and Learning at Peabody College of Vanderbilt University. His research interests include critical race theory and culturally relevant pedagogy. He can be reached at jud.laughter@vanderbilt.edu.

**Lin Lin** is Assistant Professor in Computer Education and Cognitive Systems at the Department of Learning Technologies, University of North Texas in Denton, Texas. Lin teaches undergraduate and graduate courses in instructional technology, computer applications, and multimedia design. Her research interests include new media and technology, teacher learning, and online teaching and learning.

**H. Richard Milner, IV** is Betts Assistant Professor of Education in the Department of Teaching and Learning at the Peabody College of Vanderbilt University. His research, teaching, and policy interests focus on urban education, race and equity in education; and teacher education. He can be reached at rich.milner@vanderbilt.edu.

**Barbara Morgan-Fleming** is Associate Professor in the Curriculum and Instruction Department at Texas Tech University. She teaches a wide variety of courses including undergraduate and graduate courses in literacy, educational methods, diversity, and social issues in education.

**Laurie Mullen** is Associate Dean for teacher education and an associate professor in the Department of Educational Studies at Teachers College, Ball State University. She is the editor of *The Teacher Educator* and teaches classes in teacher education and educational technology. Her research interests are in technologies in the teaching and learning process, teacher education, and curriculum.

**Claudia Peralta Nash** is Associate Professor and Chair of the Department of Bilingual Education at Boise State University. She teaches undergraduate and graduate courses in bilingual and biliteracy education, multicultural education, and multicultural literature. She is the principal investigator of a U.S. Department grant providing her the opportunity to work with graduate students in Morelia, Mexico and San Antonio, Texas.

**Chris O'Brien** is Assistant Professor in the Department of Special Education and Child Development at the University of North Carolina at Charlotte. His areas of interest and research include inclusive instructional strategies for students with high-incidence disabilities in secondary schools, innovation in research-to-practice, and school reform for struggling learners in urban schools.

**Susan R. Polirstok** is Professor of Special Education and Acting Dean of the Division of Education at Lehman College, The City University of New York. She is the author of publications on Asperger Syndrome, autism, attention deficit disorder, peer tutoring, parent training, behavioral intervention, and faculty development. She is on the editorial board of *Ciclo Evolutivo e Disabilita (International Journal of Lifespan and Disability)* and the national editorial board of *Excelsior: Leadership in Teaching and Learning.*

**Dennis Shirley** is Professor of Teacher Education at the Lynch School of Education at Boston College. He teaches courses in the philosophy, social contexts, and history of education. He is the author of *The Politics of Progressive Education: The Odenwaldschule in Nazi Germany* (Harvard University Press), *Community Organizing for Urban School Reform* (University of Texas Press), and

*Valley Interfaith and School Reform: Organizing for Power in South Texas* (University of Texas Press).

**Sarah Summy** is Associate Professor in Special Education at Western Michigan University. Her research interests include teacher preparation for children and youth with emotional and behavioral disorders, the use of seclusion and restraint in public schools, and universal design. She is currently co-directing her second U.S. Department of Education Personnel Preparation Grant.

**Karen Swan** is Research Professor in the Research Center for Educational Technology at Kent State University. Doctor Swan's research has been focused mainly in the general area of media and learning on which she has published and presented nationally and internationally. Her current research focuses on online learning, mobile computing, and on student learning in ubiquitous computing environments.

**F. Blake Tenore** is a doctoral student in the Department of Teaching and Learning at Peabody College of Vanderbilt University. His research interests include equity in education and the multicultural education of teachers. He can be reached at blake.tenore@vanderbilt.edu.

**Mark van't Hooft** is a researcher and technology specialist for the Research Center for Educational Technology at Kent State University. His research focus is on ubiquitous computing and mobile learning in K-12 education, especially in social studies. Mark holds a doctorate in Education with a dual major in Curriculum and Instruction, and Evaluation and Measurement from Kent State University.

**Roy Weaver** is Dean and Professor of Curriculum in the Department of Educational Studies, Teachers College, Ball State University. He has been a longtime advocate for school choice and technology innovation. His research interests are in policy formation and implementation related to these two areas.

**Elizabeth Whitten** is a professor in the Special Education and Literacy Studies Department at Western Michigan University where she teaches undergraduate and graduate courses in special education. She chaired the department for eight years and she has directed three federally funded teacher training grant programs. Prior to her eighteen years working in higher education, she served as a special and general education teacher, principal, and special education administrator. Doctor Whitten has been consulting with a number of school districts for the past fifteen years, providing training in areas of collaboration and teaming, research-based strategies and interventions, and differentiated instruction. She is the co-editor of the *Journal for In-*

*ternal Special Education Needs* and recently authored a book titled *Response to Intervention Toolkit for Teachers* with Doctors Kelli Esteves and Alice Woodrow. She has consulted with school districts across Michigan to implement the Response to Intervention model.

**Kenneth M. Zeichner** is Associate Dean and a Hoefs-Bascom Professor of Teacher Education at the University of Wisconsin, Madison. He has held positions as Vice President of Division K (Teaching and Teacher Education) of the American Educational Research Association (AERA) and on the Board of Directions of the American Association of Colleges for Teacher Education. He has been a member of the Board of the National Society for the Study of Education and was affiliated as a principal investigator with the National Centers for Research on Teacher Education and Teacher Learning at Michigan State University, the National Partnership for Excellence and Accountability in Teaching, the Carnegie Foundation for the Advancement of Teaching study of Teacher Education, and the AERA Consensus Panel on Teacher Education. His publications include *Teacher Education and the Social Conditions of Schooling* (1991) with Dan Liston, *Issues and Practices in Inquiry-Oriented Teacher Education* (1991) with Bob Tabachnick, *Currents of Reform in Preservice Teacher Education* (1996) with Susan Melnick and Mary Gomez, and *Studying Teacher Education: The Report of the AERA Panel on Research and Teacher Education* (2005) with Marilyn Cochran-Smith.

*To my colleagues and students at SUNY College at Oneonta*
*who shape who I am and who I am becoming as a teacher educator.*
*C.L.*

*To Diann, Rob, Holly, Jenna, and Peter*
*R.M.*

*To my daughter Whitney who keeps me youthful and inspired.*
*J.R.W.*

# FOREWORD

The chapters in this book, written by college and university teacher educators in the United States and Canada, explore many of the most important issues teacher educators in North America need to address given the current demographic and policy contexts of education and the persistent gaps in learning for students from different backgrounds that continue to undermine the goals of public schooling in democratic societies. These issues include: (a) preparing teachers to work in the current high-stakes testing and accountability-driven environment of schooling where they respond to pressures to raise standardized test scores without losing sight of the broader purposes of public education in democratic societies and the moral and ethical aspects of teaching; (b) preparing teachers to successfully teach the increasingly linguistically and culturally diverse pupils who attend North American public schools in ways that contribute to the narrowing of the achievement gaps in schools; and (c) preparing teachers to incorporate online delivery models of teaching and new and continually emerging digital technologies into their work.

Several of the chapters in the book discuss areas of needed emphasis in preservice teacher education that have been neglected for many years, such as preparing teachers in relation to conducting and interpreting assessments, working with families, and educating English learners. Several other chapters call for a rethinking of some of the major elements of teacher education, such as the conduct of field experiences, partnerships between universities and schools, and accreditation methods in light of current and future needs. There are different ways to think about each of these elements of teacher education programs and the authors unpack and explore various ways to think about each of them as part of their presentation of their own specific recommendations. This more in-depth exploration of the multiple meanings of structures and practices in teacher education is important in counteracting the negative effects of the sloganeering that has characterized the field where certain structures (e.g., school-university partnerships) and practices (e.g., preparing reflective teachers) have been uncritically embraced and have come to be defined in so many different ways that they lose meaning (e.g., Zeichner & Liston, 1996).

While the book focuses on teacher education in North America, there is an acknowledgment that the issues discussed in a North American context are international in scope and that countries all over the world are facing similar issues such as preparing enough qualified teachers to staff classrooms while maintaining reasonable standards of quality in the teaching force. There is a call in this book for a greater international perspective in North American teacher education. This is an important aspect in my view of how we can improve teacher education in North America. In adopting the kind of international perspective on teacher education advocated in this book, we can learn from others around the world, including countries in the global south, about how they are dealing with many of the same issues and tensions raised in this book. These interactions and exchanges with teacher educators around the world will mutually benefit both North American teacher education and that of the countries with whom we interact. This two-way flow of information about teacher education practices rather than the one-way importation of ideas from the global north to the global south that has been dominant historically is the kind of internationalization we should seek. This internationalization of teacher education, though, should not involve an uncritical acceptance of the agendas of agencies like the World Bank and other international development agencies that, while undoubtedly contributing some positive things to educational systems around the world, have also done much to undermine both teaching as a profession and educational quality in much of the world as they have sought to support a neo-liberal economic agenda (e.g., Carnoy, 1995; Robertson, 2000; Samoff, 1996).

Another feature of this book that is very important is the historical perspective taken by the authors toward each of the issues examined in the individual chapters. This attempt to look at particular issues as they have developed over time has been missing from much of the current discourse on teacher education, a gap that has prevented us from benefiting from what has been learned in the past.

There are two issues not discussed in this book that will affect the ability of teacher educators in North America to be able to act on the many good ideas that are proposed for improving the preparation of teachers. The first issue that is acknowledged but not really addressed is the current landscape for teacher education in the United States that involves multiple pathways into teaching including a growing number of non-college-university-based and for-profit programs (Baines, 2006; Feistritzer & Haar, 2008). In addition to colleges and universities, a variety of institutions have  become providers of pre-service teacher education programs including school districts, regional professional development centers, private companies, and community colleges (Zeichner & Hutchinson, 2008). A growing number of teachers in the United States are being prepared by teacher education programs that do not involve or only minimally involve higher education institutions.

Feistritzer (2008) has traced the growth of alternative routes into teaching over the last two decades from 1983 when eight states had authorized 12 programs to 2006 when all fifty states and the District of Columbia had authorized 485 alternative programs. While many of these alternative programs are administered and/or staffed by college and university faculty and staff (Walsh & Jacobs, 2007), the fact is that a growing number of teachers especially in certain states like Texas, California, and Florida are completing their "pre-service" teacher education while they are on the job fully responsible for classrooms of students. For example, a survey of 2007 graduates of California teacher education programs conducted in May and June 2007 indicated that about 27 percent of the 2,585 respondents completed their student teaching or internship experiences as teachers of record in California classrooms (personal communication, October, 2007).[1] The meaning of improving teacher education field experiences and the other kinds of reforms discussed in this book is very different in this kind of situation as opposed to the standard student teaching or practicum experience in a college and university-based program.

The existence of alternative pathways to teaching outside of higher education is not a new phenomenon. As Fraser (2007) notes it is only for a very brief period of time since the inception of formal teacher education programs in the mid-nineteenth century (1960 through 1990) that colleges and universities had a virtual monopoly of initial teacher preparation in the United States. Today colleges and universities are still the major but not the only providers of preservice teacher education. All types of teacher education programs, not just those run by colleges and universities, need to address the important issues that are raised in this book. Because the "preservice" preparation of an increasing number of teachers is taking place on the job rather than before it, the ways in which the issues will be addressed will be different from how they are handled in traditional campus-based programs.

Also, within college and university-based teacher preparation, there are signs of movement toward delivery of more and more of the preparation of preservice teachers to school and community contexts and of a fundamental rethinking of how teacher education institutions, schools, and communities should relate to one another in the preparation of teachers (Zeichner, 2006). More attention is being given across North America to the idea of a teacher education continuum and to greater integration and connection among the different aspects of teacher education that take place at different stages in a

---

1. These data were provided by David Wright of the California State University Chancellor's Office.

teaching career (Feiman-Nemser, 2001). The information provided in this book will be very useful to teacher educators who work at different stages in this continuum and in different institutional settings, not just to preservice teacher educators based in colleges and universities.

A second issue that is critical to whether or not the ideas that are proposed in this book will be enacted is to what extent we will begin to address long-standing problems in the preparation of teacher educators in our research universities. This issue has widespread implications for the future of teacher education in all kinds of higher education institutions. For many years, there has been clear documentation in the literature regarding the low status of teacher education in the research universities that prepare teacher educators in North America. In these universities, the reward systems for faculty and graduate students have led to low status for the work of teacher education and frequent neglect of the responsibility to carefully prepare, induct, and continually develop the teacher educators who will work with new teachers upon completion of their degrees (e.g., Labaree, 2004; Lanier & Little, 1986). Working in a teacher education program during one's graduate studies often serves primarily as a form of financial aid rather than as the basis for careful preparation and mentoring to be a teacher educator (Tom, 1997) and because of institutional priorities, the resources needed to maintain coherent programs with integrated and cumulative curricula are often not forthcoming (Featherstone, 2007).

It is absolutely essential that we begin to take more seriously the preparation of the next generation of teacher educators or the many excellent ideas set forth in this book will not be utilized. There are a number of examples of countries that have invested in careful preparation and continuous professional development of its teacher educators. We can learn much from these countries.[2] There have been recent calls for teacher education to become a central part of the mission of the education schools that prepare teacher educators (e.g., Ball, 2007), and the idea of P-12 teacher education as an important university responsibility has become a central component in several prominent teacher education reform networks such as the "Teachers for a New Era" project. These developments provide hope that the critical issue of teacher educator preparation will finally be addressed.

This book will enrich current debates about the future of teacher education in North America. Educators, policymakers, and citizens who care about the future of public education will benefit from studying it.

Ken Zeichner
Madison, Wisconsin
March 2008

---

2. Namibia (Zeichner & Dalstrom, 1999) and Isreal (www.mofet.macam.ac.il/English/) are two examples.

# REFERENCES

Baines, L. (2006). The transmogrifaction of teacher education. *The Teacher Educator, 42*(2), 140–156.

Ball, D. (April, 2007). *The case for ed schools and the challenge.* Dewitt-Wallace Readers' Digest distinguished lecture presented at the annual meeting of the American Educational Research Association, Chicago, IL.

Carnoy, M. (1995). Structural adjustment and the changing face of education. *International Labor Review, 134*(6), 653–674.

Featherstone, J. (2007). Values and the big education school. In D. Carroll, H. Featherstone, J. Featherstone, S. Feiman-Nemser, & D. Roosevelt (Eds.). *Transforming teacher education: Reflections from the field.* (pp. 203–220). Cambridge, MA: Harvard Education Press.

Feiman-Nemser, S. (2001). From preparation to practice: Designing a continuum to strengthen and sustain teaching. *Teachers College Record, 103*(6), 1013–1055.

Feistritzer, E. (2008). *Alternative teacher certification: A state by state analysis.* Washington, DC: National Center for Education Information. College Press.

Feistritzer, E., & Haar, C. K. (2008). *Alternative routes to teaching.* Upper Saddle River, NJ: Pearson Education Inc.

Fraser, J. (2007). *Preparing America's teachers: A history.* New York: Teachers College Press.

Labaree, D. (2004). *The trouble with ed schools.* New Haven, CT: Yale University Press.

Lanier, J., & Little, J. W. (1986). Research on teacher education. In M. Wittrock (Ed.) *Handbook of research on teaching,* 3rd edition. (pp. 527–569). New York: Macmillan.

Robertson, S. (2000). *A class act: Changing teachers' work, the state and globalization.* New York: Falmer Press.

Samoff, J. (1996). Which priorities and strategies for education? *International Journal of Educational Development, 16*(3), 249–271.

Tom, A. (1997). *Redesigning teacher education.* Albany, NY: SUNY Press.

Walsh, K., & Jacobs, S. (September, 2007). *Alternative certification isn't alternative.* Washington, DC: Thomas Fordham Foundation.

Zeichner, K. (2006). Reflections of a university-based teacher educator on the future of college and university-based teacher education. *Journal of Teacher Education, 57*(3), 326–340.

Zeichner, K., & Dahlstrom, L. (1999) (Eds.). *Democratic teacher education reform in Africa: The case of Namibia.* Boulder, CO: Westview.

Zeichner, K., & Hutchinson, E. (in press). The development of alternative certification policies and programs in the U.S. In P. Grossman & S. Loeb (Eds.). *Taking stock: An examination of alternative certification.* Cambridge, MA: Harvard Education Press.

Zeichner, K., & Liston, D. (1996). *Reflective teaching.* Mahwah, N.J: Lawrence Erlbaum/Routledge.

# PREFACE

In this edited volume by experts in the field of teacher education, *Current Issues in Teacher Education* combines forces from the United States and Canada to present and discuss positions on current topics and concerns in the field of teacher education. It provides an overview and multiple perspectives of issues rather than one author's position or viewpoint. This will allow the reader to reflect on multiple perspectives and to form his or her opinion and route for further action or discussion. Written in a reader-friendly style with accessible language, the book avoids the use of highly technical jargon-like language.

Divided into four parts, Part I looks at overarching issues, such as preparing for the realities of teaching imposed by state and federal mandates, curriculum delivery models, and worldwide issues. Part II explores issues related to the teacher education institution, such as preservice teacher placement, accreditation, and partnerships. Part III contains chapters on training teachers in multicultural education, technology, assessment, special needs, and family involvement. And, in Part IV, leaders from the American Association of Colleges for Teacher Education propose ideas for the future of teacher education.

Each chapter includes a section on the implications for teacher education and a look to the future. Review questions to prompt thinking or discussion complete each chapter. Teacher educators who work in the field and/or are involved with professional organizations related to the field will find the book to be useful at the college or university level. Policymakers, administrators, and other leaders in the field will also find the book to be an important addition to their library.

# ACKNOWLEDGMENTS

We would like to thank our contributors for their commitment to producing this unique resource, the staff and management at Charles C Thomas Publishers for their support and guidance, and Amanda Merritt for her help with proofreading.

—Cindy, Bob, and Jerry

I thank Millah Musungu for her help with my chapter.
—Heidi Andrade

I would like to acknowledge Professor Kensuke Chikamori and Professor Yumiko Ono of Naruto University of Education in Japan for their help in understanding teacher education in Japan and Africa.
—Carol Merz Frankel

I would like to thank the Rockefeller Study and Conference Center in Bellagio, Italy, for providing me with a residency in 2005 that enabled me to study the philosophies that I described in the chapter.
—Dennis Shirley

# CONTENTS

# CURRENT ISSUES IN
# TEACHER EDUCATION

# INTRODUCTION: WHAT ARE THE CURRENT ISSUES IN TEACHER EDUCATION?

ROBERT J. MICHAEL, JERUSALEM RIVERA-WILSON, AND CYNTHIA A. LASSONDE

*Teacher education is the Dodge City of the education world. Like the fabled wild west town, it is unruly and chaotic.*
(Levine, 2006, p. 109)

There are numerous issues, controversies, and debates in teacher education today. The introductory quote comes as no surprise to those who work and teach in higher education. Many discussions about issues in teacher education exist in the current literature (Ravitch, 2007), thus creating the Dodge City image of chaos in which everyone is waving a gun and shouting to be heard. Among the perspectives mentioned in current literature include:

- teaching in urban schools (Hollins, 2006; Obidah & Howard, 2005; Watson et al., 2006);
- challenges in the first years of teaching and the implications for teacher education (Liston, Whitcomb, & Borku, 2006; Mandel, 2006);
- professional development (Anderson & Olsen, 2006; Intrator & Kunzman, 2006);
- teacher evaluation (Goldstein & Noguera, 2006);
- traditional versus nontraditional teacher education programs (Good et al., 2006);
- teacher education program accreditation (Anderson, Spooner, Calhoun, & Spooner, 2007; Murray, 2005; Wise, 2005);
- gender issues (Sadker & Silber, 2007);
- teacher qualifications and quality (Kennedy, 2006; Lasley, Siedentop, & Yinger, 2006);

- politics of teacher education (Cochran-Smith, 2005b; Fraser, 2005; Gay, 2005; Hess, 2005; Michelli, 2005; Yinger, 2005; Zimpher & Howey, 2005);
- testing, accountability, and uses of data (Abrutyn, 2006; Asp, 2000; Berliner, 2005; Wineberg, 2006);
- diversity and teacher education (Gay, 2000; Ladson-Billings, 2005; Salend, 2005); and
- uses of professional development schools (Castle, Fox, & Souder, 2006).

As McLeskey and Ross (2004) noted, ". . . teacher education has become a 'front burner' political issue in Washington, DC and in most state houses" (p. 342). In a review of more than 300 research reports on teacher preparation, Wilson, Floden, and Ferrini-Mundy (2001) noted there are major disagreements about what should constitute good teacher preparation. In addition to this issue, the authors made note of the questions concerning areas such as subject matter and pedagogical preparation, clinical training, policy influences, and alternative certification. The debate also continues on how best to prepare teachers for our schools. In light of time, expense, convenience, and incentives, alternative certification programs have attracted a great deal of attention as well (Johnson, Birkeland, & Peske, 2005).

No Child Left Behind (NCLB) has the educational community focused on its implications for schools and teacher education. However, as Sobol (2006) has noted, there are many other equally important educational issues that need our attention:

> In short, we need to find ways to attract able and effective people into the profession of teaching, to educate teachers well in both the content and methods of their work, and to support practicing teachers with professional development linked to their daily work with standards and students. (p. 38)

Controversy and criticism surround NCLB. There are implications for teacher education drawn from this law, such as the definition of highly qualified teachers, annual yearly progress by students on tests, and accountability goals for subgroups of students (Cochran-Smith, 2005a).

As noted in the literature, "the multilingual, multicultural classroom is an American reality in the twenty-first century" (Costa, McPhail, Smith, & Brisk, 2005). There is a strong need for teachers to have training in working with English language learners. Results of studies have challenged teacher educators to be critical and thoughtful about the use and interpretation of high-stakes testing data (Escamilla, Charez, & Vigil, 2005). Indeed, they found data did not support the idea that students with language differences created a school achievement gap.

There are serious concerns but, also, significant accomplishments in the field of teacher education. Cochran-Smith (2006) noted positive trends in teacher education but also called attention to major potential problems in the future that may undercut the advancements made. The author stated, "teaching does not simply involve transmitting bits of information, and learning does not simply consist of receiving information that can be tested" (p. 24). The use of test scores to define teacher quality and student learning is far too simplistic, according to the author. She also warns about the dangers of ignoring other variables, such as resources and leadership, that impact student learning. Lastly, there is a need to understand that the purpose of education is much more than creating workers for the labor force. Among other purposes, we need to remember the goal of preparing individuals to live and work in a democratic society.

In light of these reports, it comes as no surprise that there is a myriad of issues in teacher education. We need to address the issues in teacher education but, first, identification and greater exploration are needed. It is the intent of the co-editors that this book represents a step in that direction as we explore relevant issues in teacher education. This book is designed to provide teachers, teacher educators, and individuals involved in policy and reform with current research and practical guidelines.

## OVERVIEW OF THE BOOK

It is important and interesting to note how the parts of this volume evolved. Initially, the co-editors developed a list of potential issues to include. This list was based on the editors' experience and interaction with educators from across the United States through their work and hands-on involvement in professional organizations and in editing the New York Association of Colleges for Teacher Education's state journal. Next, the co-editors invited teacher education leaders to write particular chapters based on their expertise. While working with these potential contributors, many of them suggested issues that were relevant in their region that we hadn't necessarily included. Some contributors proposed new ideas or reshaped the ones we had presented. In short, the framing of this book became a collaborative effort among the co-editors and thirty contributors from Washington State to New York State and from Florida to Canada.

The result of this collaboration is an edited volume that consists of four parts. *Part I: A Broad Perspective* provides an eclectic group of chapters that look at the overarching issues of teaching and learning, such as preparing for the realities of teaching imposed by state and federal mandates, curriculum delivery models, and worldwide concerns. The issues examined in these chapters include:

- How do we navigate and negotiate the chartered waters of high-stakes testing and accountability in the classroom?
- What is the role of distance education in providing alternative, nontraditional options for the preparation of teachers?
- How do educators teach globally?

*Part II: Institutional Perspectives* looks at concerns related to the teacher-education institution. These chapters reveal some of the obstacles and challenges that teacher-education programs face. These topics include the moral aspects of learning, developing and sustaining collaborative relationships, advantages and disadvantages of stadards-based teacher-education programs, and the complexities of student-teaching placements. This part examines questions such as:

- How do we groom "better-educated" teachers and provide for the development of their moral character?
- Where does the knowledge to teach come from and who is best suited to teach it?
- What are the advantages and disadvantages of accreditation?

Each chapter in *Part III: Educating Tomorrow's Teachers* is unique. These chapters tackle the knowledge and skill set needed of today's teachers in multiculturalism, technology, special education, and family engagement. In particular, Part III addresses the following questions:

- What is multicultural competence?
- What essential digital tools (i.e., toolkits) are needed to teach in

today's classrooms?
- What should teachers know about assessment?
- What instructional methods and strategies are needed to work with students with disabilities?
- What are family engagement practices?

Although critical topics for all teachers to know, unfortunately, due to time constraints, this information is sometimes inadequately communicated or completely neglected in teacher-education programs. Each chapter outlines the importance of the topic and suggestions for classroom and program implementation.

Finally, *Part IV: The Future of Teacher Education* draws upon the previous chapters in this volume. In this part, leaders from the American Association of Colleges for Teacher Education propose ideas for the future of teacher education from the following perspectives: tensions and challenges, factors shaping teacher-education programs, teachers for tomorrow's schools, and the survival of teacher education.

In this edited volume, experts in the field of teacher education have combined forces to present and discuss positions on current topics and concerns in the field of teacher education. This book offers an overview and multiple perspectives of issues rather than one author's position or viewpoint. The book aims to inform instructors, administrators, and others involved in teacher education using accessible language rather than highly technical jargon.

Leaders from across the United States and from Canada have committed to sharing their research, their knowledge, and their experience with readers. Chapter contributors represent membership and leading roles in organizations such as the American Association of Colleges for Teacher Education and the American Educational Research Association with long-term experience as professors in teacher education. The reader need only visit our Contributors and About the Editors pages to be convinced that this volume is well represented by experts in the field who are passionate about present circumstances and future developments of teacher training.

While each chapter focuses on a different issue, consistency among chapters is maintained through the structure of its features. Each chapter begins with a relevant quote and introduction to draw the reader in and preset the topic. Then a timeline feature provides background information on the history of how the issue has evolved in teacher education over the years. Following the body of the chapter, end-of-chapter features include a section on the implications for teacher education and a look to the future. Reflective questions to prompt thinking or discussion complete each chapter, followed by complete references in APA format.

Besides the structural features of the volume, the most remarkable feature is that this book represents discussion of relevant current issues in teacher education as explored by experts from across the United States and Canada. It will allow the reader to reflect on multiple perspectives and to, as a result, form his or her opinion and route for further action or discussion.

## REFERENCES

Abrutyn, L. S. (2006). The most important data. *Educational Leadership, 63*(6), 54–57.

Anderson, K. M., Spooner, M., Calhoun, M. L., & Spooner, F. (2007). Reviewing and refining: A professional education unit's journey toward accreditation. *Teacher Education and Special Education, 30*(2), 57–66.

Anderson, L., & Olsen, B. (2006). Investigating early career urban teachers' perspectives on experiences in professional development. *Journal of Teacher Education, 57*(4), 359–377.

Asp, E. (2000). Assessment in education: Where have we been? In R. S. Brandt (Ed.), *Education in a new era* (123–157). Alexandria, VH: Association for Supervision and Curriculum development.

Berliner, D. C. (2005). The near impossibility of testing for teacher quality. *Journal of Teacher Education, 56*(3), 205–213.

Castle, S., Fox, R. K., & Souder, K. O. (2006). Do professional development schools (PDS's) make a difference? A comparative study of PDS and non-PDS teacher candidates. *Journal of Teacher Education, 57*(1), 65–80.

Cochran-Smith, M. (2005a). No Child Left Behind: Three years and counting. *Journal of Teacher Education, 56*(2), 99–103.

Cochran-Smith, M. (2005b). The politics of teacher education and the curse of complexity. *Journal of Teacher Education, 56*(3), 181–185.

Cochran-Smith, M. (2006). Ten promising trends (and three big worries). *Educational Leadership, 63*(6), 20–25.

Costa, J., McPhail, G., Smith, J., & Brisk, M. E. (2005). Faculty first: The challenge of infusing the teacher education curriculum with scholarship on English language learners. *Journal of Teacher Education, 56*(2), 104–118.

Escamilla, K., Chavez, L., & Vigil, P. (2005). Rethinking the "gap": High-stakes testing and Spanish-speaking students in Colorado. *Journal of Teacher Education, 56*(2), 132–144.

Fraser, J. W. (2005). Notes toward a new progressive politics of teacher education. *Journal of Teacher Education, 56*(3), 279–284.

Gay, G. (2005). Politics of multicultural teacher education. *Journal of Teacher Education, 56*(3), 221–228.

Gay, G. (2000). Culturally responsive teaching. New York: Teachers College Press.

Goldstein, J., & Noguera, P. A. (2006). A thoughtful approach to teacher evaluation. *Educational Leadership, 63*(6), 31–37.

Good, T. L., McCaslin, M., Tsang, H.Y., Shang, J., Wiley, C. R. H., & Bosack, A. R. (2006). How well do 1st year teachers teach: Does type of preparation make a difference? *Journal of Teacher Education, 57*(4), 410–430.

Hess, F. M. (2005). The predictable, but unpredictable, personal politics of teacher education. *Journal of Teacher Education, 56*(3), 192–198.

Hollins, E. R. (2006). Transforming practice in urban schools. *Educational Leadership, 63*(6), 48–52.

Intrator, S. M., & Kunzman, R. (2006). Starting with the soul. *Educational Leadership, 63*(6), 38-42.

Johnson, S. M., Birkeland, S. E., & Peske, H. G. (2005). *A difficult balance: Incentives and quality control in alternative certification programs.* Harvard Graduate School of Education: Project on the next generation of teachers.

Kennedy, M. M. (2006). From teacher quality to quality teaching. *Educational Leadership, 63*(6), 14–19.

Ladson-Billings, G. J. (2005). Is the team all right? Diversity and teacher education. *Journal of Teacher Education, 56*(3), 229–234.

Lasley, T. J., Siedentop, D., & Yinger, R. (2006). A systemic approach to enhancing teacher quality: The Ohio model. *Journal of Teacher Education, 57*(1), 13–21.

Levine, A. (2006). *Educating school teachers.* Washington, DC: Education Schools Projects. Retrieved December 20, 2007 from http://www.edschools.org/pdf/Educating_Teachers_Report. pdf

Liston, D., Whitcomb, J., & Borko, H. (2006). Editorial: Too little or too much: Teacher preparation and the first years of teaching. *Journal of Teacher Education, 57*(4), 351–358.

Mandel, S. (2006). What new teachers really need. *Educational Leadership, 63*(6), 66–69.

McLeskey, J., & Ross, D.D. (2004). The politics of teacher education in the new millennium: Implications for special education teacher educators. *Teacher Education and Special Education, 27*(4), 342–349.

Michelli, N. M. (2005). The politics of teacher education: Lessons from New York City. *Journal of Teacher Education, 56*(3), 235–241.

Murray, F. B. (2005). On building a unified system of accreditation in teacher education. *Journal of Teacher Education, 56*(4), 307–317.

Obidah, J. E., & Howard, T. C. (2005). Preparing teacher for "Monday morning" in the urban school classroom: Reflecting on our pedagogies and practices as effective teacher educators. *Journal of Teacher Education, 56*(3), 248–255.

Ravitch, D. (2007). Major address: Challenges to teacher education. *Journal of Teacher Education, 58*(4), 269–273.

Sadker, D., & Silber, E. (Eds.) (2007). *Gender in the classroom.* New York: Erlbaum.

Salend, S. J. (2005). *Creating inclusive classrooms.* (5th ed.). New Jersey: Pearson.

Sobol, T. (2006). Beyond no child left behind. *Education Week,* September 20; 42, 38.

Watson, D., Charner-Laird, M., Kirkpatrick, C. L., Szczesiul, S. A., & Gordon, P. J. (2006). Effective teaching/effective urban teaching: Grappling with definitions, grappling with difference. *Journal of Teacher Education, 57*(4), 395–409.

Wilson, S. M., Floden, R. E., & Ferrini-Mundy, J. (2001). *Teacher Preparation Research Center: Current knowledge, gaps and recommendations.* US Department of Education and the Office for Educational Research and Improvement.

Wineberg, M. S. (2006). Evidence in teacher education: Establishing a framework for accountability. *Journal of Teacher Education, 57*(1), 51–64.

Wise, A. E. (2005). Establishing teaching as a profession: The essential role of professional accreditation. *Journal of Teacher Education, 56*(4), 318–331.

Yinger, R. J. (2005). A public politics for a public profession. *Journal of Teacher Education, 56*(3), 285–290.

Zimpher, N. L., & Howey, K. R. (2005). The politics of partnerships for teacher education redesign and school renewal. *Journal of Teacher Education, 56*(3), 266–271.

# PART I
# A BROAD PERSPECTIVE

# Chapter 1

# NO PRESERVICE TEACHER LEFT BEHIND: PREPARING FOR THE HIGH-STAKES TESTING CLASSROOM

Hansel Burley and Barbara Morgan-Fleming

> . . . testing is fast usurping the role of the curriculum as the mechanism of defining what schooling is about in this country. . . . It seems that the aims of education, the business of our schools, and the goals of educational reform are addressed not so much in terms of curriculum—the courses of study that are followed—as they are in terms of standardized tests. It is testing, not the official stated curriculum, that is increasingly determining what is taught, how it is taught, what is learned, and how it is learned.
>
> (Madaus, 1988, p. 83)

## INTRODUCTION

High-stakes testing, the No Child Left Behind Act of 2001 (NCLB), and new notions of educational accountability have changed the very nature of teaching in United States public schools. These three factors affect all aspects of teaching, even legally redefining what we mean by the term *learning*. However, the response of teacher preparation programs (TPPs) has been to prepare new teachers in much the same way they always have, as if these new emphases did not exist.

As teacher educators we find ourselves in the midst of contradictory rhetoric. How do we use our knowledge of research and our own teaching experiences to help preservice teachers prepare themselves for the opportunities and pressures of this new way of thinking about education and teaching? How do we prepare them to handle the complex political, pedagogical, and social conflicts surrounding high-stakes testing in K-12 settings? It is tempting in the context of higher education to prepare teachers to teach in only an ideal world. This leaves the hard work for the novice teacher who must try to apply "ideal-world" knowledge and skills in less than forgiving real-world settings.

We do not want preservice teachers to abandon the ideal, nor do we want to prepare cynics. Morgan-Fleming attacks this dilemma by telling preservice teachers that she has a list of things that will be different when she has total power (e.g., When I have total power, there will be no racism). She also acknowledges that acquiring total power may not happen this week; therefore, she must come up with a Plan B that will get as close to that goal as possible given current conditions. High-stakes testing can also be considered in this context. Former preservice teachers need not feel helpless because the ideals they learn in preservice courses seem to evaporate in a high-stakes testing culture.

To TPPs, schools, school districts, policymakers, and teachers, we recommend the adoption of a Plan B as an approach to dealing with high-stakes testing, a plan that recognizes the complex nature of the roles schools play in our society. All should recognize what these tests can and cannot do. First, tests do not teach; teachers do. Second, tests can and do focus attention on educational problem areas. Third, and most importantly, we need to behave in the best interests of the child. Ultimately, this means teachers galvanizing themselves to use tests to aid learning and instruction. Additionally, teachers can help educate policymakers and their constituents on the effective and ineffective uses of high-stakes testing programs. In short, teachers should own the tests.

To that end, in this chapter we discuss the importance of school culture and how high-stakes tests affect that culture. We suggest that TPPs need to be heavily involved in helping teachers understand the complexity of the educational enterprise in the United States, particularly when high-stakes tests become part of the equation. In fact, at the close of this paper we will argue that the skills and dispositions needed for dealing with the impact of high-stakes testing in schools must be formally addressed as a key part of preservice learning experience.

**TIMELINE**

- **1900s**. Nineteenth-century schools tested both students and teachers. If students failed tests, it was their fault (Ravitch, 2002).
- **1910s**. Top universities developed entrance examinations, leading to the creation of the College Entrance Examination Board (Ravitch, 2002).
- **1910s**. By the early twentieth century, immigrants took newly developed standardized tests. Performance on these tests could determine whether they were accepted into the United States (Amrein & Berliner, 2002).
- **1920s**. In the early twentieth century, the field of educational psychology developed with a strong emphasis in educational testing (Ravitch, 2002).
- **1930 through 1950**. Edward Thorndike's work on testing supported the progressive education movement of the 1930s and 1940s (Ravitch, 2002).
- **1950s**. Social promotion developed as an effort to protect children from the job market. Progressive education was more concerned with students' psychological well-being and social adjustment than subject matter, discipline, and grades. There is little literature from the 1930s and 1940s on using tests to hold students or teachers accountable (Ravitch, 2002).
- **1960**. By the late 1950s and early 1960s policymakers and concerned citizens openly began discussing using the new *Standard Admissions Test* as a tool for evaluating schools (West & Peterson, 2003).
- **1966**. Real interest in accountability began in with James Coleman's report, entitled *Equality of Educational Opportunity*. Commonly called the *Coleman Report*, this document shifted the focus of schools from inputs to results with a focus on how school resources affected achievement. While educators advocated for additional re-sources, policymakers and families began considering structural changes for educational systems (Ravitch, 2002).
- **1970 through 1980**. The 1970s saw the development of many new tests, including the so-called gold standard nation's report card, the *National Assessment of Educational Progress* (NAEP).

Despite the fact that more students than ever were taking the tests, many saw the decline in test scores as evidence that schools were failing (West & Peterson, 2003). See the Institute of Educa-tion Sciences website at http://nces.ed.gov/nations reportcard.

- **1983**. In 1983 *A Nation at Risk: The Imperative for Educational Reform* from the National Commission on Excellence in Educa-tion announced that "a rising tide of mediocrity . . . threatens our very future as a Nation and a people" (National Commis-sion, 1983, p. 9). It questioned the heavy emphasis on teaching methods in teacher preparation courses and pointed the way toward a standards-based movement. Read the report at http://www.ed.gov/pubs/NatAtRisk/index.html.
- **1995**. Berliner and Biddle (1997) reviewed the research that supported *A Nation at Risk* (National Commission, 1983) and found it seriously wanting, setting the stage for arguments against its conclusions in A Nation at Risk.
- 2001. The No Child Left Behind Act radically extended the Elementary and Secondary Education Act, which was first rati-fied in 1965, tying federal funding to student performance on standardized tests. Read NCLB online at http://www.ed.gov/policy/elsec/leg/esea02/index.html.

## KEY TERMS RELATED TO TESTING POLICY

For better or worse, testing drives pedagogy, and as history shows, testing can be the force behind both successful and less-than-success-ful social policy. Since many school-related performances and behav-iors are tested, we must first discuss key classifications of tests and test-ing programs.

Madaus (1988) classifies testing programs in two ways: internal/ex-ternal and high stakes/low stakes. Schools carry out internal testing programs under the control of a local school educator. They range from off-the-shelf standardized tests to teacher-made tests. Outside authorities control external testing programs; and increasingly, these outside authorities are state boards of education and legislatures.

Testing programs can also be classified as either high stakes or low stakes. Madaus (1988) says that high-stakes tests are usually linked to important decisions like graduation, educator evaluation, resource allocation, and school accreditation. Those taking these tests see them as having singular importance and automatic sanctions. On the other hand, low-stakes tests do not have rewards or sanctions attached to them. Typically, educators can ignore the results or use them diagnostically. Any actions are not perceived of as automatic. In sum, when teachers have the authority over the assessment tool, they may use it in various ways. When external forces control the test, educators will shape nearly all educational experiences in accordance with the specific objectives of the test.

## EXTERNAL HIGH-STAKES TESTS AND SCHOOL CULTURE

Pai and Adler (2001) describe a culture as a set of patterned knowledge, skills, behaviors, attitudes, material artifacts, activities, symbols, and beliefs that are transmitted from one generation to another. Culture includes everything from art, science, and music to behaviors and beliefs in a wide range of situations. Further, these beliefs are shared among all those in the group. It also includes shared goals and a vision for the future and can affect the most mundane aspects of life, such as how one perceives time to the idea of what it means to be educated. Culture is also a system of norms and control (Pai & Adler 2001), and it is a powerful determinant of all kinds of outcomes, behaviors, and performances.

Subgroup cultures, such as a school culture, work in similar fashion. Each school has its own group of deep-rooted shared beliefs and mores that can profoundly affect behavior. For example, if teachers share a belief that all students can be prepared to pass an external high-stakes test when given enough time, the organizational culture of the school and of individual classrooms will reflect this broadly held value. Such a school will seek to create opportunities to extend teaching time and students' learning-engaged time. This could include before-school, after-school, and even possibly Saturday-school instructional periods—all in an effort to increase the amount of time teachers have to instruct and students have to learn. Additionally, those teachers who violate the tenets of this culture face ostracism, isolation, or dismissal. External high-stakes testing can change the culture of a school.

## A Powerful Positive Impact of Testing

In an examination of the high-stakes testing movement in Texas, Burley, Butner, Marbley, Bush, and Fleming (2001) showed that the state was finding some success with standardized tests. First, the state-held school districts and schools accountable for the performance of all students on statewide examinations. They describe how, prior to accountability driven by high-stakes tests, the culture in many schools allowed the most effective teachers, usually those with the longest tenure, to teach students with few academic or socioeconomic challenges. Students performing least well on tests often had year after year of poorly performing or inexperienced teachers. Therefore, these students had fewer opportunities to learn foundational material. These students typically came from low-income families and were ethnic minorities. Also, the accountability rules required that ethnic and gender groups perform similarly at a state-mandated level. This new rule tied to the high-stakes tests resulted in some positive cultural shifts, such as school districts and building principals finding ways to get effective teachers into classrooms with students who had greater needs. As a result, test scores in Texas rose swiftly and rose in the most unlikely places.

## Negative Effects Outweigh Positive

The Texas standardized tests measured only math, reading, and one particular type of writing. Therefore, resources (e.g., time, money, and teachers) concentrated on math, reading, and that particular type of writing. In so doing, several areas of knowledge highly valued in society (e.g., history, geography, and science) seemed to disappear from classrooms. McNeil (2000) argues this is the result of teaching in a controlling high-stakes assessment environment. She calls this "defensive teaching." The defensive teacher will control the content by omission, excluding both controversial and difficult topics because these take more time to explain or study in depth, thus interrupting the pacing of the course.

Teachers and administrators wishing to increase test scores often teach to the test and use academic time for subjects on the tests only (Darling-Hammond, 2003). McNeil (2000) found that teachers demystified the content, reduced complex subjects to simple lists (e.g., facts, names, dates, formulas, or terms), or found other methods to simplify the subject. The goal was to focus on the examination while minimizing student resistance to the instructional approach.

If disproportional instructional time is spent practicing for tests, is there a corresponding reduction of time on tasks associated with learning (Fisher & Berliner, 1985)? Our practice as teacher educators provides one anecdotal example. A preservice teacher said that nineteen of the twenty-six children in the third-grade class where she was assigned had failed the Texas Assessment of Academic Skills pretest in reading. (One collateral effect of high-stakes testing environments is plenty of pretests and practice tests used to benchmark students prior to the actual examination. In some school districts, this can occur once a reporting period, as many as four times a year.) Therefore, instead of using their reading time to read, the third-grade students spent their reading time learning test-taking skills. We asked, "So the students can read; they just don't understand the presentation of the test questions?" The student teacher replied, "Oh no, they can't read." While such strategies may help with raising test scores, students may not be meeting the real goals of the examination (viz., reading) while simultaneously losing out on subjects typically not on tests like science, music, art, and physical education.

We should not be surprised when teachers, whose status and pay may be tied to high scores, choose to teach in schools with a history of high test scores. According to a recent Louisiana Department of Education analysis, "Teachers with high scores on professional exams tend to find jobs *not* [italics added] in schools judged unacceptable under state performance standards, but in high-achievement schools, according to an analysis of personnel and testing records of more than 31,000 teachers" (Warner, 2003, p. 1). Experienced, sought-after teachers and administrators may congregate in schools with past success on exams. While it would make sense for struggling schools to get the best educators, the current cost/benefit system makes that unlikely.

Perhaps the most disappointing effect of high-stakes testing is cheating. In the late 1990s, the Houston Independent School District (ISD) appeared to have made the dream reality in what was called the "Texas miracle" because of soaring test scores and disappearing dropout rates. According to Haney (2000), the miracle was a mirage. Perhaps the worst examples of cheating involve how the district treated students considered at risk of failing the state exam. In the mid 1990s, only 26 percent of Houston's tenth graders were passing the state mathematics test, but by 2000 nearly 99 percent were reported as passing. According to a *Washington Post* article (Dobbs, 2003) students at risk of failing were retained at the ninth grade, allowing only the most competent students to take the high school exit test during the tenth-grade year. The state evaluated schools and school districts on the performance of tenth-grade students. This more academically superior and homogenous tenth-grade cohort made the school district appear to have made great academic gains in a short time. Meanwhile after the year had passed, those retained in the ninth grade were "caught up"–moved from the ninth grade to the eleventh, so they had no tenth-grade test scores to report. Schools administrators could then use the doctored passing rates to attract students who had consistently passed exams prior to the exit exam. Like its neighbor Enron, one employee exposed Houston ISD's reputed excellence as fraud, the result of systemic cheating.

In Houston and statewide, problematic students were transferred to competing campuses or encouraged to drop out and take the *General Equivalence Exam.* In other cases, educators actually changed marks on answer sheets. Most of the cheating happened in the old-fashioned way, one student copying from another. The reported ways to cheat are too numerous and discouraging to recount completely. Of course, what drives the cheating is that school reputation, educator contracts and bonuses, and student grade advancement and graduation are tied to test scores.

## IMPLICATIONS FOR TEACHER EDUCATION

As teacher educators we must deal with the current high-stakes testing situation on four fronts while helping preservice teachers develop the skills to do the same. We must help preservice teachers by providing them with the pedagogical, statistical, ethical, and political skills and knowledge needed to practice successfully in the current environment. If we fail here, preservice teachers will be at risk of succumbing to irresistible pressure to behave unethically. Their students and the nation will be poorly served. In this section we offer some suggestions for teacher education programs on how to help preservice teachers deal with the culture of testing.

## Pedagogical

Teacher educators must redouble their efforts to impart the most effective pedagogy we know. Therefore, we must acknowledge the power of high-stakes tests and help preservice teachers understand how to prepare students for these tests. We must also impart that "drill-and-kill" teaching and other shortcuts to raising test scores must be avoided. In fact, we admit being deeply troubled by school districts that have resorted to whole curricula delivered by teacher scripts.

Some teacher educators may argue that the tests are inherently bad; therefore, they passive aggressively fail to mention high-stakes testing in teacher preparation courses. The result we have seen is simple resentment from former preservice teachers who feel completely unprepared for the values, language, and teaching behaviors of a culture shaped by high-stakes assessments. Our ignoring how high-stakes tests shape a school's culture is no option.

One thing teacher educators can do is require that for each practice lesson two plans be prepared, one for helping students on the tests and the other for preparing students to perform in the real world. Another pedagogical strategy is to require that preservice teachers involve themselves in support roles. These can include activities like tutoring, proctoring, standing-in, and mentoring. For example, a preservice teacher could stand in for a teacher by teaching a lesson to a whole class, while the classroom teacher focuses attention on students needing extra help.

## Statistical

New teachers must have an understanding of key aspects of test-related statistics. Typically, preservice teachers have scant training on how statistics apply to testing, assessment, and evaluation. Topics that need to be integrated into teacher education programs include those from introductory statistics and test and measurement courses. For example, prior to certification, all preservice teachers should have examined a high-stakes test, conducted an item-analysis, checked the validity and reliability of a portion of the test, and disaggregated data from a school. They should be able to apply what they have learned about the statistics from a test to improve classroom instruction. We must provide these opportunities to engage the statistics of testing prior to entry into the classroom.

## Ethical

Dewey (see Archambault, 1964) reminds us that "there cannot be two sets of ethical principles . . . one for life in the school, and the other for life outside of the school" (p. 108). Concentrating on test preparation and statistics teaches students and preservice educators that only the knowledge that can be tested and rewarded by an external, standardized agent is of value. Just as preservice teachers must be better aware of statistical validity, they should also understand consequential validity; that is, they must understand the consequences produced by high-stakes tests and the consequences of our reactions to the tests. For instance, in Texas, the prototype of NCLB, a *Dallas Morning News* front-page article decried the discovery of 50,000 cases of cheating on the statewide exams (Benton & Hacker, 2007). Is the rigor of the test worth the consequences?

We believe that there are several other questions that we must help preservice teachers understand, if not answer. In a high-stakes testing culture, how do we prepare students to use their curiosity and creativity to invent new knowledge or to challenge current interpretations? If teachers are considered ethical models, then what is the result of rewarding teachers and administrators who manipulate students and answer sheets to increase test scores? When is it ethical to devote large amounts of class time to teaching only the content covered by the test? In preparing preservice teachers to engage in ethical practice we must help them consider their conduct, "not simply with reference to the person who does it, but with reference to the whole living situation into which it enters" (Dewey, in Archambault, 1964, p. 110).

To that end, we must help preservice teachers prepare to negotiate the boundary between what the tests measure, and what the teacher knows to be learning. For example, preservice teachers will need to know how to rally school, district, and community resources to help students learn. This can include learning enough about the rules to appeal scores and knowing enough about test construction to identify and report bad and biased questions. Further, we must help preservice teachers recognize and resist cheating—plain and simple. We must help preservice teachers bring a new assertiveness to engaging all aspects of the school. The exemplar would be a preservice teacher who could identify malignant problems and plan constructive solutions.

## Political

It is insufficient to prepare teachers who only understand educational decision-making in the context of schools and school districts. Decisions that affect the education of the children in their charge are made in political contexts at the local, state, and national levels. It is important that preservice teachers learn to communicate with and work with individuals and groups at all political levels, articulating their knowledge and experiences. In essence, the pedagogically, statistically, and ethically astute preservice teacher (and inservice teacher, for that matter) must also be politically organized.

We must help preservice teachers leave behind the passive, co-dependent behavior that characterizes educators in warped high-stakes testing environments. For example, some educators have so accommodated themselves to the culture of high-stakes tests that they helped support systemic cheating. Instead of accommodation, we need to help preservice teachers better organize themselves to advise politicians and policymakers. We need to coach preservice teachers to be politically aware and involved, even if that means only writing a letter to an area representative. We must help preservice teachers find service opportunities on state-level committees that help design the tests and develop venues for all educators to advise education regulators on both the positive and toxic effects of the high-stakes tests.

In the last four weeks as we write this chapter, front-page Texas newspaper stories have screamed the following: 40,000 seniors blocked from graduating (TAKS Failure, 2007), soaring dropout rates continue (Story, 2007), and widespread cheating uncovered (Benton & Hacker, 2007). In the birthplace of NCLB and with daily news stories about the preceding issues, the Texas legislature voted to replace its one-shot high school exit exam with a system of end-of-course tests. The results of these tests will be combined with teacher course grades to determine whether a student has passed a course. Also, high-school graduation will be based on the combination of course credits earned and the number of subject matter tests passed over a four-year period, rather than performance on one examination. This appears to be a positive, but imperfect, first step, to be credited in large part to the perseverance of politically savvy teachers. Linda Darling-Hammond (2007) outlines the next steps in a paradigm shift from testing to investing. For example, she calls for a Marshall Plan that recruits many new teachers with service scholarships, strengthens TPPs by funding for many more professional development schools, and provides novice teachers with mentoring support for their early years of teaching.

## WHERE DO WE GO FROM HERE?

First, TPPs have been effectively neutralized because NCLB has placed them in competition with each other and with various other teacher-certifying entities. We need to rally the National Council for Accreditation of Teacher Education (NCATE) and other related organizations to prepare unified nonacademic responses, such as rallies and informational meetings. If we failed at anything prior to the advent of widespread high-stakes tests, we failed at telling our stories about education. Second, TPPs must join forces with other teaching entities to lobby statehouses and Congress for moderation of the draconian aspects of NCLB and to implement the paradigm shift recommended by Darling-Hammond (2007). Third, TPPs must be part of local efforts to ameliorate the effects of the testing culture. Fourth, TPPs must play an extended larger role in the national educational economy, now completely dominated by large textbook publishing companies.

## QUESTIONS TO PROMPT DISCUSSION

We offer these questions to help you think about the issues presented in this chapter.

1. How do TPPs balance the hegemony of accountability programs with their own autonomy?
2. How do TPPs create alternative accountability systems while helping stakeholders cope with current systems?
3. How can TPPs provide in-service instruction to help teachers meet test-based objectives without sacrificing real learning?
4. Are there theoretical models that may lead to better understanding of student and teacher behavior in high-stakes testing situations?

## REFERENCES

Amrein, A., & Berliner, B. (March 28, 2002). High-stakes testing, uncertainty, and student learning. *Education Policy Analysis Archives, 10*(18), 1–74. Retrieved October 10, 2006 from http://epaa.asu.edu/epaa/v10n18.

Archambault, R. (1964). *John Dewey on education: Selected writings.* Chicago: University of Chicago Press.

Benton, J., & Hacker, H. (June 3, 2007). Analysis shows TAKS cheating rampant. *Dallas Morning News*, p. 1A.

Berliner, D. C., & Biddle, B. J. (1997). *The manufactured crisis: Myths, fraud, and the attack on America's public schools.* Reading, MA: Addison-Wesley.

Burley, H., Bunter, B., Marbley, A., Bush, L., & Fleming, F. (2001). Standardized testing: For richer or poorer, for democracy or meritocracy? *Connections: Journal of Principal Development and Ppreparation, 3*, pp. 15–19.

Coleman, J. S. (1966). *Equality of educational opportunity (Coleman) study.* Washington, DC: US Department of Health, Education, and Welfare.

Darling-Hammond, L. (February, 16, 2003). Standards and Assessments: Where we are and what we need. *Teachers College Record.* Retrieved October 10, 2006 from http://www.forumforeducation.org/resources/index.php?page=28&item=151.

Darling-Hammond, L. (May 21, 2007). Evaluating No Child Left Behind. *The Nation.* Retrieved June 14, 2007 from http://www.thenation.com/doc/20070521/darling-hammond.

Dobbs, M. (Nov. 8, 2003). Education miracle has a math problem. *Washington Post*, p. 1.

Fisher, C. W., & Berliner, D. (Eds.). (1985). Perspectives on instructional time. New York: Longman.

Haney, W. (2000). The myth of the Texas miracle in education. *Education Policy Analysis Archives, 8*(41). Retrieved October 10, 2006 from http://epaa.asu.edu/epaa/v8n41/.

Madaus, G. F. (1988). The influence of testing on the curriculum. In *Critical Issues in Curriculum.* L. Tanner. (Ed.). 87th Yearbook of the National Society for the Study of Education, part 1, 83-121.

McNeil, L. M. (2000). *Contradictions of school reform: Educational costs of standardized testing.* New York: Routledge. Retrieved April 12, 2007, from Questia database: http://www.questia.com/PM.qst?a=o&d=103329920.

National Commission on Excellence in Education. (1983). *A nation at risk.* Retrieved October 11, 2006 from http://www.ed.gov/pubs/NatAtRisk/risk.html.

Pai, Y., & Adler, S. (2001). *Cultural foundations of education.* (3rd ed.). Upper Saddle River, NJ: Merrill/Prentice-Hall.

Ravitch, D. (Fall, 2002). A brief history of testing and accountability. *Hoover Digest*, 4. Retrieved October 10, 2006 from www.hooverdigest.org/024/ravitch.html.

Story, J. (March, 2007). *Defining and solving the Texas dropout crisis.* Austin, TX: Center for Education Policy.

TAKS failure blocks 40,000 seniors from graduating. (May 13, 2007). *Lubbock Avalanche Journal.* Retrieved July 16, 2007 from httpTPP://lubbockonline.com/

stories/051307/sta_051307121.shtml.

Warner, C. (February 3, 2003). Study links teachers, failing students: Give profes-
    sional tests more weight, it says. *The Times-Picayune*, p. 1.

West, M., & Peterson, P. (2003). The politics and practice of accountability. In P.
    Peterson & M. West, (Eds.). *No Child Left Behind?: The politics and practice of school
    accountability.* Washington, D.C.: Brookings Institution Press.

# Chapter 2

# PREPARING FUTURE TEACHERS FOR ONLINE DELIVERY MODELS: A NEW TEACHER EDUCATION?

Laurie Mullen and Roy Weaver

*In the professional preparation of teachers, the medium is the message.*
(Grossman, 2005, p. 425)

## INTRODUCTION

Marshall McLuhan's now oft-quoted phrase "the medium is the message" is found in a recent publication by the American Educational Research Association, *Studying Teacher Education* (Cochran-Smith & Zeichner, 2005) to exemplify that "how one teaches is part and parcel to what one teaches" (Loughran & Russell, 1997 cited in Grossman, 2005, p. 425). Grossman's chapter outlines various pedagogies used in teacher education and the effect of these approaches on what future teachers learn about teaching. The context for McLuhan's original usage for the phrase, however, was not for teacher education, but for understanding the effects of media on culture and society. According to McLuhan, "personal and social consequences of any medium—that is, of any extension of ourselves—result from the new scale that is introduced into our affairs by each extension of ourselves, or by any new technology" (McLuhan, 1964, p. 7).

In this chapter, we posit that the gestalt of social, educational, and economic roles of computer technologies in concert with today's

27

youth culture requires an earnest exploration on the future of new delivery models and curriculum emphases for teacher education. Education in the future will require teachers who are literate with rich pedagogical skills that incorporate and employ advanced technologies as both an aspect of curriculum and as a delivery vehicle. A major challenge for teacher education programs is to infuse technology in the context of teacher education curriculum in ways that ultimately transform teaching and learning (Cochran-Smith & Fries, 2005) and in which the computer is not just a tool but rather an extension of the environment in which preservice teachers live, work, think, and communicate. It is this extension of the environment that we address in this chapter. The imperative lies in the reality that the world that current and future students inhabit in relation to media and technology bears little resemblance to that of earlier generations.

> A new youth culture is emerging, one which involves much more than just the pop culture of music, MTV, and the movies. . . . But most importantly, it is a culture that is stemming from the N-Gen use of interactive digital media. We should pay attention because the culture [that] flows from their experiences in cyberspace foreshadow the culture they will create as the leaders of tomorrow in the workplace and society. (Tapscott, 1998, p. 55)

Driven by a proliferation of distance education and online delivery systems, the embrace of technology-driven delivery systems by teacher education is likely to produce profound educational reform (Beilke & Mullen, 2007). Given the fact that the United States Department of Education has estimated that the country will need an additional 2.5 million teachers by 2010, we may be at the cusp of dramatic change and growth in how we provide preparation for classroom teachers (Maddux, Sprague, Ferdig, & Albion, 2007). In this chapter, we pursue the following questions: *If the medium is the message, what does it mean to learn to teach in primarily online environments? How might the socialization of future teachers change in the context of web-based curriculum delivery and interaction?*

## TIMELINE

Distance education is an area of tremendous growth (McBride, McFerrin, Gillan, & Monroe, 2006). The evolution of distance education technologies contributes in part to this growth and diffusion (Appelberg, Bruillard, Downes, Katz, O'Brianin, Offir, Passey, & Passig, 2000). Appelberg and colleagues outline how the first generation of delivery systems included printed material, mail, and telephone while the second generation moved to audio recordings, radio, and television broadcasts. The third generation of delivery systems, which include web technologies, interactive environments, graphics, and communication systems, comes closer to real-time instruction. In higher education, the movement toward distance education models is already an accepted aspect of inservice teacher professional development, master's degrees, and some doctoral programs. In a recent survey of over 2,400 colleges and universities in the United States, the following information regarding online or distance education emerged:

- Sixty-three percent of schools offering undergraduate face-to-face courses also offer undergraduate courses online.
- Sixty-five percent of higher education institutions report that they are using primarily core faculty to teach their online courses compared to 62 percent that report they are using primarily core faculty to teach their face-to-face courses.
- The overall percentage of schools identifying online education as a critical long-term strategy grew from 49 percent in 2003 to 56 percent in 2005.
- Overall online enrollment increased from 1.98 million in 2003 to 2.35 million in 2004.
- In 2003, some 57 percent of academic leaders rated the learning outcomes in online education as the same or superior to those in face-to-face. That number is now 62 percent.
- The proportion that believe online learning outcomes are superior to those for face-to-face is still relatively small but has grown by 40 percent since 2003, from 12.1 percent in 2003 to 16.9 percent.
- Although online education continues to increase in all types of institutions, a relatively stable minority of Chief Academic Officers (28% in 2003 compared with 31% in 2005) continues to believe that their faculty fully accepts the value and legitimacy of online education (Sloan Foundation, 2006).

Growth in online programming is occurring in elementary and secondary schools as well. A report by the National Center for

Educational Statistics (NCES) shows increases in the availability of courses delivered by distance education for public schools in the United States. The report indicates that students in one-third of the nation's public school districts, approximately 328,000 enrollments, took courses via distance education technologies (NCES, 2005). The K-12 education landscape increasingly includes alternative delivery systems as an option for a wide range of students. As of July 2005, there were twenty-one states with statewide online learning programs, cyberschools, or district-level online programs (Watson, 2005). Political, economic, and social forces drive the increase in online opportunities for school-age children with programs experiencing a 50 to 100 percent increase per year. Setzer and Lewis (2005) provide a breakdown of 2002 to 2003 distance education enrollments per content area. The largest enrollments were in the social sciences (23%), English language arts (19%), and mathematics (15%). In terms of virtual schools, the Utah Electronic School boasts the largest enrollments at 35,000 with the Florida Virtual School at 21,000.

The North American Council for Online Learning (NACOL) recently published a comprehensive overview of online learning titled "A National Primer on K-12 Online Learning." The report outlines the multiple ways that online learning is being used. Examples that suggest the range of possibilities include:

- Expanding the range of courses available to students, especially in small, rural, or inner-city schools, beyond what a single school can offer;
- Providing highly qualified teachers in subjects where qualified teachers are lacking;
- Providing scheduling flexibility to students facing scheduling conflicts;
- Affording opportunities to at-risk students, elite athletes and performers, dropouts, migrant youth, pregnant or incarcerated students, and students who are homebound due to illness or injury; allowing them to continue their studies outside the classroom;
- Addressing the needs of the millennial student;
- Increasing the teaching of technology skills by embedding technology literacy in academic content; and
- Providing professional development opportunities for teachers,

including mentoring and learning communities (NACOL, 2007, p. 5).

## A NEW TEACHER EDUCATION?

Over thirty-five years ago, Smith (1971) framed the issue of under-standing the process of deciding the components of an effective teacher education curriculum as logically determined by the nature of the teaching tasks for which they are being prepared. The nature of the contemporary teaching task is shaped by the startling growth of digital media, computer technologies, and distance education delivery systems, accompanied by society's expectations of these technologies as an important role for both a goal and a support for curriculum (Darling-Hammond et al., 2005). A conceptualization of teaching, conscious or unconscious, explicit or implicit, is basic to the development of a design for a program of teacher education and is shaped by social, cultural, and political milieu of the times. However, an effective teacher education curriculum is more than a collection of courses. In a chapter on the design of coherent and effective teacher education programs, Ken Howey (1996) reminds us that the challenge in designing more potent programs is to focus on how the curriculum is "experienced by prospective teachers in pedagogically powerful ways" (p. 145).

However, what constitutes a teacher education curriculum when coursework migrates from an institution-bound location to an online experience? Our goal is to problematize this term by presenting various conceptions and purposes in hopes of demonstrating the issues involved. These complexities may unveil more substantial tensions than what are part of current public discourse regarding teacher education and online delivery. Teacher education, while commonly heard and used, can assume very different meanings and interpretations. Specific conceptions of what teacher education should do is reflected in teacher education curricula with these dominant conceptions having the force of paradigms, by defining for specific groups the core meaning of the enterprise itself (Zeichner, 1983). Knowledge and progress in one paradigm can be viewed as superstition and as retrogression in another (p. 5).

The following orientations for teacher education emerged from the extant literature on traditional institution-bound programs. Though not a comprehensive overview of all such orientations, we present them for discussion regarding the manner in which online environments should consider theoretical or conceptual orientation as a key feature of program design. According to Doyle (1990), "teacher education consists of a loosely coordinated set of experiences designed to establish and maintain a talented teaching force for our nation's elementary and secondary schools" (p. 3). Doyle identifies five major paradigms or themes underlying proposals for teacher education programs. They are (a) the good employee, (b) the junior professor, (c) the fully functioning person, (d) the innovator, and (e) the reflective professional. Feiman-Nemser (1990) describes teacher education programs in terms of their conceptual orientations. These conceptual orientations include "a view of teaching and learning and a theory about learning to teach. Such ideas should give direction to the practical activities of teacher preparation such as program planning, course development, instruction, supervision, and evaluation" (p. 220).

Accordingly, teacher education programs can be labeled as academic, practical, technological, personal, or critical. Giroux and McClaren (1987) argue that "most schools and colleges in North America [serve as] institutions providing students with 'requisite technical expertise' in pedagogical functions as deemed necessary by the school communities" (p. 269). This framework, referred to as technical rationality, holds that teacher education is fundamentally a process of training candidates "to conform to acceptable patterns" of teaching behavior. Technocratic rationality in teacher education programs is manifested as competency-based teacher education, competency testing of teachers, apprenticeship-based clinical teacher education, and behaviorist psychologies. In these programs teaching is separated from its ethical, political, and moral roots. Preservice teachers view practices they observe as what is possible and are accepted as natural and right. As a result, becoming a teacher becomes a problem of mastering the particular body of skills distributed in teacher education.

The assumption that appropriate conceptual orientations to professional education automatically transfer to online environments without careful consideration of instructional design and theoretical intent is the concern. As increasing numbers of traditional universities and the new for-profit universities move to online delivery formats for larger portions of certification programs for initial licensure in teacher education curriculum, we cannot assume that this happens in a pedagogical vacuum. A brief description of some prominent online universities and programs for initial teacher education in the United States provides a context for discussion. Following are some of the few available online programs for initial licensure.

- At Drexel University, the School of Education provides an online Bachelor of Science program approved by the Pennsylvania Department of Education (Drexel e-learning, 2007). The K-6 certification program requires 130 hours of in-school pre-student teaching experience and twelve weeks of student teaching leading to certification in elementary education. The two-and-a-half-year program is organized so students interact with the curriculum materials on their own or in discussion groups. In addition, two post-baccalaureate programs for initial certification are available online. Intended for students who already have a Bachelor's degree, these programs result in either initial licensing only or a Master's degree and licensure. As with most teaching certificates, graduates from these programs can use interstate reciprocity agreements to teach in other states.
- Western Oregon University offers a hybrid delivery model for a Master's of Teaching degree for initial licensure in select secondary programs. Students come to campus one Saturday per month on average.
- The Pennsylvania Department of Education granted authority to award specialized associate degrees to Penn Foster Career School, a distance education provider (Penn Foster, Inc., 2007). Students can earn an Associate in Specialized Business (ASB) Degree in Early Childhood Education and work as classroom aides. The program runs for four semesters and is formatted as independent study using online and print materials.
- Western Governors University (WGU) was created from a $10 million grant from the United States Department of Education. The WGU Teachers College offers a Bachelor of Arts in Mathematics and Science for grades five through nine or five through twelve and is the only online institution to be awarded accreditation by the National Council for the Accreditation of Teacher Education (NCATE). According to its materials, Teachers College at Western Governors was "established to create a

learning environment that fosters exploration, dissemination of knowledge and skills, and the highest level of competence for all students through its commitment to lifelong learning, equitable access, and dynamic mentoring" (Western Governors University, 2005). WGU recently was awarded a three million dollar grant to develop a new model for web-based teacher education that can be implemented on a national scale (*eSchool News*, 2007).

- The University of Phoenix is an exclusively online institution of higher education accredited by The Higher Learning Commission (HLC) and a member of the North Central Association (NCA). According to its website, The University of Phoenix is the nation's largest accredited university, boasting of over 17,000 highly qualified instructors, 170 campuses, and Internet delivery worldwide. Phoenix is expected to graduate its largest class ever in 2008. Its founder, John G. Sperling, has said he wants it to enroll 500,000 students by 2010. Initial licensure in teacher education is available. Everything can now be delivered to students entirely online, including reading materials and some 600 e-books that have been written solely for the university.

Internationally, countries utilize a range of distance education models. In a report sanctioned by the United Nations Educational, Scientific, and Cultural Organization (UNESCO), case studies of nine countries describe the need for qualified teachers and how distance education helps fill that need (UNESCO, 2001).

## BARRIERS FOR IMPLEMENTATION

Both policy and implementation issues exist that currently serve as barriers to online delivery models for teacher education. Some state education agencies, colleges, and universities may present barriers to providers who wish to offer degree programs and licenses through alternative delivery models. As a result, such providers may not be recognized by state agencies for offering such programs. In other instances, while commercial providers may be accredited, students are required to attend to additional procedures, such as a transcript audit, to be licensed. Such an audit may result in additional coursework for students. Colleges and universities may not accept course credits from commercial providers; hence, students may not be able to transfer their work for licensure or degree programs at traditional colleges and universities. Coursework may not be viewed as comparable in quality. Whether accurate or not, this perception of coursework delivered through alternative models may influence decisions about awarding credit for transfer purposes. School districts that use course credits as a basis for salary increases, in some instances, may choose to not recognize courses from some providers that use alternative delivery models.

The financial impact of increasing numbers of providers of alternative delivery models will force colleges and universities to be more competitive in terms of their services. Traditional institutions will reorganize how they register, enroll, and make materials available to be more efficient and easy. Delivery models will emphasize access and flexibility in regard to when, how, and where courses are delivered and when and how student performance is captured and assessed.

## IMPLICATIONS FOR TEACHER EDUCATION

Teacher education has always been conceptualized and shaped by the political and professional contexts of the time (Darling-Hammond et al., 2005). Consider the following realities: (a) the United States Department of Education has estimated that the country will need an additional 2.5 million teachers by 2010; (b) the existing milieu of improving interactive environments for content delivery; (c) generations of learners who are comfortable with learning in online environments; and (d) stiff competition for institutions of higher education for student enrollments. The intersection and convergence of such realities charts a path for a distinct change in preparing future educators. Teacher educators should not assume that these changes are neutral. It is quite possible that initial online preparation of educators yields positive outcomes. However, if as Grossman (2005) suggests that in the professional preparation of teachers, the medium is the message, the field needs research for better understanding of this phenomenon. Pedagogy must be concerned with what is taught, how it is taught and how it is learned, and more broadly with the nature of knowledge and learning. An understanding of online pedagogy is needed that recognizes knowledge is produced, negotiated, transformed, and realized in the *interaction* between the teacher, the learner, the context, and the knowledge itself.

Certain licensure areas may prove beneficial to online programming due to hiring demands. Benavides and Midobuche (2004) outline the role of online technologies via student perceptions for those seeking certification in English as a second language. Other high-need areas such as special education, math, and science hold promise for access to potential candidates who currently do not have access to teacher certification programs.

Other potential implications include an increase of political pressure on state agencies and legislators in states where perceived obstacles are placed in the way of accepting alternative delivery models. School districts as well will be challenged when they do not accept course credits and licensure and degree programs for salary increases. More and more colleges and universities that choose not to move to alternative delivery models will be faced with declining enrollments and subsequent decreases in funding. Inevitably, some programs could be eliminated as a result of the inability to be competitive.

For future teachers to engage in a competitive, technologically rich environment, the content of teacher preparation programs will need to include formal coursework on instructional practices in online environments (Thompson, 2003). An understanding of how students, born into such an environment and who use technologies with ease as a natural part of their daily lives, will be key. Creating and delivering curricula that is simply an extension of how these students live their lives will capture their imagination and enhance the potential for learning. Knowing how to enable students to take responsibility for their learning in a less controlled, collaborative, and creative online environment will be necessary. The ability to readily assess students' performance and respond quickly to their learning needs will be as critical.

## WHERE DO WE GO FROM HERE?

The rapid growth in distance learning and online education, proliferation of programs, and competition for students demands several important decisions.

- Professional organizations and educational associations must examine and shape policy issues aimed at allowing open exploration of online approaches, while protecting the quality of instruction for learners and make it a high and urgent priority.
- A sound, theory- and research-based conceptual orientation must serve as a framework for student experiences in online environment design.
- Recognition of and respect for student learning that occurs unconventionally through various technologies must be accorded, prized, and encouraged.
- Models and ideas for online delivery must be disseminated openly and broadly to encourage an evolving constructive criticism and debate about most effective strategies.
- Successful innovative programs that result in exemplary performance must be studied, recognized, and replicated.

## QUESTIONS TO PROMPT DISCUSSION

We offer these questions to help you think about the issues presented in this chapter.

1. How will the socialization process of preservice teachers change as the medium of delivery changes?
2. What will be the effects of certification and licensure experiences in an online environment on teacher quality?
3. What online interactions best serve the development of quality teacher preparation?
4. Given current technologies for course delivery, what new forms of content production and delivery are needed?
5. What is the role of commercial vendors in teacher education?

## REFERENCES

Appelberg, L., Bruillard, E., Downes, T., Katz, Y., O'Brianin, T., Offir, B., Passey, D., & Passig, D. (2000). *Teacher education for distance learning.* Presentation to the Information and Communications Technologies and Sciences. Conference Proceedings 276–282. Retrieved on October 14, 2006 from http://www.ifip.org/con2000/iceut2000/iceut09-03.pdf

Beilke, J. R., & Mullen, L. (2007). Problematizing pedagogy in the new scene of teaching. In *At the interface/probing the boundaries.* David Seth Preston. (Ed.). Amsterdam, The Netherlands/New York: Rodopi Press.

Benavides, A., & Midobuche, E. (2004). Online preservice teacher education programs: Issues in the preparation of bilingual education and ESL teachers. *National Association for Bilingual Education Journal of Research and Practice, 2*(1), 45–55.

Cochran-Smith, M., & Fries, K. (2005). Researching teacher education in changing times: Politics and Paradigms. In M. Cochran-Smith & K. Zeichner (Eds.), *Studying teacher education: The report of the AERA panel on research and teacher education* (pp. 69–110). Mahwah, NJ: Erlbaum.

Darling-Hammond, L., Banks, J., Zumwalt, K., Gomez, L., Gamoran Sherin, M., Griesdorn, J., & Finn, L. W. (2005). Educational goals and purposes: Developing a curricular vision for teaching. In L. Darling-Hammond & J. Bransford, (Eds.), *Preparing teachers for a changing world: What teachers should learn and be able to do.* (pp. 169–200). San Francisco, CA: Jossey-Bass.

Doyle, W. (1990). Themes in teacher education research. In W. R. Houston (Ed.), *Handbook of research on teacher education,* (pp. 3–23). New York: Macmillan Publishers.

Drexel e-learning. (2007). *Bachelor of Science in education.* Retrieved June 1, 2007 from http://www.drexel.com/online-degrees/education-degrees/bs-ed/index.aspx

*eSchool News.* (2007). $3 million grant to aid online teacher education. *eSchool News.* April.

Feiman-Nemser, S. (1990). Teacher preparation: Structural and conceptual alternatives. In W. R. Houston, M. Huberman, & J. Sikula (Eds.), *Handbook of research in teacher education,* (pp. 212–233). New York: Macmillan Publishers.

Giroux, H., & McClaren, P. (1987). Teacher education as a counter public sphere: Notes toward a redefinition. In T. Popkewitz (Ed.), *Critical studies in teacher education,* (pp. 266–297). Philadelphia: Falmer Press.

Grossman, P. (2005). Research on pedagogical approaches in teacher education. In M. Cochran-Smith & K. Zeichner (Eds.), *Studying teacher education: The report of the AERA panel on research and teacher education* (pp. 425–476). Mahwah, NJ: Erlbaum.

Howey, K. (1996). Designing coherent and effective teacher education programs. In J. Sikula. (Ed.). *Handbook of research in teacher education,* (pp. 143–170). Macmillan: New York.

Maddux, C., Sprague, D., Ferdig, R., & Albion, P. (2007). Editorial: Online education, issues and research questions. *Journal of Technology and Teacher Education. 15*(2), pp. 157–166.

McBride, R., McFerrin, K., Gillan, R., & Monroe, M. (2006). Back to the future: A review of current trends, best practices and future applications in distance education. In C. Crawford et al. (Eds.), *Proceedings of society for information technology and teacher education international conference 2006* (pp. 431–437). Chesapeake, VA: AACE.

McLuhan, M. (1964). Understanding media: The extensions of man. New York: McGraw Hill.

National Center for Educational Statistics. (2005). *Distance education courses for public elementary and secondary school students: 2002–2003.* United States Department of Education. NCES 2005-010.

North American Council for Online Learning. (2007). *A national primer on K-12 online learning.* Evergreen, CO: Evergreen Consulting Associates.

Penn Foster, Inc. (2007). *Early childhood education: Associate degree.* Retrieved on June 28, 2007 from http://www.pennfostercollege.edu/earlychilded/ProgramOutline.html.

Setzer, J. C., & Lewis, L. (2005). *Distance education courses for public elementary and secondary school students: 2002–05* (NCES 2005-010). Washington, DC: National Center for Education Statistics. Retrieved on October 4, 2005 from http://nces.ed.gov/pubs2005/2005010.pdf

Sloan Foundation, A. P. (2006). Growing by degrees: Online education in the United States. Retrieved on June 3, 2007 from http://www.sloan-c.org/publications/survey/index.asp.

Smith, B. O. (Ed.) (1971). *Research in teacher education: A symposium.* Englewood cliffs, New Jersey: Prentice-Hall, Inc.

Tapscott, D. (1998). *Growing up digital: The rise of the net generation.* New York: McGraw-Hill.

Thompson, A. (2003). Distance teaching experience: Requirement for teacher education students? *Journal of Computing in Teacher Education, 19*(3), pp. 98–112.

United Nations Educational, Scientific, and Cultural Organization. (2001). *Teacher education through distance learning.* Report to the Higher Education Division, Teacher Education Section. Paris, France.

University of Phoenix Online. *The University of Phoenix Online: About us.* Retrieved on October 11, 2006 from http://www.uopxonline.com/aboutus.asp

Watson, J. (2005). *Keeping pace with K-12 online learning: A review of state-level policy and practices.* Learning Point Associates: North Central Regional Educational Laboratory: Naperville, IL.

Western Governors University. (2005). Becoming a licensed teacher through the Teachers College at WGU. Retrieved June 30, 2007 from http://www.wgu.edu/education/teaching_license.asp.

Zeichner, K. (1983). Alternative paradigms of teacher education. *Journal of Teacher Education, 34*, 3–9.

# Chapter 3

# TEACHER EDUCATION ISSUES WORLDWIDE

Carol Merz Frankel

*To improve teacher education is to improve teaching; to improve teaching is to improve the schools; to improve the schools is to strengthen the next generation; to strengthen the next generation is a social duty of the first magnitude.*
(Commission on Teacher Education, 1944, p. 24)

## INTRODUCTION

Schools are one of the primary tools societies have used to improve their way of life. Deciding what the members of a society should know has been and continues to be a major curriculum question, but it leads quickly to the questions of who can teach this body of knowledge and how it should it be taught. These questions are as relevant today in the most technologically sophisticated countries as they are in countries struggling to develop agricultural techniques to ensure a basic food supply.

This volume has chosen to look at the issues in teacher education historically. Doing so gives us an opportunity to compare the development of education in societies throughout the world. In our timeline we will look at these steps as they occurred in the major twentieth-century post-industrial societies of Western Europe and North America. We can then apply our observations to the world of the twenty-first century in which we find societies at various stages of development facing a complicated mix of issues.

The development of teacher education, like education in general, often relates to a country's economic and social development, following a fairly predictable pattern as society changes over time. Challenges in teacher education around the world generally fall into four categories: (1) ensuring the availability of teachers; (2) maintaining high standards in the teaching force; (3) ensuring that teachers have the skills and dispositions to teach children with a variety of needs, including children from various ethnic or cultural groups; (4) ensuring that teachers have the skills and dispositions to teach a changing curriculum. Agrarian, industrial, and post-industrial societies face certain problems that occur in a historical sequence, but the picture can become complicated as countries include groups at various stages of development. For example, today in India and the People's Republic of China, groups strive to achieve a basic elementary education for each child, as other groups seek education that will ensure its members success in the international economic and technological marketplace (Gutek, 2006; Waldman, 2005). Another variation can occur in former colonies as the development of an educational system becomes a means of repudiating a colonial past (e.g., Erickson, 2002).

Increases in availability and quality of education in a country can cause problems of its own: If the country succeeds in increasing raising the level of social and economic development, curriculum must change to meet the demands of new jobs in new industries. As various ethnic groups are brought into the educational system, the country faces the issue of recognition of indigenous and minority languages and social customs (e.g., Morales & Caballero, 2002). This challenge is most visible in developing countries but exists in some form in all education systems. Schools must change their curriculum to serve new populations, and teachers must be able to teach students whose culture is unfamiliar to them.

## HISTORICAL TIMELINE

*Agrarian Societies*: Education for the Elite, Basic Skills for Others (for example, the United States and Western Europe before the nineteenth century):

- Education is tied to religious and social class structure. Teachers are selected for their religious position or affiliation with a prestigious institution.

- Teachers in rural settings usually teach only to a level considered appropriate for their pupils. There are no competency measures or certifications.

*Industrial Urban Societies*: Systems and Standards (for example, Western Europe from the nineteenth to the mid-twentieth century):

- Urban school systems develop to accommodate large numbers of immigrants.
- Education focuses on preparation for vocations.
- States gradually assume responsibility for educational systems and teacher preparation. States begin to issue teaching certificates to ensure appropriate teacher preparation.

*Post-industrial Societies*: Changing Curriculum, Competition, and New Students (for example, the United States and Western Europe in the mid-twentieth century and today):

- Widespread education of women becomes a standard, and women enter the work force in increasing numbers.
- Minority groups, including recent immigrants, demand access to education.
- Worldwide economic competition increases as scientific advances, global trade, and off-shore jobs change economic and social patterns.
- Nations compare educational achievement through international tests as a means of assessing their ability to compete economically.

## TEACHER EDUCATION IN RELATION TO ECONOMIC AND SOCIAL DEVELOPMENT

In this chapter we will look in turn at the four issues in teacher education in societies at varying stages of economic development. We will look briefly at their history in the United States and Western Europe, but we will concentrate on societies currently experiencing these challenges.

## Agrarian Societies and the Developing World

In agrarian societies, formal education tends to be limited to the upper classes and is often provided by religious institutions, rather than the state. This was true in the United States, much of Western Europe, and parts of Asia (e.g., Japan) prior to urbanization and industrialization. Education for the non-elite usually offered only enough reading and arithmetic to allow children to read scriptures and calculate as needed for farming and simple commerce. Under these circumstances of low demand for education, a small cadre of teachers served the population adequately. They tended to be trained by religious institutions or existing academic institutions. Teachers in the non-elite schools usually had no specific pedagogical preparation and were simply required to have the skills to which their students aspired. This is still true today in areas of Africa, the Middle East, and parts of Asia. For example, in Afghanistan, only 80 percent of the current teaching force of 135,000 teachers has completed secondary school to grade 12 (Islamic Republic of Afghanistan, Ministry of Education, 2006.)

Traditionally in agrarian societies, attending school has been difficult for non-elite families. It can mean that children must travel far from home and pay fees for tuition, uniforms, and books. Families frequently cannot afford these costs; but more importantly, they often cannot do without the labor of the children. Families who cannot educate all their children will often choose to educate their sons, whom they see as more likely to get jobs as a result of their education. Girls often stay home to care for younger children and to do household chores. As a consequence, the literacy rate is often usually lower among women than men in developing countries.

The goals of a free elementary education for all children and gender equity in education have become important goals today in developing countries. These goals were originally established by The World Bank, one of the major vehicles for providing aid to developing countries (Education for All, 2006). The World Bank originally set these goals to be met by 2015. They coincided with existing efforts in developing countries, especially in Africa where several countries were already attempting to drop school fees and encourage girls to attend school (Samoff, 1999). As a result demand for education has increased to a level that is hard for developing countries to meet, as will be seen in the upcoming example of Kenya.

Even in China, India, and Mexico, where there are thriving economies with technology and manufacturing, rural areas have many of the problems of less-developed agrarian societies (Gutek, 2006; Waldman, 2005). Birthrates remain high, and providing education to great numbers of children is a challenge to these countries. For example, 31 percent of the Mexican population is under age 15. In India, 36 percent of the population is under 15 (Population Under Age 15, 2005). If languages other than the official national language are spoken in rural areas, instruction at least in the early years is often in two languages.

Providing teachers in developing countries will be one of the major challenges in achieving The World Bank's goal of universal, free primary education by 2015. It is often difficult to find teachers who are willing to teach in remote areas. It is even more difficult to find teachers who speak local languages as well as the official language. Even if enough teachers of appropriate skills were to be found, developing countries often do not have the financial resources to pay the teachers (Dugger, 2004; Samoff, 1999). Classes can be very large, and countries are caught between providing enough teachers and maintaining standards for teachers. Standards are often fragile as young governments struggle to assume the responsibility that was previously carried out by religious institutions or colonial powers.

Nigeria is an example of a country struggling with education in this context. As a former British colony, Nigeria's early education history is one of Christian missionary schools in the south and Koranic schools in the Islamic north. In the late nineteenth century, the British began establishing state-supported schools. For the first half of the twentieth century, Nigeria had an education system based on the British model. With independence, Nigeria's first educational priority was to rid the educational system of the colonial influence. In a new nation of 250 ethnic groups and languages, however, the system became chaotic (Gutek, 2006).

As in other developing countries, the population of Nigeria is young; 43 percent of the population is 14 years old or younger. Today, 32 percent of the population is illiterate, and including 60 percent of women. As in India, English was the official language that linked the many ethnic groups and gave one status and economic success. At independence, languages of the major tribes—Hausa, Fulani, Yoruba, and Igbo—were declared to be the national languages of Nigeria. These languages are not only regional but represent strong and competing cultural identities. Today, strong religious differences, as well as language and cultural differences, continue to exist between regions (Gutek, 2006).

In Nigeria today, 98 percent of children of primary school age are reported to be enrolled in school. The actual number of children attending is probably much lower, especially in rural areas and among girls (Gutek, 2002). The vernacular language of the area is used for the first three primary years, although children are expected to learn Hausa, Igbo, Fulani, or Yoruba. English is used for the last three years of primary school, but many children will have dropped out by the time English is taught. It is difficult to find teachers with appropriate pedagogical preparation and linguistic ability. Many rural schools have teachers with only primary education themselves. In the Koranic schools prevalent in the Muslim north, memorization of the *Koran* and reading Arabic is emphasized. Teachers are selected for their knowledge of the *Koran* and often have no pedagogical preparation.

Acquired immune deficiency syndrome (AIDS) has become an educational issue in Africa. Children fail to attend school because of their own illness and many have to leave school to care for sick family members. Orphaned children must frequently leave school to work. Teachers themselves have been hit hard by AIDS. In 2002, The World Bank reported that AIDS was killing teachers faster than the nations of southern Africa could train new teachers (Schemo, 2002).

The most pressing issue in teacher education for these developing countries is simply finding enough teachers. In Kenya, where the abolishment of school fees caused class sizes to swell a single teacher often teaches a classroom of 125 primary pupils in the morning and another 125 pupils in the afternoon (Dugger, 2004). Teachers who have education themselves often may not want to return to the villages where they are needed, nor can teachers easily shift around from region to region because of the language policies requiring primary instruction in the local language.

In their attempt to build a well-prepared teaching force, developing countries are sometimes able to send teachers and teacher educators to model countries. Several African countries have sent teachers to Japan's Naruto University at the invitation of the Japan International Cooperative Agency (Y. Ono, personal communication October 5, 2006).

## Industrial Urban Societies

Urbanization and industrialization usually lead to the establishment of a school system in which children are grouped for instruction in an organized way. Instruction becomes standardized, with uniform curriculum goals and a standard course of preparation of teachers. By recalling the development of education during industrialization and urbanization in the contexts with which we are most familiar, namely the United States and England, we can understand the challenge to countries that are in the midst of industrialization today.

As countries move to a manufacturing economy, vast numbers of rural dwellers move to the cities. Dickens wrote vividly about the social problems of London when numbers of people moved to the cities for work, living in dense slum dwellings and taxing the social and health service systems. Urban poor children received lessons as well as food and clothing at charity schools where teachers were much the same as those who taught in small rural schools—no formal training and skills only at the level to which their pupils aspired. It was not until the late nineteenth century that the government began to take over the responsibility for universal education in England.

In the United States, the schools had been established and controlled by the community since colonial times. Nevertheless, urban schools were severely stretched as waves of immigrants came to the cities in the late nineteenth and early twentieth centuries. A first wave of immigrants was from eastern and southern Europe, bringing their many languages. This wave was followed by another of American rural poor from the South.

Teachers were not prepared to deal with the task of educating the children who filled their classrooms, and schools underwent a painful process as they developed systems to meet the challenges they faced. As students began to be sorted in classes by age in buildings later to be known as "egg-crate schools," systems were developed to regularize education; these included organized supervision, standard textbooks, and teacher training. Schools developed a system of testing whereby students could be identified and grouped for more efficient education. (For a thorough history of this era, see Tyack, *The One Best System*, 1974.)

As another way of regularizing instruction, teacher education institutions came into existence in the late nineteenth century; and systems of teacher certification followed. Few questioned the purposes or methods of the schools, which were the structures for introducing children to a new society. At this stage of urbanization and industrialization, our second challenge of establishing standards for teachers compounded our first challenge of finding enough teachers.

Today, cities around the world are experiencing a huge influx of people from rural areas. This influx stretches the established school systems just as in the cities that first underwent industrialization. In Mexico and China, for example, economic success has raised expectations even among the rural poor. In both these countries, solid systems of education take children from preschool to higher education. Each country has teacher preparation programs, examinations, and certification to ensure teacher quality. However, neither country can provide the same quality of education in rural areas as they do in urban areas, nor can they provide education to the number that floods into the cities (Erickson, 2002). Many of those coming to the city have little education and often speak a language other than the official one. In Mexico, as an example, about half the population lives in the capital city, with thousands more arriving each day. The middle-class city is surrounded by dusty slums with poor roads and little water or sanitation.

In the second half of the twentieth century, Mexico developed a large manufacturing industry and trade with the United States that created many jobs. Although Mexico has traditionally had an agricultural economy, only 20 percent of the population is now en-gaged in farming. Many of these farms are still small, with fields plowed by donkeys or horses. Today, 55 percent of Mexicans are *mestizos* (mixed Indian and European), 15 percent are of European heritage only, and 29 percent are Indian (Gutek, 2006). The Indian population lives largely in the southern unindustrialized areas of Mexico and many speak an Indian language such as Zapotec, Mixtec, or Nahua. Some speak no Spanish.

Mexico, like many countries industrializing today, faces entirely different expectations than those of the first countries to industrialize. Whereas the United States formed an efficient system of schools to teach acculturate immigrants to America, in Mexico colonialism left strong class divisions still evident in expectations today. In the 1970s a growing middle class came to expect wide-spread access to higher education; and by 1986 higher education was taking 32 percent of the education budget, compared to 27 percent for primary education (Gutek, 2006). To many Mexicans, especially those of Indian heritage, this disproportion echoes the colonial system, in which Mexicans of European heritage got the larger part of the resources. Officially, 98 percent of the primary-age children are enrolled in school; but drop-out rates are high. A system of normal schools provides three or four years of post-secondary education for primary teachers and four or five years for secondary teachers. Despite a well-organized education-al system, there are vast differences between rural and urban schools; and the schools are severely challenged to provide education for the growing population. Indigenous groups, particularly in the south, pres-sure schools to recognize their cultures and languages. They want to participate in determining curriculum and instruction. They expect the teaching force to represent their culture and be able to instruct in their language (Morales & Caballero, 2002). A teachers' strike in Oaxaca, based on issues of indigenous representation, played a big role on the national presidential election of 2006; and in the unrest that followed (McKinley, 2006).

Rising expectations affect all segments of society in these countries today where they create three of our original four challenges. Not only are these countries challenged to provide enough teachers who meet national standards of teacher preparation, school systems are expect-ed to mirror the population of the country, and not reflect a colonial hegemony. As industrializing countries become wealthier and experi-ence increases expectations, it becomes an even greater challenge to ensure that all segments of their population benefit from education and participate in the increasing wealth.

## Post-Industrial Society

As national boundaries become more permeable and goods and ser-vices are traded worldwide, educational systems experience our fourth challenges related to the rate of change in the society they serve. We will look at four aspects of this change. First, as societies move from manufacturing to service economies, jobs for which they have previ-ously prepared students are no longer available. Students need a whole battery of new skills to be prepared for employment, and the curriculum must be changed to provide this. Second, international economic competition leads to comparison of schools among nations as a means of becoming more competitive; standards may need to be raised. Third, many post-industrial societies experience an influx of foreign immigrants seeking greater economic opportunities, so schools are challenged to teach children of other languages and cultures. Fourth, as widespread education becomes the societal norm necessary for economic well-being, all segments of society demand schools that are equally available and effective for all children, including second and third generations of immigrant families.

## New Curricula

The idea of education as an accumulation of facts was been criticized by Dickens in *Hard Times* (1854/1989) during industrialization and urbanization. However, even today the greatest difference between a post-industrial society's schooling and an industrial country's schooling is the goal of teaching cognitive skills rather than teaching facts.

Late in the twentieth century, the United States realized that its educational system had been designed for an industrialized age. Even though it was not totally fact-based, it was no longer adequate for students who would live most of their lives in the twenty-first century. Factory jobs were moved overseas to less-developed countries where wages were lower, and many of the service jobs remaining required new technologies. Computers took on a new role in education. At first, teachers struggled as they acquired computer skills. The focus of computer use in schools has now changed to fairly sophisticated applications as students come to school with more computer experience than in previous years. There remains a division of computer experience along lines of family affluence, but even this seems to disappear as low-cost computer games and music devices become available.

Computers themselves have changed education, just as they have made definitive changes in post-industrial societies. Calculations and information retrieval are now carried out at rates unthinkable a generation ago. The cognitive skills that are the goals of education are ones of managing and evaluating large amounts of data and information. Post-industrial societies debate the changes necessary for the new curricula. Witness the hot debate in the United States on math curricula and the balance between operations and problem solving. The challenge for teacher education in a post-industrial world is to prepare teachers to teach a curriculum that responds quickly enough to changing technologies, recognizing that these teachers and their students will have to continually learn new skills throughout their professional lives.

### International Comparisons

As countries compete in a global economy, they begin to compare education systems. One of the first international comparisons occurred when the United States found it lagged the Soviet Union in the "space race" after the successful launch of Sputnik in 1957. This event led to curricular reform and increased emphasis on science and mathematics instruction in the United States.

More recently, international comparisons, such as the Trends in Math and Science Study (TIMSS) and the Program for International Student Assessment (PISA), have revealed dramatic differences in instruction in various countries (National Center for Educational Statistics, 2007). These studies show differences among countries at various stages of economic development but are perhaps most revealing among nations at similar stages of development. Comparisons have spawned a considerable body of literature comparing schooling in the United States and Japan (e.g., *The Learning Gap* by Stevenson & Stigler, 1992). A range of differences became apparent. Compared to the United States, the scope and sequence of instruction are more focused in Japan; Japanese students spend more time in school and studying in "cram schools."

One of the most interesting comparative studies is the TIMSS video study analyzing teaching in Japan, Germany, and the United States (International Comparisons in Education, 2006). Teaching is clearly a part of the larger culture and is both the cause and the effect of cultural differences. Once teacher educators understood the differences in teaching methods in various countries, they began to import various techniques to improve instruction. In the United States, for example, teachers attempted Japanese-style "lesson study" in which teachers plan, teach, and refine a lesson as a group. These attempts have met with varying degrees of success, but they have given educators a new set of eyes through which to look at their teaching. Teacher educators have also seen different models of preparing teachers. For example, teachers in Japan have a relatively short period of student teaching (only a few weeks) followed by a long and supportive induction period. In the United States, teachers have a longer period of student teaching, but then assume the same duties as veteran teachers once they are hired.

The international comparisons have raised the importance of testing in all aspects of U.S. education. Despite our shock at the pressure Asian students experience from examinations, we have added a number of examinations for both our students and our teachers and have increased the importance of these tests. The results of this reform are not yet clear, nor have we dealt with the issue of how these tests may affect various segments of the teaching force.

### International Immigration

International immigration becomes an increasingly important issue for post-industrial schools. Not only do vast numbers of immigrants cross international boundaries seeking jobs, but declining birthrates in post-industrial countries means that these countries become more dependent on the labor of immigrants, both legal and illegal. This issue alone has one of the most important impacts on teacher education. As birthrates decline, school enrollment drops. Today in Japan, a country with low birthrate and a low number of immigrants, schools are consolidating and closing (Kadoya, 2004). There are more teachers than teaching jobs available. This has not been the case in the United States nor in Western Europe, where the student population has been maintained by immigration. However, in these countries teachers are facing classrooms of diversity not experienced since the large waves of migration accompanying industrialization. In many European countries, former colonial subjects flood the cities where historical ties of language and quasi-citizenship give them a variation of homeland status. Schools designed as tools of nation-building and socialization to cultural norms are challenged to accommodate immigrant cultures (Gutek, 2006).

Many of the immigrants in the United States are Latino, and mastery of Spanish is becoming an increasingly important language skill for teachers. United States school systems even recruit teachers from Mexico in an attempt to serve Spanish-speaking students (High-Grade Recruits, 2007). Because Mexican schools find it difficult to compete with the higher salaries offered in the United States, it is difficult for the country to build a teaching force to meet its needs. Nevertheless, providing appropriate education for immigrants from Latin America remains a challenge for U.S. schools. The United States also receives numbers of immigrants from Russia and various Asian countries, as well as other Central and South American groups who come directly or through Mexico.

The biggest challenge to the schools of Western Europe is posed by immigration from Muslim countries. Many of these immigrants–legal and illegal–come from former colonies where the birthrate is high and wages are low. Increasing expectations and the pall of colonialist history create difficult situations, as we have seen recently in France, England, Spain, and the Netherlands (Gilman, 2005). Today, as people move around the world for work, they are able to maintain contact with their home culture through satellite television and cell phones. Schools must address the needs of these students as never before. They must attempt to teach students effectively so they can participate in the local economy. On the writer's visit to schools in London with significant Muslim populations, it was common to see provisions made for noon prayer and accompanying ablutions, periodic fasting, and appropriately modest conditions for physical education classes. These kinds of adjustments challenge many of the underlying assumptions of the place of religion in Western culture (Bilefsky & Fisher, 2006). The schools of France were challenged in their historical assumption of secularism by the headscarf controversy. To prepare teachers who have the cultural understanding and sensitivity to teach effectively in these circumstances becomes imperative.

### *Demands for Education Equality*

Post-industrial societies see increased participation of women and ethnic groups. Equal education becomes a very visible goal as test scores and enrollments are emphasized in the media. As women enter the work force in increasing numbers, gender parity becomes the standard. In some countries, two-income families become the norm to maintain the expected standard of living. This affects teacher education in a number of ways; not only are teachers expected to teach boys and girls equally, but the teaching force is changed as society sees the importance of women in nontraditional roles as, for example, math and science teachers and administrators.

In these societies ethnic and racial minorities also demand equal access to education. For example, the United States and South Africa struck down laws requiring school segregation, even though social patterns ensured that *de facto* segregation would continue (Fiske, 2002). Schools are expected to reflect the culture of minority students and to build a teaching force that includes a wide range of ethnic and racial groups. As with the education of women, these demands for equal education mean that teachers are expected to teach racial and ethnic groups equally effectively. With increasing testing, policymakers expect that students from all ethnic groups will make the same academic progress in schools. Countries strive ultimately to create a teaching force that reflects the ethnic and racial composition of the schools and the country.

## IMPLICATIONS FOR TEACHER EDUCATION

We have seen that countries around the world are facing challenges of finding enough teachers for burgeoning populations. They are struggling with setting education standards and changing curricula. However, the most pressing issue in teacher education around the world certainly must be developing teachers who can effectively teach children who are culturally different from the teachers themselves. The United States and Western Europe must develop schools and teachers who can teach immigrants well. In newly industrialized countries, teachers who were educated in colonial models and languages must teach indigenous children with whom they may have little in common. Sometimes this means reaching out to potential teachers who have a nontraditional configuration of skills. This will challenge teacher education, a system built on rules as a way of setting high standards. Just as states even now are adopting measures that make it possible for teachers to move from state to state, they will have to recognize foreign college degrees and make possible testing of teachers for whom English is not the first language. The language issue is particularly acute in developing countries. If multiple languages are recognized, language instruction can take up most of the instructional time, leaving little time for other important subjects. Policymakers will be wrestling with language issues for many years. The efficiency of one (often colonial) language is traded for respect for indigenous cultures in a cycle that seems to become increasingly intense as widespread education raises expectations in populations previously unable to participate in schooling.

Looking at a variety of systems of education worldwide through international studies and collaboration gives educators everywhere opportunities to understand education in a cultural context as never before. This one advantage possibility may outweigh all the challenges. Teachers and teacher educators in various countries have been working together now for some decades, and have moved beyond simply attempting to emulate one aspect or another of foreign schools. For example, the Japan-United States Teacher Education Consortium (JUSTEC) has been meeting alternately in Japan and the United States for over twenty-five years. Members visit each other's schools, take student teachers abroad for visits, and conduct research in settings in the two countries. Members begin to feel at ease in each other's schools and recognize the large role culture plays in schooling. Post-industrial countries, such as the United States through the United States Agency for International Development (USAID) and Japan through Japan International Cooperation Agency (JICA), have sent teacher educators to developing countries to assist in developing new educational systems. The international educational research community has begun to look at promising practices in developing countries with very different contexts. For example, O'Sullivan (2006) from the University of Limerick has examined effective practices in primary classes in Uganda of over seventy students. Her work suggests that various models common in China, Japan, and Korea will be more useful than models common in the Western industrialized nations. She particularly mentions a focused curriculum and whole-class instruction with judicious small-group work.

## WHERE DO WE GO FROM HERE?

Teacher educators must become more aware of international educational issues, to prepare teachers who will be effective in the schools of today. This can be done through exchanges and conferences as well as raising awareness through individual reading and study. Teacher educators in post-industrialized countries must understand schools in countries with whom their country competes economically, as well as those of the countries they rely on for labor, materials, and trade.

Teacher education programs must include a window on the world for their candidates. Study of foreign languages, study abroad, or student exchanges are good additions to prerequisites for teacher education programs. If these are not financially feasible, simply participating in local immigrant cultural events or including readings of culturally different material in the curriculum can open students to other cultures.

Finally, teachers all over the world must begin looking to each other not only for answers to sticky problems but for thoughtful ways of approaching the challenges of education in today's world, the role of culture in schooling, and the pace with which all our schooling is changing. O'Sullivan's effective teaching techniques for large-size classes that were previously mentioned are an example of future work that could be based on a truly worldwide knowledge of culture and schooling. We are often hampered by our cultural stereotypes of good teaching. A broader look at schooling can move us all forward in more creative ways.

## QUESTIONS FOR DISCUSSION

We offer these questions to help you think about the issues presented in this chapter.

1. How does the role of a teacher differ in countries of varying stages of development?
2. What roles do teachers play as a society works to increase its level of social and economic development?
3. How can teachers be prepared to teach students who are culturally different from themselves?
4. How can teacher educators work across national boundaries to improve education worldwide?

## REFERENCES

Bilefsky, D. & Fisher, I. (2006, October 11) Across Europe, worries on Islam spread to center. *New York Times* (electronic version).

The Commission on Teacher Education. (1944). *Teachers for our times*. The American Council on Education, Washington, D.C.

Dickens, C. (1854/1989). *Hard times.* Oxford University Press.

Dugger, C. (2004, October 24). In Africa, free schools feed a different hunger. *New York Times,* A1, A10-11.

Erickson, R. J. (2002). Foundations of Mexican federal educational system. *The Clearinghouse, 75*(3), 146–50.

Education for all. (2006). Retrieved October 15, 2006 from hppt://web.worldbank .org/wbsite/external/topics/education.

Fiske, E. (October 18, 2002). Nurturing expectations in life. *International Herald Tribune,* p. 21.

Gilman, S. L. (2005, April 8). The parallel of Islam and Judaism in diaspora. *The Chronicle of Higher Education,* B15–16.

Gutek, G. L. (2006). *American education in a global society.* Long Grove, IL: Waveland Press.

High-grade recruits: Texas schools are the better for having bilingual teachers from Mexico. (2007, February 26). *The Houston Chronicle,* B6.

International comparisons in education. Retrieved October 11, 2006 from nces.ed.gov/timss.

Islamic Republic of Afghanistan, Ministry of Education. (2006). *A national strategy: teacher education and professional development 2006-2008, draft document for discussion. Kabul, Afghanistan.*

Kadoya, S. (2007, June 22). Schools must attract students or face closure. *The Daily Yomiuri,* p. 16.

McKinley, J. R. (2006, August 24) Violent unrest tightens hold on Mexico City. *New York Times.*

Morales, M. R., & Caballero, J. J. (2002). Perspectives on the formation of indigenous teachers for an intercultural teacher education in Oaxaca. *Action in Teacher Education, 24*(2), 55–63.

National Center for Educational Statistics. Retrieved June 4, 2007 from http:// nces.ed.gov/timss and http://nces.ed.gov/Surveys/PISA.

O'Sullivan, M. C. (2006). Teaching large classes: The international evidence and a discussion of some good practice in Ugandan primary schools. *International Journal of Educational Development, 26,* 24–37.

Population under Age 15. (2005). Retrieved October 11, 2006 from http:// www.globalhealthfacts.org.

Samoff, J. (1999). No teacher guide, no textbooks, no chairs: Contending with crisis in African education. In R. F. Arnove and C. A. Torres (Eds.), *Comparative education: The dialectic of the global and the local.* (pp. 393–431). Lanham, MD: Rowman and Littlefield.

Schemo, D. J. (2002, May 8) Education suffers in Africa as AIDS ravages teachers. *New York Times,* p. A10.

Stevenson H. and Stigler, H. (1992). *The learning gap.* New York: Summit Books.

Tyack, D. (1974). *The one best system.* Cambridge, MA: Harvard University Press.

Waldman, A. (2005, April 29). Mystery of India's poverty: Can the state break its grip? *New York Times,* p. A4.

# PART II
# INSTITUTIONAL PERSPECTIVES

# Chapter 4

# GROOMING "BETTER-PREPARED" TEACHERS

CLAUDIA PERALTA NASH

*When education is the practice of freedom, students are not the only ones who are asked to share, to confess. Engaged pedagogy does not seek simply to empower students. Any classroom that employs a holistic model of learning will also be a place where teachers grow, and are empowered by the process.*

(hooks, 1994, p. 21)

## INTRODUCTION

Teacher preparation in the United States is enormously complex. It takes place in local and institutional communities where program structures interact. These are further influenced by the ability and experiences that future educators bring and take from these settings, and their interaction among them. Moreover, it is impacted by local and state political demands. This chapter identifies the best ingredients that should be part of a teacher preparation program whose graduates will impact in positive ways students' learning and other important outcomes. However, before delving into the ingredients it is important to know that the central focus of the current debate between teacher preparation and teacher quality is the research itself. The research informs the question of "whether there is a research basis for teacher education and if so, what that research base suggests" (Cochran-Smith

& Fries, 2005, p. 69). For this reason a historical perspective of this research over the past fifty years is outlined below, beginning in the 1950s when teacher education was recognized as a viable field of study. For a more extensive historical perspective, refer to Cochran-Smith and Fries (2005).

- The launch of Sputnik in 1957 by the Soviets prompted the public to question how well equipped our schools were to prepare the next generation of scientists. This further impacted the concern that the public had with the quality of schools after World War II. A two-year study (Conant, 1963) sponsored by The Carnegie Corporation of New York reviewed where elementary and secondary teachers received their education, concluding that the educational requirements for teachers were low. The study recommended teacher preparation programs place more emphasis on liberal arts and humanities courses and less emphasis on methods.

- During the 1960s and 1970s research focused on identifying the characteristics of teachers that were linked to effectiveness, specifically correlating the teacher's behaviors with students' achievement, also known as the process-product research. Thus, teaching was viewed mostly as a technical transmission activity; and teaching and learning were perceived as related in a linear way.

- In the 1980s, the United States was facing economic difficulties, and this influenced the concerns about American schools. *A Nation at Risk: The Imperative for Education Reform* report was published; and it demanded higher educational standards, concluding in a series of reforms. The argument was that redesigning schools would require a restructuring of a different teaching force and for some it would mean certification in the National Board of Professional Teaching Standards. In 1986 the Holmes Group, along with some 100 universities, called for improving teacher preparation, and the creation of professional development schools (PDS) so graduate schools of education could work collaboratively with K-12 settings.

- In the 1990s, The National Council for Accreditation of Teacher Education (NCATE) standards shaped the way teacher preparation programs became evaluated. The standards incorporated into the curriculum the professional knowledge base for teaching and learning. This shift prompted research to examine the kinds of knowledge, attitudes, and beliefs future educators brought with them when starting the programs; how they learned the knowledge, skills, and dispositions needed to teach; and how they interpreted the experiences provided in the teacher-preparation courses and field experiences.

- Today, teacher education has been constructed as a policy problem giving policymakers the idea that by manipulating the broad aspects of teacher preparation (e.g., subject matter requirements, entry routes, teacher tests) they can prepare well-rounded educators.

The current view of teacher education as a policy problem places tremendous emphasis on desirable outcomes, specifically on student gain or achievement tests. Even though these outcomes are important, these are not the only outcomes that teacher preparation programs emphasize. These programs prepare educators to live and work in a democratic society, and engage in civic action. Consequently, multicultural education should be in the heart of their program helping future educators understand that cultural diversity is a valuable resource and that cultural pluralism should be imbedded in every aspect of their teacher preparation program (Cochran-Smith, Davis, & Fries, 2004). This chapter attempts to explore how these assertions can permeate a teacher preparation program.

Although these developments and the subsequent shifts in teacher preparation programs reflect the dominant agenda of policymakers and powerbrokers, parallel counter-arguments were part of the debate though largely ignored (e.g., whole language, bilingual and multicultural education, feminism, etc.).

## A PLURALISTIC ACADEMIC COMMUNITY

Building a pluralistic academic community reflects the assumption that diversity enhances the learning of all students. Teaching is a moral and political act, and educators play a key role in facilitating social change (Darling-Hammond, French, & García-Lopez, 2002). Preservice teachers should be challenged to think, create, reflect, and examine their own philosophical ideas and teaching experiences in pursuit of pedagogical practices that empower the diverse children of tomorrow's schools. Four theoretical perspectives should inform the practices of those involved in teacher training:

1. Education either liberates or domesticates;
2. Teaching is a political act, with potent ethical ramifications;
3. Learning is most effective when it occurs in the context of a community of practice; and
4. Teaching is an act of inquiry and reflection.

## Education Either Liberates or Domesticates

An education that domesticates perpetuates the status quo. For many years, preservice teachers have been educated in a way that has prepared them to acquiesce to the mandates of authority figures, consume information uncritically, and feel no obligation to question or act. A domesticating education rarely inspires them to pause to ask themselves how their lives or the lives of others have been restricted by the cultural, social, and political contexts of their teaching. A domesticating education would not be as problematic if the world in which we live provided equal opportunities for all its inhabitants. Because this is not the case, education should be liberating rather than domesticating.

Liberatory education (Freire, 2004) proposes that we help preservice teachers question the inequities perpetuated in schools, disempowering students whose race, income, language, sexuality, or learning disability is not the norm. Because the majority of the teaching force is White and middle-class, their values, experiences, and beliefs may be very different from those of our increasingly diverse student population. The decisions, values, and perceptions of teachers have a tremendous effect on the education of diverse student populations, and lack of understanding of their experiences will negatively impact those students' education (Katz, 1999; Rodriguez, 1993). However, first-generation college students and first-, second-, and third-generation immigrants who have experienced an education in which their experiences were not validated, join the teaching force in the hope of creating a better learning space for future generations.

Creating opportunities to unfold oppression and explore life experiences are challenging acts that may be viewed by some as a way of creating separatism. However, it is important to recognize that to understand what students have in common, one must begin with personal experiences. It is critical that preservice teachers identify both their own experiences and the experiences of others to understand their students and families.

An activity to help preservice teachers reflect on how their literacy experiences have affected their success at reading and writing is to have them use only symbols (no words) to depict their earliest recollection of learning to read and write and the feelings associated with that experience. Several Latina/o preservice teachers have reflected through dialogue about how painful it was to lose their native language while learning English. Reflection of this kind encourages students to problematize knowledge.

> Some of us faced humiliations, while others were successful in our first attempts. The humiliations were created because we were all expected to learn at the same rate and in the same manner and we weren't given the flexibility or the variety of literature to motivate us to use literature as a form of entertainment. Instead, it created a sense of torment or even worse, in some of us it created a sense of accomplishment that caused us to only read what was required. After all, we had learned how to read. Wasn't that the purpose of this kind of instruction? (Selina,[1] journal, 2006)

Reflective practices can help preservice teachers become reflective practitioners and teach effectively across socioeconomic, cultural, linguistic, and gender differences. Through their own experiences, the Latina/o teachers understood that they had learned how to read, but had been denied the opportunity to learn to "read their world" (Freire, 1970) or learn how to read using their wealth of knowledge.

## Teaching Is a Political Act With Potent Ethical Ramifications

Teaching is a political and ethical act: every decision a teacher makes will affect each student differently, and schools deny or afford opportunities to students that may affect their futures negatively or positively. For example, linguistically different students are often sent to remedial classes to help them learn English, reflecting the deficit view that these students must be "fixed" to measure up to their

---

1. Pseudonyms are used for all proper names.

counterparts. The labels given often stay with such students through-out their schooling. Moreover, such placement decisions may shape how these students see themselves and their role in the world.

Curriculum is also a part of what has been called a selective tradition (Sleeter, 2005). That is, from all of the vast knowledge that could be taught, only some knowledge is considered to be the "official" knowledge (Apple, 2000). What and how a teacher decides to teach confirms particular types of knowledge, practices, or experiences as worth knowing. For example, if students of color never read the works of authors who look like the students themselves, they may not see themselves as potential authors.

Educators who understand teaching as a political and ethical act demonstrate the importance of preparing preservice teachers who are able to act as transformative intellectuals (Giroux, 1988). Helping pre-service teachers to understand that schools are social institutions that mirror society's beliefs, values, and norms is key to helping them understand how their decisions will affect their students. Preservice teachers should have opportunities to explore the social context that produces inequalities and to understand how opportunities, or lack of opportunities, get played out at school.

Appreciating the cultural circumstances within which students develop and learn is an important component of understanding students' success or failure. Yet, unless schools support the values presented by parents, tension between the home and school may affect their performance and interest (Valenzuela, 1999). In order to improve the education of culturally and linguistically diverse students, it is fundamental that teachers understand the relationship between pupils' home culture and their school learning.

Adjustment to a new language, culture, and way of life can be overwhelming for children. Teachers need to recognize the importance of incorporating into the curriculum the knowledge, interests, and experiences students bring into the classroom (Freire, 1970; Hayes, Bahruth, & Kessler 1998; Ladson-Billings, 1994; Lapp et al., 1996; McCaleb, 1997; Valdés, 1996; Zentella, 2005). Effective teaching in culturally and linguistically diverse communities requires exposure to the lives and points of views of children (Kailin, 1994; Sleeter, 1992; Veléz-Ibañez & Greenberg, 1992). Exposure should include a deep understanding of teaching practices in children's homes and communities. Preservice teachers should engage in a dialogue with parents to understand not only the parents' educational vision for the child, but also the child's learning styles.

An example of a preservice teacher's understanding of a child's responsibilities outside the school came through a parent-teacher interview between Emily, a preservice teacher, the mother of her student, Mario, a recent Philippine immigrant. Mario spoke little English. His mother believed that learning English would be the key to her son's success; however, she understood that this was something he had to do on his own because she herself could not speak English. Emily learned that Mario was responsible for getting ready and walking to school every morning, as his mother left for work before dawn. After school, Mario was to come straight home and wait for her phone call. Having this information helped Emily understand Mario's reluctance to participate in after-school programs and homework clubs. Emily understood that, at a young age, Mario was responsible for much more than his school life and learning English.

## Learning in Communities of Practice

"The work of justice requires acknowledging the impotency of the isolated individual and the danger of the closed door classroom" (Huebner, 2005, p. 304). The call for justice may be answered in many ways: teachers need to come together and gain their voices; collisions must occur among teachers and with students; and curriculum materials, grading, and grouping must be examined from the viewpoint of oppression. An example of the struggle for justice is painfully explicit in Selina's final action plan for a class in which she was enrolled (2006). She shares her struggle of being compliant with the rules while trying to be faithful to her calling as an educator.

> I will continue to be "faithful" to the program . . . but I will "enhance" the program by providing different learning opportunities and expanding the activities to challenge the students. I will introduce them to literature that they can see themselves in and allow them to write freely in their journals. . . . (Selina, Action Plan, 2006)

Any community of practice is formed of members with a range of experience and expertise. Most preservice teachers have experienced traditional ways of learning, but critical or radical pedagogy must insist that all members of the community be present and participate. This involvement cannot be demanded but must be demonstrated through nurturing ways and genuinely valuing everyone's presence (hooks, 1994). The dynamic of the classroom must include a true recognition that all members of the community must be given opportunities to engage in valued activities and to be viewed as resources. Without opportunities to engage, one is more likely to remain a peripheral member of the community.

Another way of building community is by practicing what hooks (1994) calls "engaged pedagogy" (p. 21). Educators who share their own narratives with preservice teachers and bring to the classroom their own personal experiences reveal to students their willingness to take risks, linking their own experiences to academic discussions. An example of this may be seen in the "Mexican American Traditions and Culture" class I teach. In my introduction to the class, I share that I am not Mexican, Mexican American, or Chicana, but rather Uruguayan. Even though I am a Latina I recognize that my experiences of oppression in this country are very different from the Mexican experience. I share that when I worked as a cashier in a small market in northern California, people always assumed that I was from Europe because their only frame of reference to the Spanish language was Mexican Spanish. My accent was viewed as different, but "cute." "Different" meant not being labeled Mexican. I did not have to experience some of the hidden racism harbored against Mexican people. However, I can share my struggles upon arriving in this country as a foreigner and how by cleaning houses I earned the money to attend English as a Second Language classes at a junior college. By sharing our stories, we participate more centrally in the activities that we value.

At the beginning of teacher training, preservice teachers often participate at the periphery; but through engaged participation and sharing of experiences they may move to the center. This perspective on learning allows more established members of the learning community to use their positions to facilitate or impede the learning of necessary knowledge, skills, or dispositions (Sleeter et al., 2005).

One way to build the community is to conduct a "tea party" activity on the first day of class. Students form two circles, one inside the other. Members from the inside circle face members of the outside circle, taking turns asking questions that will help them understand each other's schooling experiences. Student evaluations of the course reflect that this activity has proven to be invaluable.

## Teaching Is an Act of Inquiry and Reflection

Teaching as an act of inquiry should include engagement, understanding, and performance (Shulman, 2004). Inquiry means that we are interrupting our thinking to ask questions such as: How did I arrive here? What am I going to do next? Shulman calls this the "overtly emotional and moral component of learning and development" (p. 58). Perhaps we need to stop asking ourselves questions about how people learn and develop and ask instead what gets in the way of that great journey (Huebner, 2005). In a class I teach on parent involvement in education, the final assignment is a reflection paper. One of the questions to which students are asked to respond is: "What do you think would be the response of the parent(s) on the action plan developed?" José, a Chicano student, reflects on his beliefs and values after receiving an education in the United States. The following is a translation because his paper was written in Spanish.

> My goal in receiving a degree was to use my resources in helping students with Latin descent. Of course, this will also mean that I would have the chance to work with the parents of my students. In my mind I set out to "educate the parents." This phrase was what I used when referring to the work I was doing with the parents. It was not until I took this class that I realized that I was imposing my way of thinking as the "right way." Because I had been successful, I wanted to share the recipe with them, but I completely forgot that every family brings values and beliefs when they arrive in this country. I totally forgot that each family has an array of knowledge that they pass on to their children. I forgot to respect the parent's culture. (José, final paper, 2006)

In this piece José reflects on something that he had not realized before. In his rereading of the world, he recreated what it meant to be a teacher, not from repeating the dominant ideology, but by taking back his responsibility as a member of the Latino community (Freire, 2004).

Teacher preparation programs need to prepare preservice teachers to work in linguistically and culturally diverse classrooms. Engagement in reflection is paramount if we want teachers to be successful in accomplishing change. It is well documented that once preservice teachers join the work force, they will most likely fall back to their own comfort zone, using the same strategies and models of teaching used by their teachers (O'Loughlin, 1995). Therefore, if we fail to engage preservice teachers in considering how the practices of the dominant ideology have influenced their behaviors, likes, dislikes, and learning opportunities, we have accomplished little. (We have reinforced that same dominant ideology.)

Learning to teach is a lifelong commitment and preparing preservice teachers is a tremendous responsibility. Learning to teach can be guided by a set of principles to empower educators who are well grounded in teaching strategies, theory, and teaching experiences in culturally and linguistically diverse settings. See Chapter 6 of *Literacy con Cariño* (Hayes, Bahruth, & Kessler, 1998).

## IMPLICATIONS FOR TEACHER EDUCATION

*Tough Choices or Tough Times: The Report of the New Commission on the Skills of the American Workforce* (National Center on Education and the Economy, 2007) reports that public education is not servicing the public, and it should be turned over to private managers. This idea has several implications for teacher education. Many in the business community believe that teachers unions are the cause for the low performance in the public schools and agree that without unions schools would be high-performing organizations. Weakening the unions means weakening the salaries that teachers receive. Thus, teachers are not motivated to further their education. Another implication already in place in the Denver public schools is the pay-for-performance arrangement, paying teachers with bonuses linked to students' test scores (Mauricio-Lopez, 2000). Policies that reduce or eliminate professional requirements to teach increase the number of applicants and reduce the pressure on the government to spent money on education (e.g., salaries, working conditions, etc.). Many educators understand the implications of these recommendations. They recognize that "The goal of greater social justice is a fundamental part of the work of teacher education in democratic societies, and we should never compromise on the opportunity to make progress toward its realization" (Zeichner, 2006, p. 337).

## WHERE DO WE GO FROM HERE?

We must help future educators realize the importance of understanding society, the structures within it and how to respond to social powers. Many educators seem to fall under what intellectuals of the twentieth century define as "spectator democracy" where a specialized class of the population identifies what common interests are, and think and decide accordingly. This theory of democracy declares, ". . . that common interests elude the general public and can only be understood and managed by an elite group" (Ross, 2008, p. 372). Educators understand that effective education means helping students bring their lives into the classroom and take what they learn into their homes and communities. It is our responsibility to help future educators understand that this applies to their lives. They should be made aware that the dialectic relationship between their beliefs, actions, and place of work can have a tremendous impact on the top-down initiatives prevalent in current reforms. Future educators need to make their voices beyond their classroom walls heard if we are to believe that education is a social responsibility.

## QUESTIONS TO PROMPT DISCUSSION

We offer these questions to help you think about the issues presented in this chapter.

1. How do we build equitable access to high-quality, intellectually rich, culturally affirming teaching?
2. Why and how might we help future teachers understand the power their voices have in today's educational climate?

## REFERENCES

Apple, M. W. (2000). *Official knowledge: Democratic education in a conservative age.* NY: Routledge.

Cochran-Smith, M., Davis, D., & Fries, K. (2004). Multicultural Teacher Education. In James A. Banks and Cherry M. Banks, (Eds.), *Handbook of research of multicultural education* (3rd ed., pp. 931–975). San Francisco, CA: Jossey-Bass.

Cochran-Smith, M., & Fries, K. (2005). Researching Teacher Education in Changing Times: Politics and Paradigms. In Marilyn Cochran-Smith & Kenneth M. Zeichner (Eds.), *Studying teacher education. The report of the AERA panel on research and teacher education* (p. 69.). Washington, DC: American Educational Research Association & Mahwah, New Jersey: Lawrence Erlbaum Associated.

Conant, J. (1963). *The education of American teachers.* New York: McGraw-Hill.

Darling-Hammond, French, J., & García-Lopez, S. P. (2002). *Learning to teach for social justice.* NY: Teachers College Press.

Freire, P. (1970). *Pedagogy of the oppressed.* New York: Continuum.

Freire, P. (2004). *Letters for Christina.* Boulder, CO: Paradigm Publishers.

Gay, G. (1993). Building cultural bridges: A bold proposal for teacher education. *Education and Urban Society, 25*(3), 285–289.

Giroux, H. A. (1988). *Teachers as intellectuals.* South Hadley, MA: Bergin & Garvey.

Hayes, C. W., Bahruth, R., & Kessler, C. (1998). *Literacy con cariño.* Portsmouth, NH: Heinemann.

hooks, b. (1994). *Teaching to transgress: Education as the practice of freedom.* London: Routledge.

Huebner, D. (2005). Education and spirituality. In H. S. Shapiron & D. E. Purpel (Eds.), *Critical social issues in American education.* (pp. 309–324). Mahwah, NJ: Lawrence Erlbaum Associates.

Kailin, J. (1994). Anti-racist staff development for teachers: Considerations of race, class, and gender. *Teaching and Teacher Education, 10*, 169–184.

Katz, S. R. (1999). Teaching in tensions: Latino immigrant youth, their teachers, and the structures of schooling. *Teacher College Record, 100*(4), 809–840.

Ladson-Billings, G. (1994). *The dreamkeepers: Successful teachers of African-American children.* San Francisco, CA: Jossey-Bass.

Lapp, D., Flood, J., Tinajero, J., Lungren, L., & Nagel, G. (1996). Parents make a difference. Padres hacen la diferencia. *The Journal of Educational Issues of Language Minority Students Special Issue, 16*, Summer Issue, 263–280.

Mauricio-Lopez, C. (2000, January 3). *Neoliberalism and teachers. A summary of Carlos Mauricio Lopez's report on the effects of neoliberalism on education in Central America.* Retrieved November 17, 2007 from http//www.vcn.bc.ca/idea/neolib.htm.

McCaleb, S. P. (1997). *Building communities of learners. A collaboration among teachers, students, families, and community.* Mahwah, New Jersey: Lawrence Erlbaum.

National Center on Education and the Economy. (2007). *Tough choices or tough times: The report of the New Commission on the Skills of the American Workforce.* San Francisco, CA: Jossey-Bass Publishers.

O'Loughlin, M. (1995). Daring the imagination: Unlocking voices of dissent and possibility in teaching. *Theory into Practice, 34*, 107–116.

Rodgriguez, L. J. (1993). *Always running: La vida loca. Gang days in L.A.* Willimantic, CT: Curbstone Press.

Ross, E. W. (2008). Social Studies education. In David Gabbard (Ed.), *Knowledge and power in the global economy. The effects of school reform in a neoliberal/neoconservative age* (2nd ed., p. 372). NY: Lawrence Erlbaum Associates.

Shulman, L. S. (2004). *Teaching as community property: Essays on higher education.* San Francisco, CA: Jossey-Bass.

Sleeter, C. E. (1992). *Keepers of the American dream: A study of staff development and multicultural education.* Washington, DC: Falmer Press.

Sleeter, C. E. (2005). *Un-standardizing curriculum: Multicultural teaching in the standards-based classroom.* New York: Teachers College Press.

Sleeter, C. E., Hughes, B., Laughlin, P., Meador, E., Rogers, L., Whang, P., Blackwell, K. & Peralta Nash, C. (2005). Working an academically rigorous, multicultural program. *Equity and Excellence in Education, 38*(4), 290–299.

Valdés, G. (1996). *Con respeto. Bridging the distances between culturally diverse families and schools. An ethnographic portrait.* New York: Teachers College Press.

Valenzuela, A. (1999). *Subtracting schooling: U.S. Mexican youth and the politics of caring.* Albany, NY: SUNY Press.

Veléz-Ibañez, C. & Greenberg, J. B. (1992). Formation and transformation of funds of knowledge among U.S.-Mexican households. *Anthropology and Education Quarterly, 23*(4), 313–335.

Zeichner, K. M. (2006). Reflections of a university-based teacher educator on the future of college- and university-based teacher education. *Journal of Teacher Education, 57*(3), 326–340.

Zentella, A. C. (2005). *Building on strength: Language and literacy in Latino families and communities.* New York: Teachers College Press.

# Chapter 5

# THE MORAL CHARACTER OF LEARNING: A NEGLECTED DIMENSION IN THE PREPARATION OF TEACHERS

Dennis Shirley and Randall Lahann

*Of all of the many-sided things, it is the one with the most sides.*
(John Stuart Mill, 1931, p. 32, on education)

## INTRODUCTION

Picture this: You are a beginning teacher at an elementary school in close physical proximity to the community in which you grew up. You are a third-grade teacher, and your first weeks on the job, while demanding, give you plenty of evidence that you chose the right profession. You are forming solid relationships with your colleagues, you are able to establish the right balance of fun and firmness with your students, and you have even received a couple of warm thank-you cards from families who have noticed the extra effort you have made to differentiate your instruction to best serve children with special needs.

All goes well until a Friday afternoon in late September when one child suddenly strikes out at another while lining up to come back to the classroom. One child curses another with a rapid-fire burst of profanity, a shouting match ensues, and before you know it you have twenty-five little pairs of eyes looking up to see how you will respond.

Or, imagine this: You enter high school English teaching, thrive in your first year in the classroom as you try out all kinds of hands-on, creative activities that you learned in your preservice teacher education program. You know you have connected with your ninth graders when even the students with the toughest reputations begin handing "high fives" out to you when you meet in the hallway. Convinced you are on the right path, you work away at refining your curricula over the summer.

Disappointingly, in the fall when you return to school, your principal reprimands you because the school did not make annual yearly progress and your students seemed to be especially problematic. You know the enthusiasm and sense of excitement you brought to the class was a major attraction for students on the edge even to come to school, but you are shaken by your principal's adversarial tone. Perhaps it is time to tailor your curriculum more to the test as some of your more senior colleagues have done? Or, should you dig in, keep creating curricula that your students seem to thrive on, and vow to weather the storms that you are certain will lie ahead for you?

These first two vignettes are drawn from experiences that beginning teachers with whom we have worked recently have experienced. The vignettes are intended to illuminate the inescapable moral reality of teaching as a profession. How should teacher educators prepare preservice teachers to respond to the scuffles and fights that seem endemic to so many classrooms and schools? Should we teach preservice teachers that a teacher's first responsibility is to one's pupils or to the school system in which they are placed? How should we help preservice teachers to make difficult moral decisions, in which the advantages and disadvantages of different resolutions are opaque and admit of no simple answer, but only layer upon layer of shifting shades of gray?

In addition, how should we help our preservice teachers to resolve common dilemmas in school systems that contain features that many teachers find morally suspect? Recent survey data indicate that a majority of teachers indicate that the high-stakes testing reforms of recent years have led them to teach in ways that they do not believe are in the best interests of their children (Pedulla et al., 2003). Nine out of every ten teachers believe their state's standardized tests do not reflect what their students who are English language learners know (Pedulla et al., 2003). Ever since the *Coleman Report* (Coleman, 1966), we have known that students' social and economic status are highly correlated with their levels of academic achievement; yet, efforts to rectify funding disparities have generally been modest. Virtually no one argues that rich and poor children in the United States have equal opportunities to learn challenging curricula.

Make no mistake about it, teacher educators must help future teachers to make difficult choices about ethical matters they will face dozens of times every single day. How teachers should prepare lessons with the right amount of challenge and support; how they should handle conflicts between pupils or among colleagues; how they should help struggling learners who crave extra attention while not neglecting others—these are matters of tremendous import to pupils and families today. We all remember teachers who made huge differences for the better in our lives, just as we regret those who left lasting scars we hope will heal one day. Yet, how should one help preservice teachers to think about complex moral dilemmas? And, how can preservice teacher education programs help to prepare future teachers for these challenges?

## TIMELINE: AN HISTORICAL PERSPECTIVE

- **1789.** Thomas Jefferson proposes a Bill for the Diffusion of Knowledge among the People to the Virginia legislature. The Bill would establish public schools for all free boys and girls. The Bill is defeated by the legislature, which rejects state-level control of local education.
- **1830s.** Common School Reform Movement begins in New England establishing a system of tax-funded public schools, a Superintendent of Education, and normal schools for the preparation of teachers.
- **1865.** The Fourteenth Amendment to the United States Constitution proclaims that everyone who is born in the country, regardless of racial status, is a United States citizen and subject to equal protection under its laws.
- **1916.** John Dewey published *Democracy and Education*, linking the flourishing of education to equality of social conditions in an age of rapid industrialization and demographic change.

Although various sketches to create public schools were developed by Americans such as Thomas Jefferson, Benjamin Rush, and Noah

Webster during the revolutionary and early national periods, none of these ideas really materialized until the 1830s, when Horace Mann, Henry Barnard, and other New England reformers succeeded in organizing public school *systems* rather than isolated schools supported by a haphazard mixture of local taxes and private subscriptions (Katz, 1987).

If one rereads the writings of the early "common school reformers," as they were called in their day, one is struck by the blend of Christian evangelical zeal, confidence in progress, and public spiritedness that marked their speeches (Cremin, 1957; Filler, 1965). The common school reformers wanted public schools to serve as the "great equalizer of the social conditions of men–the balance wheel of social machinery" (Mann cited in Cremin, 1957, p. 87) that would literally *create* a public where hitherto disparate factions of citizens faced one another. When combined with Horace Mann's fiery abolitionism, his insistence on humane treatment of the mentally disabled and his support for women's rights, public school reform became linked with a whole ensemble of antebellum social movements. Small wonder, then, that Southern states, where laws against teaching slaves to read and write were widespread, resisted the common school movement. Although there were a few pockets, mostly in seaport urban areas, where public schools in the South began before the Civil War, they really did not develop as systems until Reconstruction.

In the first two-thirds of the twentieth century, educational historians typically portrayed common school reformers as champions of liberty and equality, an assessment that was based upon their confidence in the ability of education to rectify social injustices such as the divide between social classes. By and large this assessment was accurate, and very few people today believe that the nation would have prospered as well as it has without a strong public school system. However, the very success of the common school reformers contained a number of unintended consequences for the moral education of American children. Acknowledging the power of diverse religious groups in American society, Mann, Bernard, and their allies exhorted teachers to try to find a common-sense middle ground on complex moral and religious issues. This stance of apparent neutrality did not work for many groups. They especially did not work for immigrant Catholics, who did not want their children to learn relativism and compromise, but rather the doctrine of the faith as a creed not to be challenged

(Ravitch, 1974). Likewise, African Americans found themselves compelled to wage court battles to test whether the common schools really were open to all as integrated settings (Schultz, 1973), and Native Americans lost much of their cultural heritage when their children were shipped off to distant boarding schools to be stripped of their native languages, clothing, and beliefs (Adams, 1995).

Hence, public schools came to have two different sides to them—the promise of a progressive opening for all citizens on one hand, but conformity to a dominant pan-Protestant, European heritage and capitalist culture on the other. The nation's first preservice teacher education programs, New England institutions adapted from French and German antecedents, reinforced this new political construction of the public realm. Our earliest records of teaching in the "normal schools," as they were then called (from the *ecole normale* for the teaching of norms in France), reflect the middle-class virtues of sobriety, punctuality, individual achievement, and cleanliness that were to be inculcated by generations of schoolmarms intent on promoting the formal education and moral uplift of the American people.

This premise of the public school as a central community setting for the inculcation of moral values basically dominated the entire history of American education until the 1960s. Public schools took on the daunting tasks of socializing new immigrants to American culture and rituals, such as pledging the allegiance to the flag, that were considered beyond question as strategies for building national unity. Yet, the 1960s challenged the assumptions that had animated many public school practices. During that tumultuous decade, a variety of social protest movements disputed what might be deemed a the triumphalist narrative of continual progress based on individualism, materialism, and Protestantism, and a variety of hitherto marginalized groups fought for greater inclusion in the body politic.

Simultaneously, several Supreme Court decisions reinforced the First Amendment's "disestablishment clause" articulating the separation of church and state, and the use of schools to inculcate values embedded in Christian theology was rendered unconstitutional (Fraser, 1999). As a consequence, schools and the teacher education programs that served them increasingly became sensitive to criticisms of indoctrinating young people with particularistic values. Many teachers of social studies and history, rather than enter into uncertain terrain, opted to drop the study of world religions and other potentially divisive topics from their curricula altogether.

These challenges to the explicit formation of character and values in the public schools have also had their ramifications in the area of teacher education. Efforts by teacher educators to address social injustices in American society, for example, have met with protest from thinkers on the conservative side of the political spectrum, who have charged teacher educators with ideological proselytizing. These polemics recently became so fierce that the National Council for the Accreditation of Teacher Education (NCATE), a professional organization involved in the accreditation of over six hundred teacher education programs, abruptly dropped their social justice standards in June 2006. While numerous teacher education programs (such as our own, at Boston College) maintained their social justice orientation, faculty associated with such programs found themselves on the defensive, caught uncomfortably in the spotlight of public opinion.

## NEW CONTEXTS, PERSISTENT DILEMMAS

How should teacher educators prepare future teachers in a conscientious, thoughtful, and fair way to deal with the moral dilemmas encountered by teachers and pupils in today's increasingly contentious environment? In general, teacher educators as a profession have been compelled to follow policymakers' quest for "hard" data about pupil achievement. The most comprehensive study of teacher education to date, *Studying Teacher Education: The Report of the AERA Panel on Research and Teacher Education* (Cochran-Smith & Zeichner, 2005), a tome of over eight hundred pages, reveals just how fully issues of moral education have been pushed to the margins of the profession. Not only is there no chapter dedicated to moral education as a component of teacher education, but the terms *ethics* and *moral education* do not even appear in the index. Instead, policymakers' push for the "basics" in education–as expressed through pupil academic achievement–forms the center of the research review.

In spite of this lacuna from the side of research, issues involving ethics and morality form an inescapable reality of teachers' daily experiences. Consider some of the following problems that teachers we work with have recently reported:

- A middle-school pupil says "F- -k you!" to his teacher, is sent to the principal's office, and is back in the classroom five minutes later with no consequences;
- A colleague routinely makes disparaging remarks about students in the faculty lounge, in some instances using racially charged language;
- A teacher is told by a literacy coach in his building to modify his science instruction to help to prepare pupils for the state's standardized test in reading and writing;
- First-year teachers find themselves assigned to a school's "instructional leadership team" because more experienced faculty either doubt their own abilities to influence school policies or do not want to take on the extra work; and
- All kinds of pupil misconduct occurs on school buses on the way to and from school each day, with bullies terrifying the smaller children; yet no decisive adult intervention is forthcoming.

Such problems must be tackled by educators if we are to provide learning environments in which children cannot only cope with the many stressful challenges they encounter but also flourish in a new information age that in many ways is the most exciting epoch in human history. How can teacher educators help their future teachers develop the skills and sensitivity entailed in the resolution of moral dilemmas to take on these problems?

## A SCUFFLE WHILE LINING UP: AN OPPORTUNITY FOR MORAL EDUCATION

Perhaps the saddest by-product of the "standards stampede" (Hargreaves, 2003, p. 176) of American education today is the way in which everyday problems that arise in school are now often viewed as obstacles to learning rather than points of departure for group reflection and individual growth.

All group settings—whether in the family, the elementary school classroom, or the offices of attorneys or lawyers—are inherently conflicting. Learning how to cope with and learn from disagreements without their escalating into adversarial relationships, simple-minded name-calling, or violence is a key task for all human beings, from the smallest of children to the most powerful of politicians.

From developmental psychology we know that a wide variety of teaching practices and forms of group interaction promote children's moral growth (Damon, 1988). Children need structured opportunities to understand and to elaborate rules of conduct for getting along with one another, and they need skillful adult guidance to cope with individual transgressions, counterproductive forms of peer pressure, and wounded feelings. Their emotions are deeply engaged with any events that strike them as unfair, and they seek out adults who can serve as moral exemplars to help them to realize their own potential in ways that will enhance their self-esteem and moral standing.

Because many forms of moral reasoning developed by philosophers are highly abstract and decontextualized, teacher educators who prepare teachers to educate young children may find many ethical theories of limited utility for their settings. Recognizing this limitation, Nel Noddings (1984) in particular has sought to articulate an ethical theory centered upon *caring* as the foundation for a humanistic philosophy of education. From Noddings' perspective, today's educators typically become too focused upon the transmission of academic content knowledge; a more generative point of departure for creating a positive learning environment is to insist that "The student is infinitely more important than the subject matter" (1984, p. 176). Nodding contends that educators should not only be interested in their students, as advocated by progressive educators from John Dewey (1902/1990) to Deborah Meier (2002), but positively experience "engrossment" (1984, p. 17) with them. Only from this state of deep emotional engagement with and attachment to learners, Noddings suggests, could teachers model for students the centrality of empathy and caring for others, not as isolated classroom management strategies, but as a personalized and verbally explicit way of being in the world that will exert its own moral pull on students.

Noddings' (1984) philosophy of caring was daring when it was first articulated in the 1980s, because it seemed to argue that moral reasoning evolved out of existential engagement with and even emotional absorption in the world, rather than from the more detached and analytical perspectives traditionally favored by Anglo American and continental philosophers from the Enlightenment to the present. For Noddings, a teachers' response to a classroom scuffle around lining up should not so much be the immediate response of restoring order and rebuking the adversaries as it should be creating activity settings such as "morning meeting" sessions or small group mediations in which children have opportunities to discuss conflicts and to help one another to learn how to resolve them. This need not involve a reluctance to bring what William Damon (1988, pp. 13–30) has described as "the early moral emotions" of not only empathy, but also shame and guilt, into play. Without a firm sense of boundaries, children are likely to experience a sense of uncertainty that can easily invite acting out in any number of counterproductive ways. The key idea for our deliberations here, however, is that out of the very everyday stuff of pupil interactions teachers can develop opportunities for moral reflection—and that philosophers of education such as Nel Noddings offer points of departure for helping teacher educators and teachers to tackle complex ethical issues that arise in classrooms and schools.

## STRIVING FOR INTEGRITY IN TEACHING IN AN AGE OF HIGH-STAKES TESTING

When the No Child Left Behind (NCLB) legislation was under review by Congress in 2001, overwhelming majorities of both the Democrats and Republicans found much to applaud in the legislation. Annual testing of pupils in grades three through eight, it was argued, would generate data that teachers would use to close the achievement gap between White and Asian students on the one hand and Black and Hispanic students on the other. Billions of additional dollars would increase desperately needed financial resources that would flow to Title I pupils living in poverty. Children in failing schools would have opportunities to transfer to high-achieving environments, many of which were thought to exist only miles away but were blessed with talented principals and highly qualified teachers. Specialized educational services offered outside of the usual school environment would help students to receive tutoring support and life-skills training.

Several years later, the achievement gap has proven stubbornly persistent in the nation as a whole, even though there have been sporadic successes in individual districts and states. Military interventions in Afghanistan and Iraq have drained $480 billion from the nation's economy, with the consequence that promised NCLB expenditures have failed to materialize. Children in failing schools usually are in districts with few high-achieving schools into which they can transfer. Only a tiny amount of funding has found its way to the specialized educational services supported by NCLB.

The negative sanctions on schools–holding them accountable, in the official parlance–have remained, generating phenomenal pressure on superintendents and principals to boost up pupil achievement on standardized tests. In the case of special education students, this pressure appears to have been successful, as principals and superintendents have found that NCLB guidelines prohibit them from concealing underachievement by special education students in aggregate gains (National Center for Learning Disabilities, 2007). Other research, however, argues that measured gains may be the result of "teaching to the test" and neglecting formerly sacrosanct components of general education such as science, social studies, foreign languages, and the arts (Booher-Jennings, 2005). As of this writing, a debate is raging among educators and policymakers about what components of NCLB should be adjusted–or even whether NCLB should be reauthorized at all–to prevent these kinds of curricular distortions.

From a philosophical perspective, however, what is most striking about the NCLB debate is the truncated manner in which moral and ethical deliberations inform public discourse. Perhaps because of the widespread willingness to suspend moral judgment entirely–best captured in the acronym DDDM for data-driven decision making–even bringing moral concerns into play has become a heterodox anomaly. Nonetheless, for educators such as the high-school English teacher described in the second vignette at the opening of this chapter, the ethical dilemma posed in abandoning his creative and engaging curriculum for test preparatory activities is a real one. To be "driven" by the data, in this case, would appear to run the risk of "driving" the at-risk students out of his class and out of their school. How could ethical theory help such a teacher, and how should teacher educators draw on ethical theory to prepare their preservice teachers for such challenges?

As was the case with Nel Noddings' (1984) utility for the elementary school teacher in the first vignette, ethical theory provides numerous resources to help a struggling teacher such as the English teacher described in the second vignette. As an illustration of this capacity, consider Immanuel Kant's famous "categorical imperative" to "Act so that you use humanity, as much in your own person as in the person of every other, always at the same time as end and never merely as means" (Kant, 1785/2002, pp. 26–27). In advancing this "formula of humanity as an end in itself" (p. xviii) Kant sought to develop the cornerstone of his moral theory–that those acts are most moral that lead us to act against our self-interest to serve the interests of others as ends in themselves. Kant did not mean to imply that we should never act in our self-interest, but he was acutely aware that it is human nature to advance our own interests while claiming to act in the interests of others. "Everywhere we run into the same dear self, which is always thrusting itself forward," he quipped (p. 23). He wanted to establish a rigorous ethical theory that would allow for such action, but remove the shield of moral virtue from it, reserving that for the special kind of ethical conduct that puts the interests of others ahead of one's own.

Kantian ethics have been debated for centuries, primarily because Kant focused on an individual's intentions, while many philosophers (dubbed "consequentialists" rather than "intentionalists") have preferred to examine the results of moral deliberations. One can see how Kantian ethics might help a struggling second-year teacher make moral decisions about curriculum. The teacher might inquire after the self-interest of the principal who is pushing him to raise test scores and might ascertain whether the principal would receive a bonus if test scores rose significantly. The teacher might also note how his self-interest in terms of job security is influencing his curricular decisions. Putting the students first, from the standpoint of Kantian ethics, would lead our English teacher to continue with his creative curriculum because using the students to make the school look good on tests would be to reduce them to *means* rather than *ends*–an approach strictly forbidden under Kantian ethics.

It would, of course, be too facile to suggest that Kantian ethics necessarily is this straightforward. Kant provided several different formulations of the categorical imperative, which indicate that he well knew that in real life we are often faced with a plurality of different ends and that we need a compass for moral philosophy that is not rigid but allows for endless variation and adaptation. Hence, one could argue that the right application of Kantian ethics in the present case would be for the English teacher to present the curricular dilemma he faced to the students in a professional and respectful manner (omitting reference to the principal) so they achieve greater clarity about their own situation and gain insight into the teacher's moral reflections. Students themselves could be invited by the teacher to create a community of discourse with him that is engaged in moral reflection and action. While the teacher should maintain ultimately responsible for his decisions, there is no *a priori* compelling reason why students should be excluded from participation in group deliberation about their learning. Indeed, Kantian ethics, which insist upon the latent moral and rational capacity of every single human being, invites this kind of participation in a community of discourse and practice. Inven-tive teachers often are able to mediate between external mandates and prescriptions and the on-the-ground realities of the classroom. While not easy, it is possible; and on occasions it indicates how progressive instructional practices can blend with high levels of pupil achievement on standardized tests (Scheurich, 1998; Shirley, 1997).

## IMPLICATIONS FOR TEACHER EDUCATION

Teacher educators today are faced with continual demands to collect evidence that their programs are producing graduates who will go on to add value to pupils' learning on standardized tests (Cochran-Smith, 2006). Older forms of accountability—such as interviews with school district personnel who hire teacher education graduates, review of course syllabi, and study of preservice teacher education graduates' portfolios—increasingly are viewed as tangential and lacking rigor in the push to raise pupil achievement. This instrumentalization of teacher education is introducing numerous distortions into the process of teaching and learning that will only be relieved by the evolution of a new paradigm of post-standardization (Hargreaves & Shirley, in press). One may hope this paradigm will recover much of the flexibility, inventiveness, and personalization that have been compromised in the current era of standardization and accountancy.

In the interim, teacher educators might wish to become more assertive and to view moral education not as secondary to basics such as literacy and math but rather as an essential cornerstone of any humanistic and democratic education. We cannot elude the multifaceted dimension of education to which John Stuart Mill referred in the citation that graces the outset of this chapter. Moral issues could animate and enrich all of teacher education, from the very first introduction to education course to the final after-school reflections between a student teacher, a cooperating teacher, and a university-based supervisor. Such a change of course would involve considerable controversy and debate, which are phenomena that should be welcomed as evidence of an introspective, self-scrutinizing, and intellectually engaged profession.

## WHERE DO WE GO FROM HERE?

One premise is that nothing (or at least, very little) can be done until teachers are in some measure relieved of the multiple pressures placed upon them. Only then can they develop new forms of group work and collaborative reflection that will enable them to share and resolve the many issues they confront on a daily basis. It is now well-established in the research on teachers' workplace cultures that whenever teachers fall into entrenched patterns of individualism, conservatism, and fixation on daily survival (what sociologist Dan Lortie, 1975, called "presentism") forms of mental habituation take place that undermine serious deliberation about moral issues.

For teachers who are working in stressed and underresourced settings, such as almost all American urban schools, even the creation of professional learning communities may not suffice as an intervention to create a framework for moral deliberation and action for teachers. The reason for this is because urban systems have developed in such a way that they are overly bureaucratized and hierarchical, shaping teachers' workplace cultures. They commonly doubt their own efficacy and come to rely more on high-stakes outcomes (such as pupil achievement on today's standardized tests) than on their day-to-day interactions and formative assessments of children's learning. In such environments, there is often the need for partnership with a third party—drawn from a community-based organization, a business partner, or a university—to question taken-for-granted assumptions that prevent innovative and responsive reflection and collaboration in schools.

This, then, is an arena in which preservice teacher educators can be especially helpful in our collaboration with classroom teachers. Preservice teacher educators have a crucial role to play in what Lave and Wenger (1991) described as "legitimate peripheral participation" (p. 29)—that is, as "critical friends" who both manifest "radical collegiality" (Fielding, 1999, p. 26) with teachers and yet are also willing to offer detached, and even challenging statements that help teachers overcome habituated forms of thinking and acting that do not promote moral reflection and action. Furthermore, preservice teachers need to see that university-based teacher educators are not "ivory tower" sages remote from the messiness and needfulness of schools but are learners engaged in a lifelong process of "sustained interactivity" (Huberman, 1993, p. 291) with teachers and pupils.

Even the development of school and university partnerships is not likely to suffice to develop schools as places in which moral development attains its proper status unless they have a variety of philosophical lenses at their disposal to enable preservice teachers to engage in serious ethical inquiry into their teaching. The dilemma of the current age is that reformers increasingly attempt to apply technical solutions to complex human and moral problems. Instruction in assessment and measurement largely has crowded out topics related to ethics and reflective judgment in teacher education course curricula (Ludlow, Shirley, & Rosca, 2002). Furthermore, in a time of relentless "academic capitalism" (Slaughter & Leslie, 1999, p. 8), faculty has learned to pursue grant-funded activities to boost their school of education rankings, making mindful criticism of policy trends more difficult.

Nonetheless, one can argue that the need to make moral decisions is ontological—that is, an inescapable dimension of our common human identity—and even if one might wish to bracket moral issues out of teacher education, they will nonetheless be encountered on a daily basis by practicing teachers working in real classrooms in real schools. While space considerations make it impossible to explore these topics in all of their scope and relevance here, one may nonetheless return to the two vignettes described at the outset of this chapter to illustrate the importance of moral reasoning in teacher education today.

## QUESTIONS TO PROMPT DISCUSSION

We offer these questions to help you think about the issues presented in this chapter.

   1. How do you prepare your preservice teachers to think about

moral issues in teaching and learning? Is this an explicit part of your teacher education curriculum?

2. How do you prepare your preservice teachers to lead group problem-solving sessions dealing with such issues as justice, fairness, compassion, and respect for others?

3. How do you help your preservice teachers to recognize "teachable moments" for discussing and resolving conflicts and teasing out their moral ramifications?

## REFERENCES

Adams, D. W. (199574). *Education for extinction: American Indians and the boarding school experience*, 1875–1928. Lawrence, KS: University Press of Kansas.

Booher-Jennings, J. (2005). Below the bubble: Educational triage and the Texas accountability system. *American Educational Research Journal, 42*(2), 231–268.

Cochran-Smith, M. (2006). *Policy, practice, and politics in teacher education.* Thousand Oaks, CA: Corwin.

Cochran-Smith, M., & Zeichner, K. M. (2005). *Studying teacher education: The report of the AERA panel on research and teacher education.* Mahwah, NJ: Lawrence Erlbaum.

Coleman, J. S., et al. (1966). *Equality of educational opportunity.* Washington, DC: U.S. Office of Education.

Cremin, L. (1957). *The republic and the school: Horace Mann on the education of free men.* New York: Teachers College Press.

Damon, W. (1988). *The moral child: Nurturing children's natural moral growth.* New York: Free Press.

Dewey, J. (1902/1990). *The school and society and the child and the curriculum.* Chicago: University of Chicago Press.

Fielding, M. (1999). Radical collegiality: Affirming teaching as an inclusive professional practice. *Australian Educational Researcher, 26*(2), 1999, pp. 1–34.

Filler, L. (1965). *Horace Mann on the crisis in education.* Yellow Springs, OH: Antioch Press.

Fraser, J. W. (1999). *Between church and state: Religion and public education in multicultural America.* New York: St. Martin's Press.

Hargreaves, A. (2003). *Teaching in the knowledge society: Education in the age of insecurity.* New York: Teachers College Press.

Hargreaves, A., & Shirley, D. (in press) The persistence of presentism. *Teachers College Record.*

Huberman, M. (1993). *The lives of teachers.* New York: Teachers College Press.

Huberman, M. (1999). The mind is its own place: The influence of sustained interactivity with practitioners on educational researchers. *Harvard Educational Review, 69*(3), pp. 289–319.

Kant, I. (1785/2002). *Groundwork for the metaphysics of morals.* New Haven: Yale University Press.

Katz, M. (1987). *Reconstructing American education.* Cambridge: Harvard University Press.

Lave, J., & Wenger, E. (1991). *Situated learning: Legitimate peripheral participation.* New York: Cambridge University Press.

Lortie, D. (1975). *Schoolteacher: A sociological study.* Chicago: University of Chicago Press.

Ludlow, L., Shirley, D., & Rosca, C. (2002). The case that won't go away: Besieged institutions and the Massachusetts teacher tests. *Educational Policy and Analysis Archives, 10*(5), December 2002, http://epaa.asu.edu/epaa/v10n50/.

Meier, D. (2002). *In schools we trust: Creating communities of learning in an era of testing and standardization.* Boston: Beacon Press.

Mill, J. S. (1931). Inaugural Address at St. Andrews, in Cavenagh, F.A. (ed.) *James and John Stuart Mill on Education*, Cambridge: Harvard University Press, p. 32.

National Center for Learning Disabilities. (2007). *Rewards and roadblocks: How special education students are faring under No Child Left Behind.* New York: National Center for Learning Disabilities.

Noddings, N. (1984). *Caring: A feminine approach to ethics and moral education.* Berkeley, CA: University of California Press.

Pedulla, J., Abrams, L. M., Madaus, G. F., Russell, M. K., Ramos, M. A., & Miao, J. (2003). *Perceived effects of state-mandated testing programs on teaching and learning: Findings from a national survey of teachers.* Chestnut Hill, MA: National Board on Educational Testing and Public Policy.

Ravitch, D. (1974). *The great school wars: New York City, 1805-1973.* New York: Basic Books.

Scheurich, J. J. (1998). Highly successful and loving, public elementary schools populated mainly by low-SES children of color: Core beliefs and cultural characteristics., *Urban Education, 33*(4), 451–491

Schultz, S. K. (1973). *The culture factory: Boston public schools, 1789-1860.* New York: Oxford University Press.

Shirley, D. (1997). *Valley Interfaith and school reform: Organizing for power in South Texas.* Austin: University of Texas Press.

Slaughter, S., & Leslie, L. (1999). *Academic capitalism: Politics, policies, and the entrepreneurial university.* Baltimore, MD: Johns Hopkins University Press.

## Chapter 6

## PLACING AND MENTORING STUDENT TEACHERS: ISSUES, CHALLENGES, AND NEW POSSIBILITIES

Finney Cherian

*Teachers need to understand the person, the spirit, of every child and find a way to nurture that spirit. And they need the skills to construct and manage classroom routines efficiently, communicate well, use technology, and reflect on their practice to learn from and continue to improve it.*

(Darling-Hammond, 2006, p. 300)

### INTRODUCTION

Irrefutably, teaching is one of the most complex of crafts; its complexity is rooted in the limitless boundaries of the human mind and soul. Darling-Hammond (2006) reminds us of the vast distances teachers have to travel in their daily work, doing everything from nurturing a child's mind and spirit to integrating technology and teaching manners—tasks that can challenge the most seasoned of veterans and paralyze the most talented of novices. Darling-Hammond's sentiments accurately describe what most faculties of education hope their programs and practicum components will help to develop within their preservice teachers.

The behemoth of the standards-based curricula movement has rumbled across the landscape of education. Local boards of education have been pressured to implement programmatic changes to meet legislated accountability requirements associated with the No Child Left Behind legislation (Goertz & Duffy, 2003). The focus on quality education has shifted to attention to the quality of teacher education. Administrators, teachers, educational researchers, and teacher educators sit in opposing camps fractured over the question: What should preservice teachers know and be able to do?

Feiman-Nemser and Rosaen's (1997) framework for guiding students addresses the aforementioned question and provides a framework that harmonizes faculty and board intentions in relation to preparation of preservice teachers. Their framework focuses on the influence between internal factors, such as dispositions and beliefs, as well as external factors, such as program philosophies and school cultures and the effect these may have upon mentor-novice relations. Their framework is composed of the following three domains: participants and their relations; goals in relation to relationships and aims of practice; and finally context and conceptual underpinnings that drive desired practices of either the cooperating teacher or preservice candidate.

Feiman-Nemser and Rosaen's (1997) provide a detailed description of each element of their framework:

- **Mentoring Relationship.** In the mentor-student teacher relationship the relationship is an important unit of analysis, particularly, to explore issues of power between mentor and novice.
- **Goals and Purposes.** The preservice teacher should be guided to (a) seek new visions and possibilities in their daily teaching; (b) implement new or novel curricular experiences and teaching strategies; (c) reflect and study their practice and those of their mentor in systematic ways through activities such as observation, conferencing, and reflective journal writing; and (d) restructure their teaching based on reflections.
- **Practices.** Cooperating teachers need to guide preservice teachers through observation, co-planning, and co-teaching.
- **Context.** The tone, tact, and character of mentorship/guidance are shaped by the contexts in which it takes place—the classroom, school, program, community, and larger culture. How these contexts constrain or support the work of beginning

teachers can prove to be of significant empirical significance for the improvement of teaching and teacher education.

• **Conceptual underpinnings.** The work of cooperating teachers and the ethos of student teaching classrooms are informed by the personal beliefs cooperating teachers bring to their work.

The process of learning to teach is a process of social relations in which the novice enters and approximates the skills and cultures of the profession in a critical and engaging manner (Lave & Wenger, 1991). Hence, the topic of placing preservice candidates is more than finding and matching willing mentors to preservice candidates; it is an exercise situated within the larger question of what is effective mentorship within student teaching. Issues associated with placing a student go beyond the binary mechanics of matching individual preservice teachers to schools and cooperating teachers willing to take one. For this reason the ensuing discussion of the complexities of practice teaching include an historical overview of this practice and a review of the liberating and constraining aspects of student teaching from student-teacher perspectives. A discussion of the issue of creating educative space, situated learning, and the work of producing transformative intellectuals for the new era in teaching are explored.

Having taught preservice teachers in Canada and the United States, the author of this chapter believes the ensuing discussion explores the issues, challenges, and new possibilities for effective mentorship in student teaching–a need both nations have in common. It is hoped that the perspectives and issues presented will spark interest and insight from teacher educators passionate about helping new teachers actualize Darling-Hammond's (2006) vision.


## TIMELINE

The brief historical overview in the following section outlines the development of formalized teacher education in the United States. The introduction and development of field experiences (the role of classroom teachers) has been an entrenched element of teacher development.

Since the conception of the republic, the ideals of democracy, justice, and the hope of social advancement have been models to the rest of the world. North American schools and universities responsible for the preparation of teachers have held at their core the commitment of preparing the nation's youth for citizenship characterized by productive engagement. Based on the historical work of Urban (1990) the following is an historical overview of milestones that have lead to the nation's current degree-granting teacher-preparation programs. I also suggest readers refer to Oakes and Lipton's (1999) book, *Teaching to Change the World*. Oakes and Lipton (1999) provide a comprehensive and succinct historical overview of America's schooling and the legislative and social trends that influence the structure and practices of the nation's schools.

- From 1776 through 1779 education for pay was available in private homes. "Dames schools" were usually run by mature, well-educated women who taught elementary subjects within their homes for those in the general population who were able to afford their services.
- The beginning of the late 1800s marked the development of what were called *schools* or *academies*.
- In the 1830s, Horace Mann actualized his vision that all Americans should be educated. For Mann, functional literacy was a right for all regardless of socioeconomic status. For this reason the 1830s marked the establishment of the first public normal school (also referred to as common) in Lexington, Massachusetts.
- From 1920 through the 1940s, according to Urban (1990), was the first time most states required student teaching and professional courses as prerequisites to certifications for both the elementary and secondary teacher candidates.
- In 2007, the National Council for Accreditation of Teacher Education (NCATE) reported that many teacher candidates spent as much as 300-plus contact hours in classrooms (pre-student teaching experiences) prior to student teaching, which can be as long as thirteen to sixteen weeks.

## THE WISDOM OF PRACTICE TEACHING:
## VISION, ISSUES, AND CHALLENGES

The value of experience in the classroom, observing, or participating has long been extolled, and student teaching is the one indisputable essential element in professional education. Learning-by-doing provided the sole education of early teachers in many cases. Dewey (1938) expressed that firsthand teaching experiences were critical to the education of teachers; however, he equally asserted that not all experiences were necessarily beneficial.

Dewey (1938) regarded all learning to be along an experiential continuum where the past shapes what follows. Dewey was, however, more concerned with shaping and interpreting experience, specifically of such interpretations of experience that led to transformative knowledge and the social world. To this Britzman (1991) writes, ". . . experience, refers to the connectedness we feel toward our social practice and activities, and whether we see ourselves as authors of, rather than as authored by, our experiences." Britzman goes on to further distinguish between routine and continuity. An experience of routinization in which preservice teachers are asked to learn technical expertise by moving students mechanistically through lessons (Goodlad, 1984) is one that undermines any opportunity to transform one's learning practice beyond a narrow set of technical practices and behaviors that numb and desensitize the practitioner to seek new alternatives to practice.

With respect to teacher education, specifically preservice teaching, what can be mined out of the assertions of these researchers is that campus courses and field experiences must work together so that preservice teachers make distinctions between lived experience and educative experiences. For many preservice teachers, their only classroom encounters have been those shaped by participation as students and their field placements (Gellego, 2001). Thus, researchers Solomon and Allen (2001) remind us that the past schooling experiences and field experiences of perspective are not independent of one another. Often the perspectives preservice teachers adopt during their field experiences are directly influenced by the past beliefs and assumptions that preservice teachers bring with them.

## Issues and Challenges

The independent works of Au (2002), Pajak (2001), Paris and Gespass (2001), and Zeichner (1996) all appeal to recurring themes concerning some common obstacles or shortcomings of preservice programs, specifically, in relation to the practicum experiences. First, most faculties satisfy their practice teaching requirements by placing students in single classrooms while ignoring any opportunity for students to metaphorically transcend the "walls" of their individual classrooms and isolated work and see schooling within a broader context of the entire school and the communities in which the schools are located. By doing so, students are often placed in classrooms where they participate in a narrow band of teaching experiences while never being prepared to work in a school with other education professionals and community liaisons. Second, preservice teachers need to be exposed to work with low-income pupils and students of color. Teachers need to work with populations in which a myriad of social, linguistic, and economic variables can influence the learning of students. Teachers, especially those from the dominant culture, need to be exposed to children other than those who look like themselves. Third, the literature (see Knowles, Cole, & Presswood, 1994; Pajak, 2001) states that, while preservice teachers are exposed to good mentorship practices by some cooperating teachers, feedback and conferences between cooperating teachers and preservice teachers indicated very little in the way of learning and teaching. Fourth, Paris and Gespass (2001), as well as Zeichner (1996) found that the evaluation of students in the practicum was very subjective on the part of cooperating teachers. Evaluation comments tended to be based on personality and social acceptability rather than on their teaching competence. Finally, Knowles et al. (1994) and Zeichner (1996) state that faculties of education and school boards must make efforts to recognize the role of cooperating teachers by creating stronger partnerships and training of cooperating teachers to fulfill their roles. This leads to the question: What are the expected roles of classroom teachers as mentors?

## EXPECTED ROLES FOR MENTORS

Wang and Odell (2002), having conducted an extensive and comprehensive literature review of the expected role of practicum teaching mentors (defined as classroom teachers responsible for observing, instructing, and in some cases evaluating preservice teachers during the student teaching component of their academic programs) in times of standards-based learning, have identified four global expectations that faculties of education currently hold for cooperating teachers:

1. Mentors need to guide and support novice teachers to pose questions about current teaching practices. They need to guide beginning educators to uncover the assumptions underlying curriculum and practices to encourage them to reconstruct curriculum and practices to suit the teaching contexts in which they find themselves.

2. Mentors are encouraged to assist novices in developing mastery of subject matter but also in connecting subject matter knowledge to meet the needs of diverse linguistic and cultural populations.

3. In the current climate of the standards-based movement, faculties want to ensure that  student teaching is not reduced to the singular focus of developing specific teaching techniques and procedures but developing a strong understanding of the relationship between teaching principles and practice.

4. Finally, mentors will not simply impart teaching knowledge to novices.  Teaching knowledge would be achieved as a product of inquiry and reflection about one's teaching. Novices need to be guided to discovery of knowledge rather than be imparted with it.

## MENTORSHIP THROUGH PRESERVICE EYES

Distilling the work of Feiman-Nemser and Rosaen (1997), Wang and Odell (2003), and Volante and Earl (2002), the following constraining and liberating factors in an educative practicum can be identified. Within these studies, the notion of an educative practice teaching experience was defined along Deweian thinking, which would define educative mentoring as a process of guidance that fosters the conditions for intellectual and social growth, which, in turn, all contribute to the enhancement of experience.

### Constraining Aspects of Mentorship

Cherian (2007) observed that cooperating teachers who did not attempt to create a collaborative democratic partnership limited the opportunity for preservice teachers to develop critical reflective teaching. Such mentors also proved ineffective in guiding preservice teachers to question and reform their beliefs and practices. In addition, Cherian (2007) reported that preservice teachers felt that some cooperating teachers were best at providing technical input but were ineffective in helping them to analyze their emerging thoughts and personal philosophies about teaching. Stanulis (1995) urges that faculties of education need to encourage mentoring teachers to see reflective-based teaching practice as a guide that helps to frame and interpret daily teaching experiences.

Brewster and Railsback (2001) described ineffective mentors as those who created an ethos of subservience in their working relations with preservice teachers by not attempting to balance the asymmetrical power relations in their roles. Such circumstances severely restricted opportunities for preservice teachers to pursue their ideals and passions for teaching. To question these imbalances of power lead to conflict situations that many preservice teachers felt would have negative consequences to their teaching evaluations (Solomon & Allen, 2001). Volante and Earl (2002) reported that preservice teachers in their study expressed frustration with not being able to experiment with issues like constructivist teaching practices as well as social justice and equity pedagogy. Pressures and attitudes directed to supporting teaching practices focused on maintaining standardized curriculum and testing procedures, contradicted the faculty's initiatives to encourage preservice teachers to create and adapt curriculum to explore issues like social justice, equity, and constructivism.

## Liberating Circumstances

Solomon and Allen (2001) reported that preservice teachers described that having an associate who was emotionally supportive and accepting of their faculty programs was crucial to helping them meet their personal teaching goals and allowing them to successfully make connections with what they were learning in the university courses. This proves to be a consistent finding in the literature (Sanders & Sinclair, 2005; Wang & Odell, 2002). Findings from these studies suggest that knowing they were welcome and wanted in their practice teaching classrooms helped preservice teachers find their sense of place in someone else's domain of authority. Knowing they were wanted in their practice teaching classrooms helped them psychologically deal with uncertainties of classroom management, lesson planning, and the anxieties of being evaluated throughout the practicum.

Volante and Earl (2002) repeatedly mention that mentoring teachers who placed a consistent emphasis on guiding them to reflect on their teaching practices through observation, conversation, co-planning, and co-teaching helped them identify problems and deepen their reflective thinking about their teaching. Feiman-Nemser's (2001) work with effective mentors defined such practices as opportunities to "co-think" about the complexities of teaching. Her study suggests that invitations for productive consultations in which mentors guide preservice teachers' thinking about their daily work through open-ended questioning in the context of safe, open conversations can move the notion of reflective practice from the realm of abstraction to that of the tangible.

During field experiences, effective mentors acted as local guides who guided them not only through their individual classrooms but the communities in which their host schools were located. These opportunities broadened the perspectives of novices to the socioeconomic and cultural influences communities place on local schools. In addition, they created opportunities for preservice teachers to envision new possibilities for educational reform that could benefit their pupils and school communities. Zeichner (1996) argues that one goal of an educative practicum is to help preservice teachers become researchers of their practice within the context of their classrooms and to go beyond the idiosyncratic confines of single classrooms to observe multiple teaching styles in a school and explore the communities within which schools are situated.

## CREATING SPACES OF HOPE

Preservice teachers need to explore the type of educational spaces faculties of education and mentoring teachers need to create to engage the preservice teachers with complexities and potentials of teaching. Brazilian educator Paulo Freire (1997) reminds us that it is important that the students be allowed to live parts of their dreams within their educational spaces. But what does it mean to create space? Palmer (1998) identifies six paradoxical tensions that help to create such classroom spaces.

1. The space should be bounded and open. Cooperating teachers and faculty personnel need to create a structure of gradual integration into a class. Student teachers need time to watch cooperating teachers teach and start with a few lessons before being thrown the keys to a classroom and told to teach. Teachers too have Vygotskian zones of proximal development. Cooperating teachers need to determine with the student what they feel ready and confident to take on independently and what requires a scaffold plan of assistance from the cooperating teacher. Cole and Sorrill (1992) describe how because of the lack of training for their roles, cooperating teachers relied on their experiences in student teaching as models for their students.

2. The space should be hospitable and charged. Palmer (1998) says, "Open space is liberating, but it also raises the fear of getting lost in the uncharted and the unknown. So the learning space must be hospitable–inviting as well as open, safe, and trustworthy as well as free" (p. 75). Working with cooperating teachers and faculty who set high standards for student teaching, while being encouraging and supportive, created a caring learning environment that stimulated many students to take risks in their teaching or to teach curriculum areas and subjects they feared or felt intimidated teaching. Nel Noddings (1996) writes, "The capacity to care may be dependent on adequate experiences in being cared for" (p. 22). The author, a faculty supervisor who evaluates preservice teachers in practicum, has observed his students consistently identify that one of the most beneficial messages they could receive from cooperating teachers and faculty supervisors is a sense that they were cared for by individuals who empathized with their challenges and anxieties as beginning teachers.

3. The space should invite the voices of the individual and the voice of the group. Learning spaces for preservice teachers need to invite students to find their authentic voices as teachers, whether what they speak is met with approval or not. Silence or being silenced out of fear suppresses ideas and emotions while nurturing confusion and ignorance and complacency. Preservice teachers felt that those associates and faculty members who encouraged talk and respected their opinions helped them reshape and refashion many of their beliefs and

misconceptions about teaching and learning. Students told the author that where there was imposed silence in their relationship with cooperating teachers and faculty, their learning stopped.

4. The space should honor the little stories of the students and the big stories of the disciplines and traditions. Preservice teachers need to teach the lofty stories of curriculum and subject disciplines but also leave room for students to explore their own stories of schooling. This is done so that stories of bad teachers, good teachers, the worst day at school, and the best day at school, become the stuff from which preservice teachers fashion new alternatives and horizons for their teaching practices.

5. The space should welcome both silence and speech. Palmer writes (1998), "Words are not the sole medium of exchange in teaching and learning—we educate with silence as well. Silence gives us a chance to reflect on what we have said and heard, and silence itself can be a sort of speech, merging from the deepest parts of ourselves, of others, of the world" (p. 77). Preservice teachers' diaries, journals, and logs need to accompany these moments of silence suggested by Palmer. Such forms of writing and recording could help identify critical moments in their learning and teaching. Keeping a record of insights gained from discerning patterns of teaching and learning in progress, for reflecting on previous reflections, could prove extremely helpful in guiding student thinking both inside and outside the practicum experience.

6. The space should support solitude and surround it with the resources of community. Isolation is an enemy of the work of a teacher. Being separated and detached from others (community) robs one of resources and strength required in a laboring effort that could be engaged in seven days a week twenty-four hours a day. The author has come to learn that there is a difference between isolation and solitude. Solitude is necessary in classroom spaces. Preservice teachers need time to think, reflect, absorb, and watch alone. Solitude needs to be situated in the context of a community of learners, where we can be left alone to think and then leave and broaden the insular and circular patterns of our thoughts by sharing them with others.

## COMMUNITIES OF PRACTICE

Educative spaces as described in the preceding section do not occur spontaneously or serendipitously. Such spaces emerge out of communities of practice in which mentors regard teaching and learning as a relational social activity. But with respect to placing preservice teachers, what are the elements of socially engaging communities of practice? Lave and Wenger's (1991) conceptual framework offers important elements that can support the development of educative spaces of hope: They define socially engaging communities of practice for preservice teachers ideally characterized by the following three dimensions: (a) community as a joint enterprise, continually renegotiated by its members; (b) within the community of practice the experienced and the novice are engaged in mutual engagement, which in turn binds members together into a social entity; and (c) within this activity the novice and the experienced share a repertoire of communal resources (routines, sensibilities, artifacts, vocabulary, styles, etc.) that members have developed over time. However, communities of practice do not spontaneously occur. They are created. Current literature on professional development schools offers possibilities for interanimation between such sites of learning.

Antonek, Matthews, and Levin (2005) regard interanimation as collaboration between university faculty and site-based schools, where members at both sites work to create mutually derived goals and objectives. In such collaborations, school teachers are seen as site-based faculty whose presence assists preservice teachers to learn and assist university faculty to blend their teaching, service, and research within the context of local schools.

## IMPLICATIONS FOR TEACHER EDUCATION

It is difficult to envisage an effective program of teacher education without a considerable emphasis in practice teaching. The placement of preservice teachers in practicum is envisioned by many faculties as an opportunity to assess their aptitude for and their commitment to teaching as a career. The opportunity to work with cooperating teachers assists preservice teachers develop and appreciation for the interrelationship between the theories and methods they encounter within their faculty programs and the situations faced in the schools. In addition, the practicum provides candidates with the opportunity to develop their distinctive teaching styles.

However, researchers like Solomon and Allen (2001) argue that in light of the standards and testing-based reforms currently in North America, practicum mentors are absorbed with standardized curriculum and teaching methods given the pressures associated with standardized testing. Such preoccupations by cooperating teachers limits the range of teaching activities of preservice teachers to following strictly standardized practices such that the discussion of the larger questions concerning the meaning of teaching and its experiences under such reforms never takes place. As a result, preservice candidates are forced on the low road of technical preoccupations. The high road of exploring teaching style–that sees education through the lens of a progressive social vision where the practice of teaching and learning are never questioned in an effort to create a more just, democratic society–is rarely traveled. But how do we assist practicum mentors to help preservice teachers travel the high road of reform and social vision?

The soul of effective mentorship is devoted to guide the novice in exploring the authenticity and meaning of teaching and regards the process of learning as committed to the larger goal of ethically and socially transforming the individual and the larger social order. For this reason faculties of education and field experience mentors need to see beginning teachers as reform-minded practitioners who consider the following ideals in their work: (a) teachers who take into account questions of language, culture, race, and the ways in which they affect a student's academic and social outcomes. A student's family, cultural, and economic background should never be seen as loci of pathology; (b) critique curriculum and introduce material that allows students to see their lives outside of school reflected in school, along with their cultural and linguistic heritage; (c) explore every aspect of the relationship between culture, politics, economics, and contemporary schooling; and (d) act as agents of change who are politically and morally protective of the histories, knowledge, and experiences of their students. Until these considerations are realized, the soul of teaching will estrange new teachers from the noblest of teaching goals, the transformation of individual lives, and the hopefulness associated with designing futures where dreams are within reach.

## WHERE DO WE GO FROM HERE?

Antonek, Matthews, and Levin (2005) suggest that the practicum is not only a time for preservice teachers to explore the complexities of classroom teaching but is a time for cooperating teachers to explore the complexities of teaching adults. Researchers need to explore the process of teacher mentoring with respect to the following issues: (a) examine the role of standardized curriculum and teaching in relation to reform-minded teaching; (b) model and challenge associates to reflect on critical moments of teaching and learning that can bring about alternative interpretations and solutions that compensate for the shortcomings and constraints of standards-based teaching; and (c) cooperating teachers need to communicate consistently and flexibly in a manner that helps preservice teachers interpret and reinterpret how current standardized teaching practices and curriculum reforms impact ideals of democratic teaching. Mentorship devoted to assisting new teachers in becoming transformative intellectuals who do not compromise the needs of their students to justify the latest educational trend is of great importance to the vision of democratic teaching.

## QUESTIONS TO PROMPT DISCUSSION

Where does the knowledge to teach come from? And who is best suited to teach the novice? Educational researchers often quibble around the edges of such questions. As a teacher educator, when I talk to my preservice teachers about their practicum experiences many sadly report playing subservient and enslaved roles to the idiosyncratic demands of individual teachers and their classroom practices. Their visions for their own teaching remain dormant. In this sense, many of my preservice teachers describe student teaching as a process of peril. But it need not be so. It needs to be reclaimed as a process of promise and potential. In light of these challenges I ask readers to consider the following questions for reflection and discussion:

1. Consider how reforms associated with the standardized-based education movement have influenced the mentorship experiences and expectations of preservice teachers in practicum.
2. The relationship between mentors and preservice teachers is complex and is shaped by different personalities and differing

expectations. It is a fine balancing act between tensions associated with themes of authority and collegiality. What can cooperating teachers do to bring balance to such tensions in their work with preservice teachers?

3. Many researchers devoted to understanding the complexities and characteristics of mentorship would argue that "good" mentorship cannot be defined within a single framework of characteristics. How would/could you articulate the notion of "good" mentorship to capture some of its essential characteristics?

## REFERENCES

Antonek, J. L., Matthews, C. E., & Levin, B. B. (2005, Winter). A theme-based, cohort approach to professional development schools: An analysis of the benefits and shortcomings for teacher education faculty. *Teacher Education Quarterly, 32*(1), 131–150.

Au, K. H. (2002). Communities of practice: Engagement, imagination, and alignment in research on teacher education. *Journal of Teacher Education, 53*(3), 222–227.

Brewster, C., & Railsback, J. (2001). Supporting beginning teachers: How administrators, teachers and policymakers can help new teachers succeed. Retrieved October 12, 2005 at http://www.nwrel.org/request/textonly/html.

Britzman, D. (1991). *Practice makes practice: Critical study of learning to teach.* Albany, New York: State University of New York Press.

Cherian, F. (2007). Learning to teach: Teacher candidates reflect on the relational. conceptual and contextual influences of responsive mentorship. *Canadian Journal of Education, 3*(1), 25–46.

Cole, A. L., & Sorrill, P. W. (1992). Being an associate teacher: A feather in one's cap? *Education Canada, 32*(3), 40–48.

Darling-Hammond, L. (2006). Constructing 21st-century teacher education. *Journal of Teacher Education. 57*(3), 300–314.

Dewey, J. (1938). *Experience and education.* New York: Collier Books.

Feiman-Nemser, S., & Rosaen, C. (1997). *Guiding teacher learning.* New York: American Association of Colleges for Teacher Education Publications.

Feiman-Nemser, S. (2001). Helping novices learn to teach: Lessons from an exemplary support teacher. *Journal of Teacher Education, 52*(1), 17–30.

Freire, P. (1997). *Pedagogy of the oppressed.* New York: Seabury Press.

Gellego, M. (2001). Is experience the best teacher? The potential of coupling classrooms and community-based field experiences. *Journal of Teacher Education, 52*(4), 312–325.

Goertz, M., & Duffy, M. (2003). Mapping the landscape of high-stakes teaching and accountability programs. *Theory into Practice, 42*(1), 4–11.

Goodlad, J. (1984). *A place called school.* New York: McGraw-Hill.

Knowles J. G., Cole, A. L., & Presswood, C. S. (1994). *Through preservice teachers' eyes: Exploring field experiences through aarrative and inquiry.* Ohio: Prentice Hall.

Lave, L., & Wenger, E. (1991). *Situated learning: Legitimate peripheral participation.* Cambridge: Cambridge University Press.

Noddings, N. (November 1996). Fidelity in teaching, teacher education, and research for teaching. *Harvard Educational Review, 56*(4), 496–510.

Oakes, J., & Lipton, M. (1999). *Teaching to change the world.* Boston: McGraw Hill.

Pajak, E. (2001). Clinical supervision in a standards-based environment. *Journal of Teacher Education, 52*(5), 233–243.

Palmer, P. (1998). *The courage to teach.* San Francisco, CA: Jossey-Bass.

Paris, C., & Gespass, S. (2001). Examining the mismatch between learner-centered teaching and teacher-centered supervision. *Journal of Teacher Education, 52*(5), 398–412.

Sanders, M., Dawson, M., & Sinclair, C. (2005). What do associate teachers do anyway? A comparison of theoretical conceptualizations in the literature and observed practices in the field. *Teachers College Record, 107*(4), 706–738.

Solomon, R. P., & Allen, A. M. A. (2001). The struggle for equity, diveristy, and social justice in teacher education. In Portelli, J. P. & Solomon, R. P., *The erosion of democracy in education: From critique to possibilities.* Calgary, Alberta, Canada: Detselig Enterprises Ltd.

Stanulis, R. N. (1995). Classroom teachers as mentors: Possibilities for participation in a professional development school context. *Teaching and Teacher Education, 11*(4), 331–344.

Urban, W. J. (1990). Historical studies of teacher education. In W. R. Huston (Ed.), *Handbook of Research on Teacher Education.* New York: Macmillan.

Volante, L., & Earl, E. (2002). Teacher candidates' perception of conceptual orientations in their preservice program. *Canadian Journal of Education, 27*(4), 419–438.

Wang, J., & Odell, S. J. (2002). Mentored learning to teach according to standards-based reform: A critical overview. *Review of Educational Research, 72*(3), 481–546.

Zeichner, K. (1996). Teachers as reflective practitioners and democratization of school reform. In K. Zeichner, S. Melnick, & M. L. Gomez (Eds.), *Currents of reform in preservice teacher education* (pp. 199–214). New York: Teachers College Press.

# Chapter 7

# A QUEST FOR MUTUALISM: THE UNIVERSITY-SCHOOL PARTNERSHIP APPROACH FOR TEACHER PREPARATION

BARBARA FINK CHORZEMPA AND AARON D. ISABELLE

*Nature does nothing uselessly.*
Aristotle (Brainymedia.com, 2007)

## INTRODUCTION

Mutualism is a relationship between two species from which both receive some benefit. There are many examples of mutual relationships in nature. For example, bees depend on the flowers for the nutrients that provide their energy; and the flowers depend on the bees to transfer the pollen to other flowers to pollinate the plants, thus exemplifying that "nature does nothing uselessly" (Aristotle, Brainymedia.com, 2007). Transferring this term to education, one can view the university-school partnership as a mutual relationship.

Education literature, more than ever, is overflowing with a multitude of reports of university-school partnerships and their role in the improvement of schools and teacher education (e.g., Dallmer, 2004; Darling-Hammond, 2000; Franklin & Semmons, 2005; Harris & van Tassell, 2005; Lee, 2005; Miller, Ray, Dove, & Kenreich, 2000). A university-school partnership can be defined as "(1) a thoughtfully created, (2) value-added and mutually beneficial relationship, (3) between consenting organizations, (4) that is nurtured over time, and (5) leads to measurable results" (Coble & Williams, 1998, Background and Context section, para 5).

University-school partnerships have become "a major focus of teacher education reform in the United States" (Van Scoy & Ebert, 2004, p. 134). The Holmes Group (now called the Holmes Partnership), National Council for Accreditation of Teacher Education (NCATE), the National Education Association's Teacher Education Initiative, American Educational Research Association, and the National Network for Educational Renewal support and encourage the development of partnerships for reasons including the potential effects they have on student learning as well as the ability to improve the quality of teaching (NCATE, 2001).

Relatively new as a model of the university-school partnership is the concept of the professional development school or PDS (Leonard, Lovelace-Taylor, Sanford-DeShields, & Spearman, 2004). Simply defined, a PDS can be viewed as "a learning organization formed through a collaboration of a university-based teacher education programme with its K-12 school partners" (Harris & van Tassel, 2005, p. 179). Created by the Holmes Group in 1986 in response to a call for educational reform (Harris & van Tassel), the PDS has been noted as the most common form of a university-school partnership for the past two decades (Epanchin & Colucci, 2002).

In this chapter, we will explore past and current issues related to university-school partnerships by further explaining the concept and providing examples of the models over time, including the more recent PDS model. We will also discuss the implications for teacher education including some of our experiences with partnership schools as well as the future of the partnership initiative.

## AN HISTORICAL PERSPECTIVE

It is important to realize that not all university-school partnerships are new: Colleges and universities have been working cooperatively with schools on staff development and preservice teacher education for years (Kirschner, Dickinson, & Blossner, 1996). Some of the most influential partnership movements, which date back to the early nineteenth century, are summarized here.

- **1836.** The first laboratory school, "The Dewey School," founded by John Dewey and his wife, Alice Chipman Dewey, opened in 1836 in Chicago. This collaborative school was an educational setting where university scholars and classroom teachers could consider a range of theoretical and practical formulations about teaching and learning (Perrone, 1994).
- **Early Twentieth Century.** The Child Study Movement, initiated in the late nineteenth century by G. Stanley Hall, became a national movement in the early twentieth century that called for the widespread scientific observation and study of children. Teachers at the elementary and secondary levels were encouraged to be documenters of children's learning and their teaching practices, being able in the process to be active contributors to knowledge and the developing field of educational psychology (Perrone, 1994). Movement leaders also sought to reform public schools and to make them more child-centered (Humphreys, 1985).
- **1930s.** In New York City during the 1930s, the Cooperative School for Teachers opened as part of the Bank Street School. A joint venture between the Bureau of Educational Experiments, created by Lucy Sprague Mitchell, and eight other local experimental schools, resulted in decades of successful collaboration among student teachers, in-service teachers, and college faculty (Perryman & Fisher, 2000).
- **1960s and early 1970s.** Various teacher exchange programs were established that consisted of visiting teachers and scholars. By having university faculty teaching on occasion in schools, and teachers from the schools teaching in the colleges and universities, more commonalities of understanding became possible. A base for constructive discourse was then established (Perrone, 1994).
- **1986.** The Holmes Group, a consortium of 96 research universities with professional education programs, was instituted in 1986 to accomplish the following goals: (a) change the way teachers are educated, (b) help construct a true profession of teaching, (c) cooperate with school personnel to transform schools, and (d) restructure colleges of education to achieve these ends (The Holmes Partnership, 2007). The Professional Development School model resulted from this work.

## THE SPECTRUM OF PARTNERSHIPS

In the spectrum of university-school partnerships (see Figure 7.1), a wide range of formats and designs have been implemented ranging from "simple episodic transactions to complex ongoing partnerships" (Coble & Williams, 1998, Background and Context section, para 4). The latter partnership model, most commonly advocated for by national organizations, is known as a PDS or PDS Collaborative. In the middle of the spectrum is the University-School Partnership Concept, which is an arrangement based upon an exchange of resources. At the other end of the spectrum (i.e., simple, episodic) is the traditional campus-based model of training preservice teachers with field experiences in preschool, elementary, and/or secondary schools. This type of arrangement usually entails what Melser (2004) called the "circuit rider approach" (p. 31) in which the university supervisor travels to different partner schools to infrequently supervise student teachers, often with minimal contact with the school or classroom. Sherman (2005) further noted a disadvantage to this type of arrangement for training preservice teachers:

> Part of the problem is that the required courses for prospective teachers are rarely, if ever, connected to authentic school-based experiences. . . . Even if they have studied the skills and strategies necessary to be successful teachers, they have not been given enough opportunities to practice and hone their skills before entering the job market. (p. 37)

According to Shen, Lu, and Kretovics (2004), "University-school partnerships can be established (1) solely to seek institutional resources (*resource-dependence theory*); (2) to exchange resources between or among organizations (*resource-exchange theory*); (3) to provide an infrastructure for bringing about renewal (*simultaneous-renewal theory*); or (4) to make a symbolic gesture (*symbolic theory*)" (pp. 186–188). Whereas the PDS model is based upon the simultaneous-renewal theory in which the focus is primarily on educational reform, restructuring, and change, non-PDS partnerships primarily adhere to the characteristics of the resource-exchange theory; that is, partnerships can "form when organizations anticipate mutual benefits or gains from the exchange which is primarily voluntary" (Shen et al., 2004, p. 189). In the following paragraphs, each of these two general types of partnerships (i.e., non-PDS and PDS) will be discussed.

Figure 7.1. Spectrum of University-School Colloration.

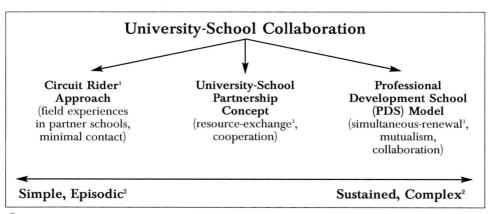

*Sources:*
 1. From "The shared supervision of student teachers: Leadership, listening, and lessons learned," by N. A. Melser, 2004, *The Professional Educator, 26*(2), p. 31.
 2. From "The partnership concept: A framework for building and sustaining university-school partnerships," by C. R. Coble & T. Williams, 1998, *Teacher Education and University Outreach to North Carolina Public Schools.* Retrieved March 20, 2007, from http://www.ga.unc.edu/21stcenturyschools/reports/partnerconcept.html.
 3. From "Improving the education of students placed at risk through university-school partnerships," by Shen, Lu, & Kretovics, 2004, *Educational Horizons, 82*(3), pp. 184–193.

## Non-PDS Partnership Models

There are many non-PDS interpretations of partnerships for school improvement. "Many of these models utilize individual strategies that tend to view the teacher and principal as change agents and involve initiatives in forms of [preservice], in-service, and management training that might influence attitudes, knowledge, or skills" (Lee, Lo, & Walker, 2004, p. 3). From the perspective of a resource-exchange theory, different types of relationships and shared resources are viewed as mutually beneficial to both universities and schools (Shen et al., 2004). Recent trends in the literature identify three major themes: (a) the development of a laboratory school environment for preservice teachers, (b) a professional development program for in-service teachers, and (c) technology acquisition and curricular infusion.

A laboratory school relationship is illustrated in the university-school partnership between Boise State University and ANSER Public Charter School in Boise, Idaho in which professors of education engage preservice teachers in a variety of hands-on teaching and learning experiences (Parrett & Willison, 2004). In the literacy component of this partnership,

One professor engages his students in weekly journaling exchange with entire classrooms of ANSER students. This partnership provides [pre-service] teachers an opportunity to observe the developmental growth of a student's writing within the context of authentic writing samples. In return, ANSER students are engaged in meaningful correspondence and partnership with an adult. Through the experience, an ANSER student will write to and receive a minimum of 15 letters from their partner. (Parrett & Willison, p. 83)

Another example of this type of relationship is a clinical supervision model for student teaching that can be observed at various laboratory school sites in the Morgan School District, in conjunction with Miami University in Oxford, Ohio (Shiveley & Poetter, 2002). In this model,

> The traditional role of the university supervisor is replaced by a group of master teachers in the school who have been trained in clinical supervision approaches by university faculty. The university liaison [who receives a one-course release from university teaching] keeps the program going, acts as a general resource, participates in periodic seminars, and provides a university presence at the site. (Shiveley & Poetter, p. 286)

The Morgan clinical supervision model reflects "a collegial, formative approach" in which "the work is much less measurement-oriented, and much more formatively evaluative" (Shiveley & Poetter, p. 286).

The second type of relationship in a university-school partnership is the development of a professional development program or PDP for in-service teachers. The rationale for a comprehensive approach to teachers' professional development reflects the need for cooperating or mentor teachers who will be able to provide student teachers with a powerful, supportive learning experience (Mun-ling & Lai, 2004). This means that "teacher education institutions must work in partnership with schools toward providing a conducive learning environment where student teachers' learning to teach can be situated in a culture which reflects the best of practice" (Mun-ling & Lai, p. 116). For example, the university-school partnership between the University of Hong Kong and local schools began by developing the Unified Professional Development Project for Teachers and Student Teachers. University and schools became close partners working cooperatively to provide a holistic school experience for student teachers through the development of a quality teacher force. This was achieved "by providing opportunities for teachers' continuing professional development at different stages of their career: from preservice teachers, to beginning teachers, and to experienced teachers" (Mun-ling & Lai, p. 118).

In another partnership model between The Ohio State University–Lima and public schools, a teacher needs-based PDP was developed "to deepen the participating teachers' conceptual understanding of mathematics content knowledge and pedagogical content knowledge by exposing them to innovative and creative approaches that necessitate active participation in developing mathematics concepts" (Lee, 2005, p. 41). Through the use of "reform PDP strategies" such as study groups, mentoring, networking, and coaching, as well as a focus on units over disconnected activities, the teachers "reported that they were not afraid of introducing innovative ways of solving mathematics problems anymore" (Lee, p. 45). Lee also noted that "the teachers adapted new pedagogical strategies and alternative ways to assess their students' understanding and learning" (p. 45).

The third type of partnership relationship is one in which the acquisition and infusion of technology for teaching and learning is of mutual benefit to both university and school personnel. According to Pohan and Dieckmann (2005),

> Most traditional teacher education programs have technology components, but these courses are often removed from real life in K–12 classrooms. Without collaboration between K–12 schools and university programs, preservice teachers are unable to observe examples of classroom teachers integrating meaningful and authentic technology projects into the content areas. (p. 22)

In a partnership between the College of Education at California State University Sacramento and Roseville City School District, a year-long project created by university-school "design teams" was implemented in an effort to increase effective integration of technology in instruction by K-8 classroom teachers (Franklin & Semmons, 2005). Each design team, which consisted of a minimum of one university faculty, one K-8 classroom technology mentor teacher, and K-8 teachers, developed various integrated technology lessons during the fall semester. During the spring semester, student teachers participated in the implementation of these lessons. The university faculty also consistently integrated technology into their methods courses in a variety of meaningful ways. As a result, the participants' technology skills improved; the preservice teachers learned how to integrate technology into the curriculum in a meaningful way; and positive attitudes and dispositions developed among both preservice and in-service teachers that supported integration of technology in teaching.

In a similar partnership titled "The Technology Fair Project," preservice teachers from the University of Cyprus and primary school students from local schools worked in a one-on-one collaborative format to find the solution to their chosen technological problem (Mettas & Constantinou, 2006). A noted benefit of the technology fair projects was that they

> provide an opportunity for interaction between undergraduate student teachers and elementary school students so that they can work as a team with shared but different goals: the child aims to solve a problem and present both the problem and the solution during the technology fair; the student-teacher aims to use the interaction as a process for helping the child develop problem-solving and decision-making skills through a systematic approach. (Mettas & Constantinou, p. 19)

According to Henderson (1990), for any university-school partnership to succeed, there must be mutual benefit (such as a focus on higher student achievement scores, improvement in the quality of programs, and increased support and services), commitment (such as formal written agreements, shared organizational values, vision, and goals), and common predispositions (such as relationships built on trust in which promises are met and an overall attitude of acceptance of the partnership on the part of the administration, faculty, and staff). If one or more of these elements are not established, difficulties can, and most likely will, occur within the university-school partnership concept. These problems mostly stem from the fact that both K-12 teachers and teacher educators are more accustomed to working independently than collaboratively with their colleagues. It is important for partners to remember that in making a decision to form a partnership "K-12 and university educators are making a commitment to learn together how to do something on shared turf that neither group necessarily knows how to do on its home turf" (Stephens & Boldt, 2004, p. 703).

From their work with university-school partnerships, Stephens and Boldt (2004) have identified four problematic areas that reflect the reality of the partnership concept: (a) within both schools and institutions of higher education, there are often tensions about which individuals should participate, who should not, and who should make such decisions; (b) although university faculty involved in partnerships need to help preservice teachers make connections between university classes and K-12 classroom practices, the reality is that there are some faculty members who have not been in a K-12 classroom in many years; (c) partners often bring to the partnership very different ideas about his/her own role and the role of the other partners; and (d) sustaining university-school partnerships is a time-consuming task that takes valuable time away from other endeavors. These complex issues do not have straightforward answers; however, in an attempt to address these issues to find plausible solutions, partnerships can succeed and teacher education can improve.

## Professional Development Schools

As the name implies, professional development schools entail much more than just providing a field experience opportunity for preservice teachers in a school linked with an institute of higher education. Castle, Fox, and Souder (2006) stated, "PDSs are clinical field sites in which the school and university partners focus together on improving teacher education and the professional development of practicing teachers as well as increasing student achievement and conducting research" (p. 65). As previously mentioned, PDSs were developed by the Holmes Group (1986) to initiate reform and were based on the medical training model of the teaching hospital (Hooks & Randolph, 2004; McKinney, Robinson, & Spooner, 2004; Wait & Warren, 2002). In a PDS environment mutual decision-making occurs, and all partners benefit from the arrangement to some degree (Marlow, Kyed, & Connors, 2005, p. 557). Mule (2005) described the link of PDSss to teacher education reform as such:

> PDSs are understood both as a place and a concept or idea (NCREST, 1993). As a place, as summarized by Abdal-Haqq (19985), PDS (1) are located in public schools, (2) are involved in reform efforts, (3) collaborate with universities and colleges, districts, and professional associations, (4) base their practice on research and experience, and inquiry-based methods are used to refine practice. As a concept, they emphasize collaboration between university and school. (p. 206)

Variations of how a PDS is designed exist (Lee et al., 2004). For example, a PDS can be organized in one school, district, or county (e.g., Melser, 2004; Wait & Warren, 2002) or in more than one district or county, such as the model Professional Development School Without Walls described by Epanchin and Colucci (2002). Criteria and standards for these partnerships at the P-12 level have been laid out by many, including NCATE. NCATE standards for PDSs include the following:

> **Standard I:** Learning Community—Addresses the unique environment created in a PDS partnership that supports both professional and children's learning.
> **Standard II:** Accountability and Quality Assurance—Addresses the responsibility of a PDS partnership to uphold professional standards for teaching and learning.
> **Standard III:** Collaboration—Addresses the development and implementation of a unique university/school community that shares responsibility across institutional boundaries.
> **Standard IV:** Equity and Diversity—Addresses the responsibility of the PDS partnership to prepare professionals to meet the needs of diverse learners.
> **Standard V:** Structures, Resources and Roles—Addresses the infrastructure that a PDS partnerships uses and/or creates to support its work (NCATE, 2001, para 3).

Epanchin and Colucci (2002) noted there is often disconnect between on-campus coursework and off-campus clinical experiences. That is, the concepts and strategies taught in the methods courses on the college campus may not reflect the practices observed by the preservice teachers during their field experiences. Thus, Epanchin and Colucci recommended that what preservice teachers need are learning experiences that allow them to attach meaning to concepts and theories, as well as opportunities to interact with others in the practice of those concepts and theories. This notably is an advantage of PDS teacher preparation programs. Other advantages of PDS models include the impact of these environments on the retention of preservice teachers in the teaching profession (Levine, 2002; Paese, 2003) and the opportunity to immerse preservice teachers into a culture of inquiry and collegiality (Levine). McKinney and Finke (2005) also noted that PDSs were designed to better prepare preservice teachers for working with students in urban areas and in high-poverty school environments when the field experiences were provided in urban PDSs (p. 52). University faculty also benefit by working in a P-12 school on a regular basis (Wait & Warren, 2002) and thus become more informed in current educational practices.

In PDS environments, teacher preparation programs are not the sole benefactor. PDS models have also been noted to improve P-12 student learning (Harris & van Tassell, 2005; Levine, 2002; Wait & Warren, 2002); lower the student-to-teacher ratio (Levine, 2002; Sherman, 2005); and allow for the sharing of knowledge, skills, and resources for all partners (Levine, 2002). Central to the mission of PDS models is professional development. So, not only do preservice teachers benefit from being part of a PDS initiative, but the practicing teachers do as well. Educators are provided with opportunities to conduct action research (Levin & Rock, 2003), teach or coteach university courses (Levine), and other professional development opportunities (e.g., use of technology) through working with university faculty (Epanchin & Colucci, 2002; McBee & Moss, 2002). Advantages to working in a PDS environment reported by practicing teachers include (a) more willing to experiment and take risks, (b) being energized and "intellectually stimulated," and (c) displaying a greater sense of power (i.e., self-efficacy) and an increased feeling of professionalism (Abdal-Haqq, 1998, p. 24).

Not unlike any partnership, there have been noted barriers to successful PDSs. In her meta-ethnographic study, Rice (2002) identified twelve themes that emerged from twenty case studies reviewed, many of which were obstacles facing the PDS partnership. These obstacles, embedded in the themes she identified, included the unwillingness to collaborate, prior relationships and negative attitudes, difficulty sustaining funding, lack of formalization, issues of parity and control, lack of support from the principal, miscommunication, intraorganizational strains (i.e., disagreement among colleagues within the same organization), conflicting goals among organizations, and initial distrust and skepticism (Rice, pp. 58–62).

As the number of PDS partnerships increases so, too, does the need to evaluate the effects of PDS versus non-PDS partnerships on teacher-education programs. Several researchers (e.g., Castle et al., 2006; McKinney et al., 2004; Paese, 2003; Reynolds, Ross, & Rakow, 2002; Ridley, Hurwitz, Hackett, & Miller, 2005; Wait & Warren, 2002) have already begun to examine this issue with somewhat mixed results, spawning the question of what impact this will have on teacher education.

## IMPLICATIONS FOR TEACHER EDUCATION

Several researchers emphasize that teacher education programs be restructured to make the transition from a university-school partnership concept to a PDS (Henderson, 1990; Kirschner et al., 1996; Van Scoy & Ebert, 2005). This transition involves an increase in trust, risk-sharing, and rewards for those involved. Transforming a university-school partnership to a PDS requires a shift from a cooperative relationship to a collaborative relationship characterized by "joint intellectual effort and mind-to-mind interactions" (Kirschner et al., p. 207). However, although several authors have noted the benefits of PDS partnerships (e.g., Epanchin & Colucci, 2002; Levine, 2002; Wait & Warren, 2002) and others recommend the shift from a partnership to a PDS, Castle and her colleagues (Castle et al., 2006) noted that

> A report by the Education Commission of the States (2003) found no conclusive evidence supporting PDS programs but did suggest the importance on strong, well-supervised field experiences that are integrated with course work and lead to a solid grasp of subject matter and pedagogy. (p. 66)

This finding leads to the question then if establishing PDSs is warranted.

In either case, whether it be a PDS or non-PDS university-school partnership, it would seem imperative for teacher educators to establish the mindset that we have just as much to learn from our colleagues in the field as do our students (i.e., the preservice teachers). In some cases, this means a complete restructuring of the teacher education program, replacing outdated methods and instruction with practices currently used in the field as explained by the resident experts, the teachers themselves. As teacher educators we present our research at conferences, but so too should we attend workshops or informational sessions held by teachers to provide us with the best practices for the students in our local environments.

## WHERE DO WE GO FROM HERE?

Like many colleges of education, as university teacher educators we have explored several ways for our teacher candidates to conduct the numerous hours of field experiences required, ranging from the "circuit rider" approach to several attempts at establishing PDSs. Both of us have had the opportunity to teach a methods course (i.e., English Language Arts and Science) onsite in an elementary setting, but with different components. In our experiences, overall we noticed the preservice teachers grasped the pedagogical concepts more quickly and were more positive about their training experiences in the PDS model than in the traditional methods course taught on the college campus.

It is our belief that teacher preparation programs should strive to include strong partnerships (i.e., mutual relationships) as part of their teacher preparation programs. As Rice (2002) stated, however, successful university-school partnerships cannot be established or maintained unless the support is available. A great deal of time and effort are needed, something we have both experienced firsthand. For teacher education programs this means an increase in the number of faculty is necessary so that teacher educators can spend more time in the field alongside the preservice teachers and fewer on-campus obligations (e.g., college-wide committees) should be required for these faculty members. Because of the tremendous increase in time and effort given by the faculty involved in the PDS, faculty members should be compensated and rewarded for their involvement. For example, when we teach the methods course on campus, each course meets for almost three hours. However, when we teach the methods course on-site in the local elementary schools, we are in the school for no fewer than seven hours every week. Therefore, we feel that those faculty involved in the PDS should also have a reduced course-load to compensate for the additional time spent with the on-site methods course. These issues need to be addressed before more faculty members become involved with PDSs, as they serve as obstacles to establishing successful partnerships.

If our aim is to prepare effective teachers, then we need to model effective instruction, and how better to do this than by instructing our teacher candidates in the settings in which they will soon find themselves? Thus, the opportunity to benefit not only the preservice teachers but the school community as well leaves us then with the quest for mutualism in the partnership approach for teacher preparation.

## QUESTIONS FOR DISCUSSION

We would like you to consider the various partnership models presented in this chapter and reflect on your teacher training program.

1. Considering the field experiences in your teacher preparation program, where do they fit on the spectrum of university-school partnerships? (Refer to Figure 7.1.) What do you see as the benefits and drawbacks to the partnerships you have encountered?
2. How have university-school partnerships prepared you to teach in today's classrooms?

## REFERENCES

Abdal-Haqq, I. (1998). *Professional development schools: Weighing the evidence.* Thous-and Oaks, CA: Corwin Press.

Brainymedia.com (2007). Brainy quote. Retrieved May 30, 2007 from http://www. brainyquote.com/quotes/quotes/a/aristotle164510.html.

Castle, S., Fox, R. K., & Souder, K. O. (2006). Do professional development schools (PDSs) make a difference? A comparative study of PDS and non-PDS teacher candidates. *Journal of Teacher Education, 57,* 65–80.

Coble, C. R., & Williams, T. (1998). The partnership concept: A framework for building and sustaining university-school partnerships. *Teacher Education and University Outreach to North Carolina Public Schools.* Retrieved March 20, 2007, from http://www.ga.unc.edu/ 21stcenturyschools/reports/partnerconcept.html.

Dallmer, D. (2004). Collaborative relationships in teacher education: A personal narrative of conflicting roles. *Curriculum Inquiry, 34*(1), 29–45.

Darling-Hammond, L. (2000). How teacher education matters. *Journal of Teacher Education, 51*(3), 166–173.

Epanchin, B. C., & Colucci, K. (2002). The professional development school without walls: A partnership between a university and two school districts. *Remedial and Special Education, 23,* 349–358.

Franklin, C. A., & Semmons, D. B. (2005). A situative perspective on a collaborative model for integrating technology into teaching. *Journal of Educational Computing Research, 32*(4), 315–328.

Harris, M. M., & van Tassell, F. (2005). The professional development school as learning organization. *European Journal of Teacher Education, 28,* 179–194.

Henderson, J. C. (1990). Plugging into strategic partnerships: The critical is connection. *Sloan Management Review, 31*(3), 7–18.

The Holmes Partnership: History & Work (2007). *The Holmes Partnership.* Retrieved on March 28, 2007, from http://www.holmespartner ship.org/history.html.

Hooks, L. M., & Randolph, L. (2004). Excellence in teacher preparation: Partners for success. *Childhood Education, 80,* 231–236.

Humphreys, J. T. (1985). The Child-Study Movement and Public School Music Education. *Journal of Research in Music Education, 33*(2), 79–86.

Kirschner, B. W., Dickinson, R., & Blossner, C. (1996). From cooperation to collaboration: The changing culture of a school/university partnership. *Theory into Practice, 35*(3), 205–213.

Lee, C. K. J., Lo, L. N. K., & Walker, A. (2004). Partnership and change for school development. In C.K.J Lee, L.N.K. Lo & A. Walker (Eds.), *Partnership and Change* (Educational Study Series). Hong Kong: The Chinese University Press.

Lee, H. J. (2005). Developing a professional development program based on teachers' needs. *The Professional Educator, 27*(1–2), 39–49.

Leonard, J., Lovelace-Taylor, K., Sanford-DeShields, J., & Spearman, P. (2004). Professional development schools revisited: Reform, authentic partnerships, and new visions. *Urban Education, 39,* 561–583.

Levin, B. B., & Rock, T. C. (2003). The effects of collaborative action research on preservice and experienced teacher partners in professional development school. *Journal of Teacher Education, 54,* 135–149.

Levine, M. (2002). Why invest in professional development schools? *Educational Leadership, 59*(6), 65–68.

Marlow, M. P., Kyed, S., & Connors, S. (2005). Collegiality, collaboration, and kule-ana: Complexity in a professional development school. *Education, 125,* 557–568.

McBee, R. H., & Moss, J. (2002). PDS partnerships come of age. *Educational Leadership, 59*(6), 61–64.

McKinney, S. E., & Finke, J. A. (2005). A comparison of the internship experience for student interns placed in different urban school environments. *The Professional Educator, 27*(1&2), 51–57.

McKinney, S. E., Robinson, J., & Spooner, M. (2004). A comparison of urban teacher characteristics for student interns placed in different urban school settings. *The Professional Educator, 26*(2), 17–30.

Melser, N. A. (2004). The shared supervision of student teachers: Leadership, listening, and lessons learned. *The Professional Educator, 26*(2), 31–37.

Mettas, A., & Constantinou, C. (2006). The technology fair project. *Technology Teacher, 65*(8), 19–21.

Miller, S. L., Ray, S., Dove, T., & Kenreich, T. (2000). Perspectives on personal professional development. In M. Johnston, P. Brosnan, D. Cramer, & T. Dove, (Eds.), *Collaborative Reform and other Improbable Dreams* (pp. 141–151). Albany, NY: State University of New York Press.

Mule, L. (2006). Preservice teachers' inquiry in a professional development school context: Implications for the practicum. *Teaching and Teacher Education, 22,* 205–218.

Mun-ling, L., & Lai, E. (2004). Quality education through quality teacher education development: The unified professional development project. In C. K. J Lee, L. N. K. Lo & A. Walker (Eds.), *Partnership and Change* (Educational Study Series). Hong Kong: The Chinese University Press.

National Council for Accreditation of Teacher Education. (2001). *Five defining characteristics of PDSs.* Retrieved, March 31, 2007, from http://www.ncate.org/public/pdswhat.asp?ch=133.

Paese, P. C. (2003). Impact of professional development schools: Preservice through induction. *Action in Teacher Education, 25*(1), 83–88.

Parrett, W., & Willison, S. (2004). Alternative, magnet and charter schools: Models for creating effective partnerships. In C. K. J. Lee, L. N. K. Lo, & A. Walker (Eds.), *Partnership and Change* (Educational Study Series). Hong Kong: The Chinese University Press.

Perrone, V. (1994). University-school collaboration in historical perspective. *On Common Ground, 2.* Retrieved March 28, 2007, from http://teachers.yale.edu/oncommonground/index.php?skin=h&page=02/02.

Perryman, A., & Fisher, P. (2000). A brief history: Bank Street College of Education. *Bank Street College of Education.* Retrieved March 28, 2007, from http://www.bankstreet.edu/aboutbsc/history.html.

Pohan, C. A., & Dieckmann, J. (2005). Preservice partnerships create classroom leaders. *Learning and Leading with Technology, 33*(1), 22–24.

Reynolds, A., Ross, S. M., & Rakow, J. H. (2002). Teacher retention, teaching effectiveness, and professional preparation: A comparison of professional development school and non-professional development school graduates. *Teaching and Teacher Education: An International Journal of Research and Studies, 18*, 289–303.

Rice, E. H. (2002). The collaboration process in professional development schools: Results of a meta-ethnography, 1990–1998. *Journal of Teacher Education, 53*, 55–67.

Ridley, D. S., Hurwitz, S., Hackett, M. R. D., & Miller, K. K. (2005). Comparing PDS and campus-based preservice teacher preparation: Is PDS-based preparation really better? *Journal of Teacher Education, 56*, 46–56.

Shen, J., Lu, X., & Kretovics, J. (2004). Improving the education of students placed at risk through university-school partnerships. *Educational Horizons, 82*(3), 184–193.

Sherman, D. B. (2005). Closing the experience gap for new teachers. *Principal, 84*(4), 36–38.

Shiveley, J. M., & Poetter, T. S. (2002). Exploring clinical, on-site supervision in a school-university partnership. *The Teacher Educator, 37*(4), 282–301.

Stephens, D., & Boldt, G. (2004). School/university partnerships: Rhetoric, reality, and intimacy. *Phi Delta Kappan, 85*(9), 703–707.

Van Scoy, I. J., & Ebert, C. (2005). Teacher development and empowerment through school-university partnerships. In C. K. J Lee, L. N. K. Lo, & A. Walker (Eds.), *Partnership and Change* (Educational Study Series). Hong Kong: The Chinese University Press.

Wait, D. B., & Warren, L. L. (2002). Reforming teacher education through professional development schools. *International Journal of Educational Reform, 11*, 228–250.

# Chapter 8

# ACCREDITATION RECONSIDERED: BENEFITS, CHALLENGES, AND FUTURE DIRECTIONS

Susan R. Polirstok and Annette D. Digby

*If teacher education is the Dodge City of the education world, teacher education accreditation bodies are weak sheriffs.*

(Levine, 2006a, p. 10)

## INTRODUCTION

In the 1950s and 1960s, the jolt that Sputnik provided to the education system in America was extraordinary, especially in mathematics and science. Heightened public awareness led to an increased focus on efficacy of schools, student achievement, and access to higher education. Additional funding became available for higher education institutions to design targeted initiatives in these areas. These efforts paid off. America found its competitive edge at the right moment in time, as evidenced by landing a man on the moon before the end of the decade of the 1960s.

A key question, however, is: What has transpired since then? National initiatives, such as the American Competitiveness Initiative announced by President George W. Bush in 2006, support the premise that the United States must provide additional supports to education to maintain its competitive edge in the world. If so, what role can and should higher education institutions and, in particular, schools and colleges of education, play in helping America maintain its competitiveness?

Without being overly dramatic, this question is quite important to American families, children, teachers, and citizens at large and can be answered with one word. That word is *accreditation*. According to the U.S. Department of Education Office of Postsecondary Education, "the goal of accreditation is to ensure that education provided by institutions of higher education meets acceptable levels of quality" as determined by an agency recognized by the U.S. Secretary of Education (www.ope.edu/accreditation). While earning accreditation may not be a panacea for all problems associated with preparing teachers and for restoring global competitiveness, it is a tool that schools of education can use to improve the quality of their preservice teachers and their teacher preparation programs.

A raging debate continues within the professional education community around the value of accreditation and whether expenses in terms of personnel and other resources are justified. Arthur Levine (2006a), in his report entitled "Educating School Teachers," expresses the viewpoint held by many teacher educators that the accreditation process is a weak way for the profession to police itself and is, therefore, not rigorous enough to provide confidence in the espoused quality of a given program or institution, thus failing to silence the critics of teacher education preparation programs. More and more, the critics maintain that the only true measure of quality teacher education programs are the academic gains students make in P–12 classrooms taught by graduates of these programs. According to Fallon (2006), "the emergence of longitudinal databases that link the performance of individual pupils with specific teachers has resulted in the emergence of a remarkable new technology, value-added analysis, that allows us to identify the results of effective teaching" (p. 151).

## ACCREDITATION: AN HISTORICAL PERSPECTIVE

While student achievement in mathematics and science has been gradually rising in the United States, America's problem is that it is not rising as quickly as it is in many other countries, including China, Japan, Indonesia, Korea, Estonia, and Hungary. Legislation such as PL 107-110, the *No Child Left Behind Act* of 2002 (NCLB) has put an intense focus on student achievement and school performance and in the process has shined a spotlight on teacher quality (Kellough & Kellough, 2007). Cochran-Smith (2005) observes, "Notwithstanding considerable debate about the meanings of *teacher quality and highly qualified teachers*, it is no exaggeration to say that the national focus on these issues rivals that of any previous period" (p. 306). Even so, the call for accountability via accreditation in higher education can be traced back approximately 100 years (Council for Higher Education Accreditation, 2006). Accreditation of education programs began in earnest in the 1950s and continues today as evidenced by key developments, including:

- The 1954 United States Supreme Court decision in *Oliver L. Brown et al. v. the Board of Education of Topeka (KS) et al.* "paved the way for diversity within and among school systems by dismantling "the legal basis for racial segregation in schools and other public facilities." (Brown Foundation for Educational Equity, Excellence, and Research, 2004).

- The National Council for the Accreditation of Teacher Education (NCATE) was founded in 1954 as an independent accrediting body, replacing the American Association of Colleges for Teacher Education (AACTE) as the agency responsible for monitoring the quality of teacher education programs (NCATE, 2007). The mission of NCATE is to "help establish high quality teacher, specialist, and administrator preparation. Through the process of professional accreditation of schools, colleges and departments of education, NCATE works to make a difference in the quality of teaching, teachers, school specialists and administrators. NCATE believes every student deserves a caring, competent, and highly qualified teacher" (NCATE, 2007, http://www.ncate.org/documents/NCATE Mission.pdf).

- The successful launch of Sputnik I on October 4, 1957, by the Soviet Union "ushered in new developments in technology, science, politics, and the military. It marked the beginning of the Space Age and the space race between the United States and the Soviet Union. This event led the U.S. citizenry to reevaluate the effectiveness of schooling, including higher education institutions, with an intense focus on science and mathematics instruction.

- On November 29, 1975, Congress passed the *Education for All Handicapped Children Act* (Public Law 94-142) "to support states and localities in protecting the rights of, meeting the individual needs of . . . infants, toddlers, children, and youth with disabilities and their families" (http://www.ed.gov/policy/speced/leg/idea/history.html). Amended in 1997, the law still continues to ensure that all students have access to appropriate educational services.

- In 1983, the National Commission on Excellence in Education released *A Nation at Risk.* Often recognized as the origin of current reform efforts, the report recommended (1) strengthening high-school graduation requirements in English, mathematics, science, social studies, and computer science; (2) adopting higher and measurable standards for performance by schools and colleges; (3) increasing the time that students spend engaged in learning activities; and (4) strengthening the teaching profession through higher standards for initial preparation and continued professional development (U.S. Department of Education, 2000).

- In 1990, Boyer's *Scholarship Reconsidered: Priorities of the Professoriate* ignited a passionate and continuing debate over the definition of scholarship and its role in teaching and learning.

- In 1997, the Teacher Education Accreditation Council (TEAC) was founded as a "nonprofit organization dedicated to improving academic degree programs for professional educators, those who will teach and lead in schools, pre-K through grade 12" by supporting "the preparation of competent, caring, and qualified professional educators" (TEAC, 2007, http://www.teac.org/about/index.asp). Specifically, "TEAC's primary work is accrediting undergraduate and graduate professional education programs in order to assure the public about the quality of college and university programs" (TEAC, 2007, http://www.teac.org/about/index.asp).

- On January 8, 2002, President George W. Bush signed the *Elementary and Secondary Education Act/No Child Left Behind Act* of 2002, which initially called for accountability and high standards for the academic achievement of all children in reading and mathematics by placing "highly qualified teachers" in every classroom (U.S. Department of Education, 2004).

- In 2006, Levine released *Educating School Teachers* with recommendations for improving what he considers to be the dismal state of teacher preparation programs (Washington, DC: Education Schools Projects, 2006). Reformation of schools of education and closure of others are among the proposed solutions discussed at length.
- On February 26, 2007, the membership of AACTE passed by a narrow margin Resolution 54 that calls for a "single, national, nongovernmental system for accreditation of educator development that is aligned with AACTE principles demonstrates impact on P-12 learners" (AACTE, 2007, http://www.aacte .org/Programs/Accreditation_Issues/resolution54.pdf).

## ACCREDITATION: CURRENT PERSPECTIVES

If teacher performance is going to be scrutinized so closely through assessments of pupil achievement mandated by NCLB, then the schools of education that prepare those teachers cannot escape that same scrutiny and accountability. How can higher education institutions that prepare teachers ensure that their preservice teachers are being held to the highest standards, that their programs are worthy of national recognition, and that the schools where preservice teachers intern and work with cooperating teachers provide optimal clinical/practical learning experiences that will shape their teaching effectiveness? Simply put, accreditation is a quality assurance process intended to answer accountability-related questions by measuring institutions and programs against a set of standards that have been field-tested by professionals over time.

### Multiple Functions of Accreditation

Many states currently require schools of education to be accredited for their preservice teachers to be eligible for state licensure. On a national level, every higher-education institution that prepares teachers must report the results of statewide licensing examinations as part of Title II. States like New York require schools of education to maintain pass rates above 80 percent to prevent losing the ability to prepare teachers and face the closure of their education programs; however, inconsistencies in accreditation requirements from state to state and differences in standards that states adhere to complicate the process of licensure reciprocity. This point is best illustrated by Wise (2005) who reported that "39 states adopted or adapted NCATE unit standards as state standards for approving teacher education institutions" (p. 328) and "22 states have chosen to delegate review of teacher education programs to NCATE for purpose of NCATE accreditation and state program approval" (p. 328).

Beyond verifying that an institution meets standards, accreditation fulfills other crucial roles. Accreditation helps consumers make informed choices about selecting higher-education institutions or programs that are of high quality. In a competitive job market, choosing a quality teacher preparation program suggests that the network of alumni and prospective employers affiliated with that institution or program can provide opportunities for mentoring and employment. Institutions or programs that are accredited may be reluctant to accept transfer credit from similar institutions or programs that have not been able to earn accreditation or have not sought accreditation.

With respect to extramural funding, if a funding agency has to choose between two institutions or programs that are competing for funds, will not the choice of the accredited school or program imbue more confidence? Similarly, to maintain one's accreditation requires adherence to standards over time. Maintenance of accreditation offers a valid reason for institutions or programs to resist undue political pressures from the community, to avoid reactionary responses to "fads of the day," to resist hiring faculty who do not meet the highest standards, and to remind administrators that failure to fund certain initiatives and infrastructure development may result in a loss of accreditation.

Accreditation also serves as one of several considerations used as a basis for determining eligibility for Federal assistance; however, the most important function of accreditation is the quality assurance process required both to achieve and maintain accreditation. Engaging faculty, staff, and students in a self-study process that targets goals for improvement, results in an overall raising of standards that ranges from simple changes in courses, to the design of new curricula, and to faculty development necessary to deliver new curricula better, can only strengthen the institution and its programs.

## The Accreditation Process

Accreditation in the United States is a process that can be applied to both governmental and nongovernmental agencies or institutions. However, the U.S. Department of Education (USDOE) is not charged with accrediting institutions of higher education or their specific programs. Rather, the USDOE is required to recognize private agencies and/or professional organizations that are deemed "reliable authorities" by the National Advisory Committee on Institutional Quality and Integrity to evaluate the excellence of an institution or its programs. The steps involved in such a recognition process, including the criteria and a list of recognized accrediting agencies regularly published by the USDOE, are published in the *Federal Register* (http://www. archives.gov/federal-register). Two well-known professional organizations nationally recognized for accreditation of schools of teacher education are NCATE and TEAC. As an option to either of the national organizations for accreditation, some states provide an alternate accreditation route for teacher education institutions or programs through state-sponsored regional accreditation processes.

The accreditation process usually takes place in the context of a peer evaluation provided by regional or national professional associations where institutions or programs are measured against a set of widely accepted standards of practice. An institution or program seeking accreditation would then undergo an intensive and comprehensive self-study, measuring and reviewing its admissions and advisements procedures, programs, faculty, graduation rates, resources, and so on against the accrediting agencies' standards. A site visit team of professionals from similar institutions or programs would then visit the institution or program seeking accreditation to verify the extent to which the standards are being met. Statements made in the self-study documents are verified in vivo by the visiting team. Questions that are asked by the visiting team provide a window into where an institution or a program may be falling short of meeting a given standard or provide insight into the fact that the substantiating evidence may not have been presented effectively.

Over time, the accreditation process has become increasingly data-based and outcomes driven. It is not enough for an institution or program to assert in a self-study document that standards are being met; hard data that are systematic, reliable, and valid must be made available to the team to document the extent to which standards have or have not been met. Moreover, "data for data-sake" is not the point of the accreditation review. An institution or program must show that the data collected are carefully reviewed by key stakeholders and used to make decisions that shape the further development of that institution or its program, as well as policy decisions. In essence, accreditation requires data collection on an ongoing basis and analysis of this data then drives program development and program quality.

Once an institution or program achieves accreditation, the process does not end there. Rather, findings from the accreditation review target areas for improvement, and provide specific timelines to address the areas of concern and make improvements. Accredited institutions or programs typically report on their progress toward standards or areas for improvement on a yearly basis, with the expectation that the areas for improvement will be completely satisfied before the next re-accreditation review takes place. Clearly, earning initial accreditation and then maintaining that accreditation across time involves an ongoing commitment to assessment, data analysis, and quality review.

## National Accreditation Benchmarks

The two major accreditation organizations for schools and programs of teacher education, NCATE and TEAC, appear similar on the surface. NCATE accredits at both the education unit and individual education program levels; TEAC accredits only at the individual program level. While some of the differences between these organizations will be explored, the strongest common link between them is the commitment to systematic assessment for the purpose of quality control. An examination of the NCATE standards and TEAC guiding principles for accreditation follows.

### NCATE Standards

The 2002 NCATE accreditation process is built around a conceptual framework that guides and informs education programs and a number of standards. The standards focus on achievement; program development, implementation, and assessment; and governance. Specifically, NCATE institutions must provide evidence of having met the following standards at least at the acceptable level as discussed at www.ncate.org.

- *Standard 1: Candidate Performance*, which is based on candidate knowledge, skills, and dispositions;
- *Standard 2: Assessment System and Unit Evaluation*, which requires systematic data collection on candidate qualifications and performance and demonstrates how that data collection informs program development, program improvement, and decision-making in the school of education;
- *Standard 3: Field Experiences and Clinical Practice*, which examines collaborations with professional development schools and the cooperating teachers on staff, and evaluates candidate performance (knowledge, skills, and dispositions) in fieldwork and student teaching/internship placements;
- *Standard 4: Diversity* focuses on the opportunities provided for preservice teachers (with diverse higher education faculty, diverse professional development school faculty, diverse preservice teachers, and diverse students in P-12 settings) to develop the necessary knowledge, skills, and dispositions needed to be successful when working in multicultural settings with diverse populations;
- *Standard 5: Faculty Qualifications, Performance, and Development*, which evaluates faculty performance as teachers themselves, as researchers, as collaborators in professional development schools, and overall as likely models for the knowledge, skills, and dispositions required of candidates; and
- *Standard 6: Unit Governance and Resources*, which measures a school of education's authority, resources, budget, personnel, and facilities including technology resources to determine the ability to prepare preservice teachers so they meet professional, state, and institutional standards (NCATE, 2002).

## *TEAC Principles*

Institutions seeking TEAC accreditation must provide evidence of having met *Quality Principles* by preparing inquiry briefs (www.teac .org). As with NCATE, the heart of TEAC is a commitment to an evidentiary process based on three guiding principles:

- *Quality Principle I* requires program faculty to provide concrete quantitative and qualitative evidence to support the student learning outcomes (depth of content and pedagogy preparation) that the program purports to develop as a function of its overall professional education curriculum and the sensitivity and caring with which that curriculum is delivered. Other content areas that the program is expected to provide concrete evidence about include multicultural sensitivity and technology.

- *Quality Principle II* requires program faculty to provide a rationale for the various assessments the program employs and that these assessments are both reliable and valid.
- *Quality Principle III* asks that program faculty analyze the data collected from the various assessments and use this information for the purpose of program review, program improvement, and policy decisions. To prove a program merits accreditation, additional information beyond the quality principles is needed to demonstrate that the program has the capacity to promote the student learning outcomes it is specifically designed to achieve. Capacity here refers to the adequacy of faculty, curriculum, budget, scholarship, student learning, counseling support services, and local school partnerships for fieldwork, student teaching, and internships.

## A Comparison of NCATE and TEAC Accreditation Processes

In comparing the process each accreditation organization requires, more similarities than differences exist. The most significant similarity, according to Murray (2005), is that "TEAC's Quality Principles I and II are virtually the same as NCATE 2000's Standards 1 and 2" (p. 309). Clearly, there are differences in the two approaches to accreditation. NCATE is more directive and scripted, requiring the alignment of the program's curriculum with state, specialty-group, and national standards (i.e., Interstate New Teacher Assessment and Support Consortium [INTASC] or National Board for Professional Teaching Standards [NBPTS]). "TEAC makes no prescriptions about what the better evidence must be, only whatever it is, it must (a) meet contemporary research standards and (b) support the claims that the graduates are competent, caring, and qualified" (Murray, 2005, p. 310). Although the nomenclatures vary, ultimately the difference between these two accreditation organizations has to do primarily with how each organization defines what is acceptable as evidence in the quality review process.

## Advantages and Disadvantages of Accreditation

Earning accreditation has many advantages for an institution or program. First and foremost, institutions or programs that are accredited are viewed as high quality because the ongoing systematic data collection process creates opportunities for program improvement and informed decision-making. Since earning accreditation is arduous, a positive result to an accreditation review evokes much professional pride on the part of both faculty and students. "The public expects that colleges of education should be professionally accredited. Eighty-two percent of the public favors requiring teachers to graduate from nationally accredited professional schools" (Public Opinion Poll, Penn and Schoen; NCATE Fact Sheet, http://www.ncate.org/docments/NCATEMission.pdf). Graduates of accredited institutions or programs may have increased employment opportunities and licensure mobility from state to state. From an institutional perspective, earning accreditation may help to leverage funds, both internally and externally, as accreditation requires certain expenditures to maintain program quality and to build partnerships and design grants to strengthen student clinical experiences.

In contrast, accreditation also carries some disadvantages. The accreditation process from preparing initial documents, to scheduling site visits, to arranging for food and lodging for site team members for several days is quite costly. Accreditation is resource intensive with respect to personnel, time, and money. Another concern about the entire process is that accreditation decisions may be somewhat subjective despite all attempts to prevent any bias. Weighing the benefits against the expenses, faculty and administrators of programs that have achieved accreditation are often at odds about whether the overall process has resulted in an improvement in program quality or increased candidate performance commensurate with the resource outlay. Moreover, can any teacher education accreditation process be rigorous enough to satisfy the critics of schools of education in this climate of increased accountability?

## IMPLICATION FOR TEACHER EDUCATION

*Educating School Teachers* (Levine, 2006a), a report that explores the effectiveness of university-based teacher education programs, proposes criteria that should be used to evaluate program quality and outlines a plan for improving teacher education programs, was released in September 2006. In essence, the report is about the reform of teacher education and the future of teacher preparation institutions. Levine's work is based on national surveys of key constituent groups: education school alumni, principals, education school deans, and faculty. Twenty-eight schools of education were visited, and their teacher education graduates were evaluated with respect to student achievement in their own teaching classrooms. Selected findings from the study excerpted from http://www.edschool.org/pdf/Educating_Teachers_Exec_Summ.pdf include:

- preservice teachers are not getting adequate preparation (not prepared for realities of today's classrooms);
- teacher education curricula are in disarray (no standard approach to preparing teachers; chasm between theory and practice);
- low admission standards plague education programs (education programs are "cash cows" lacking rigor in entrance and graduation requirements);
- insufficient quality control often characterizes teacher education programs (state and national accreditation standards for maintaining quality are ineffective because they focus on process and not substance);
- disparities in institutional quality (more than half of all teachers prepared are graduates of colleges awarding baccalaureate and master's degrees only. These colleges may lower admission standards, fewer distinguished faculty, and higher student-faculty ratios. While doctoral universities produce fewer teachers, the level of student achievement associated with doctoral university-trained teachers is higher); and
- effects on student achievement are quite limited in more than 50 percent of all teachers prepared in Master's I institutions.

According to Levine(2006a), teacher education programs must be judged with respect to their purpose (positively impacts student learning in K-12 schools), curricular coherence (supports the purpose), curricular balance (integrates theory and practice), faculty composition (consists of researchers and practitioners), admissions criteria (identifies students with capacity and motivation to be effective teachers), graduation standards (students are well prepared to teach), research (high-quality study linked to practice), finances (resources adequate to support the purpose), and assessment (systematic and ongoing for the purpose of program improvement). At the center of these criteria and the cornerstone of Levine's 2006 report is the definition of success—successful teacher education programs produce graduates who successfully impact student learning in K-12 settings as measured by scores on standardized assessments. To fully accept this statement as valid requires an understanding of value-added modeling that employs statistical formulae to control for the variability of a myriad of social factors in the Levine study that impinge on student performance.

The Levine study (2006a) concludes with five recommendations to strengthen teacher education:

1. Schools of education need to focus on school practice and should adopt a professional development school model.
2. Student achievement is the most pertinent measure of teacher quality. To effectively measure teacher quality, states will need to develop longitudinal tracking systems (not K-12 but K-16) so that student progress from year to year can be assessed for "value added." Schools of education should receive regular feedback on how effectively their graduates are performing in terms of student achievement. States including Florida, Ohio, and Delaware have been successful in developing K-12 tracking systems that may serve as models for other states.
3. Standardize teacher education program length to five years, with a strong focus on content mastery and content pedagogy.
4. Develop an effective mechanism for teacher education quality—rethink accreditation. Levine (2006a) urges the involvement of the exemplary teacher education programs he cites (Alverno College, Emporia State University-The Teacher's College, University of Virginia Curry School of Education, and Stanford University Teacher Education Program) in the development of new accreditation standards and compliance procedures.
5. States must also be asked to develop common, outcomes-based requirements for certification and licensure.
6. Close failing teacher education programs. Provide incentives for talented students and career changers to enter teacher edu-

cation at doctoral universities.Education schools whose graduates do not impact positively on student achievement using a value-added model should be closed to limit the damage that low-performing teachers can cause year after year.

## ACCREDITATION: WHERE DO WE GO FROM HERE?

AACTE, at its national meeting in February 2007, offered a proposal for membership endorsement that would establish a unified system for national accreditation, integrating both the NCATE and TEAC philosophies and practices. For example, NCATE requires each program to complete a specialty professional association review to determine if a given program can provide evidence that it meets the appropriate professional association's standards. According to Murray (2005), "these program reviews could be immeasurably improved, for example, if they were verified by a TEAC audit of the evidence cited in the program-review document" (p. 316).

As the focus continues on raising the quality of teacher preparation and student achievement in classrooms, a merger of these two separate accreditation organizations that brings the strengths of each model to the accreditation process of teacher education institutions in conjunction with strong state partnerships can be a very powerful tool for education reform. Wise (2005) states, "A profession is an occupation that seeks to regulate itself by (a) developing a consensus concerning what its practitioners must know and be able to do and (b) developing an accreditation and licensing system to ensure the transmission of that knowledge and skill. An occupation becomes a profession when organizations such as universities, states, and the public accept that system" (p. 318).

## QUESTIONS FOR DISCUSSION

This chapter has provided background information and a context for understanding the current issues swirling around accreditation of teacher education programs. The questions that follow will provide you with an opportunity to integrate and apply the material addressed in this chapter.

1. In his report entitled *Educating School Teachers* (2006a), Arthur Levine offers five recommendations for strengthening teacher education, including "The measure of a teacher education program's success is how well the students taught by its graduates perform academically" (http://www.edschool.org/pdf/Educating_Teachers_Exec_Summ.pdf). To what extent do you agree with this statement within the context of *NCLB?* To what extent is this view rather simplistic, given all the factors that impinge on performance and are outside the control of school personnel?

2. In reflecting on the material in this chapter, to what extent is the accreditation process an effective mechanism for ensuring the quality of teacher education preparation? If you do not perceive accreditation as an effective quality control measure, what alternative(s) would you recommend?

3. Think about the educational setting in which you work. To what extent are data collected, analyzed, and used for program development/improvement or policy decisions. How can such a data-based approach improve your setting?

## REFERENCES

*American Association of College for Teacher Education.* (2007). Retrieved July 11, 2007, from http://www.aacte.org.

*Accreditation in the United States.* (n.d.) Retrieved October 27, 2006, from http://www.ed.gov/print/adminis/finaid/accred/accreditation.html.

*American Competitiveness Initiative.* (2006). Retrieved July 10, 2007, from http://www.whitehouse.gove/stateoftheunion/2006/aci.

Boyer, E. (1990). *Scholarship reconsidered: Priorities of the professoriate.* San Francisco: Jossey-Bass.

*Brown Foundation for Educational Equity, Excellence, and Research.* (2004). Retrieved June 10, 2007, from http://www.brownvboard.org/summary/.

Clifford, G. J., & Guthrie, J. W. (1988). *Ed school: A brief for professional education.* Chicago: University of Chicago Press.

Cochran-Smith, M. (2005). The new teacher education: For better or for worse? *Educational Researcher, 34*(7), 3–17.

Council for Higher Education Accreditation. (2006). *Talking points: The value of accreditation.* Retrieved June 10, 2007, from http://www.chea.org.

Darling-Hammond, L. (6 September 2002). Research and rhetoric on teacher certification: A response to Teacher Certification Reconsidered. *Educational Policy Analysis Archives, 10*(36).

Education Commission of the States. *Teacher quality sources.* Retrieved October 31, 2006, from http://www.tqsource.org/prep/policy/.

Efforts to improve teacher quality. (5 January 2006). *Education Week: Quality Counts 2006*, pp. 86–90.

Fallon, D. (2006). The buffalo upon the chimneypiece: The value of evidence. *Journal of Teacher Education, 57*(139), pp. 139–154.

Graham, P. A., Lyman, R. W., & Trow, M. (1995). Accountability of colleges and university. Retrieved October 31, 2006, from http://www.teac.org/literature/acu.asp.

Kellough, R. D., & Kellough, N.G. (2007). *Secondary school teaching: A Guide to Methods and Resources* (3rd ed.). Upper Saddle River, NJ: Pearson, Merrill, Prentice Hall.

Levine, A. (2006a). *Educating school teachers.* Washington, D.C.: Education Schools Projects.

Levine, A. (2006b). *Educating school teachers: Executive summary.* Retrieved October 15, 2006, from http://www.edschool.org/pdf/Educating_Teachers_Exec_Summ.pdf.

Murray, F. B. (2005). On building a unified system of accreditation in teacher education. *Journal of Teacher Education, 56*(4), 307–317.

National Aeronautic and Space Administration. (19 January 2007). *Sputnik and the dawn of the Space Age.* Retrieved July 11, 2007, from http://history.nasa.gov/sputnik/.

National Archives and Records Administration (2007). *Federal register.* Retrieved July 27, 2007 from http://www.archives.gov/federal-register).

The National Commission on Excellence in Education. (1983). *A nation at risk: The imperative for educatinal reform.* Washington D.C.: The United States Department of Education.

*National Council for the Accreditation of Teacher Education.* (2007). Retrieved April 10, 2007, from http://www.ncate.org.

*NCATE Fact Sheet,* http://www.ncate.org/documents/NCATEMission.pdf

*No Child Left Behind Act of 2002, Public Law No. 107-110-2002.*

*Quality counts at 10: A decade of standards based education.* (2006). Retrieved October 31, 2006, from http://www.edweek.org/sreports/qc06.

*Teacher Education Accreditation Council.* (2007). Retrieved April 10, 2007, from http://www.teac.org.

U. S. Department of Education. (2000). *Special education and rehabilitative services archived: A 25-year history of the IDEA.* Retrieved July 9, 2007, from http://www.ed.gov/policy/speced/leg/idea/history.html.

U. S. Department of Education. (2004). *No Child Left Behind: A desktop reference.* Retrieved July 11, 2007, from http://www.ed.gov/admins/lead/account/nclbreference/index.html.

Weglinsky, H. (13 February 2002). How school matters: The link between teacher classroom practices and student academic performance. *Education Policy Analysis Archives, 10*(12).

Wise, A. E. (2005). Establishing teaching as a profession: The essential role of professional accreditation. *Journal of Teacher Education, 56*(4), 318–331.

# PART III
# EDUCATING TOMORROW'S TEACHERS

## Chapter 9

## PREPARING TEACHERS TO SUPPORT QUALITY FAMILY ENGAGEMENT IN SCHOOLS

Jerrell C. Cassady, Anne T. Henderson, Molly M. Jameson, and Jacqueline R. Garvey

*Coming together is a blessing;*
*keeping together is progress;*
*working together is success.*
(Henry Ford, n.d.)

### INTRODUCTION

Decades of controlled research studies and centuries of wisdom have demonstrated that parents and families play a critical role in their child's educational lives. The evidence has consistently supported the assertion that family engagement has a positive and meaningful impact on student achievement, achievement motivation, and children's satisfaction in educational settings. Furthermore, highly successful schools and schools that demonstrate dramatic positive gains in academic competence often report a strong family-school collaboration or partnership. Those schools that are successful in promoting engagement in families at various levels serve as models of best practices and generally can base their successes on the committed efforts of all stakeholders. A broad view of the stakeholder in this complex relationship is imperative to promote strong implementation of effective family-school-community partnerships that reproduce the positive effects of those exemplary models. Often, ecological systems theory provides a meaningful framework for representing the multiple spheres of influence that interact when discussing family engagement. In this way, the roles of teachers, families, students, community members, school administrators, and other relevant stakeholders are represented and respected as meaningful partners. Systems theories have also supported the development of several models of family engagement that appreciate the diverse contributions that families can make to school communities. Again, recognition of the family-school partnership as multifaceted and not cast in only a traditional "bake sale support" mode helps schools and families negotiate mutually beneficial relationships that ultimately support the child.

Consistent with the growing attention to promoting collaborations and partnerships among schools, families, and communities, teacher education programs have received some pressure to promote attention to preservice teachers' knowledge, dispositions, and performances relative to family influences in the school environment. For instance, in the Interstate New Teachers Assessment and Support Consortium (INTASC) standards, there are allusions as well as direct references to recognizing the role of diverse family backgrounds in student learning and attention to demonstrating the ability to communicate effectively with families from diverse settings. While innovative programs at select universities and colleges have demonstrated positive gains in promoting knowledge and skills related to promoting quality family-school partnerships, these programs typically are transient or isolated.

Thus, while there is clarity and consensus in the literature regarding the benefits of adopting family engagement models that are multidimensional, and the primary role that teachers serve in developing and supporting quality programs of family engagement in local schools, there continues to be a pervasive absence of systematic training in teacher education programs on proven strategies to develop and maintain family engagement in schools. This discusses the needs to include as part of the systemic nature of teacher education programs deliberate instruction on models of family engagement, strategies for promoting family-school partnerships, and developing family-friendly environments. Part of this discussion will include the presentation of leading models of family engagement, noted successes in promoting awareness and skill in developing teachers with strong family engagement strategies and promising practices that have begun to emerge as potential models to replicate in providing quality instruction.

## TIMELINE

- **1897.** National Congress of Mothers formed, holds first meeting in Washington, DC. Organization changed name to National Congress of Parents and Teachers, then The Parent Teacher Assocation (PTA).
- **1969.** Center for Law and Education founded at Harvard University, which is now a national presence for promoting student rights and family-school coordination.
- **1973.** National Committee for Citizens in Education (NCCE) formed to "put the public back in the public schools." The stated aim was to challenge the entrenched power of teachers' unions, administrator organizations, and the federal and state education bureaucracies. Strategies and infrastructure included national hotline, publishing house, national projects, and lobbying.
- **1973.** The Institute for Responsive Education (IRE) was founded at Boston University, with the mission of achieving "a more equitable distribution of educational opportunities and achievement for all children across lines of race, ethnicity, language, religion, gender, economic conditions, and geography" (http//www.responsiveeducation.org). From its university base, IRE conducted research, developed publications on partnership and shared responsibility, and offered professional development to educators on forming school, family, and community partnerships through its League of Responsive Schools.
- **1973.** Children's Defense Fund is established.
- **1981.** NCCE published the first in a series of research reviews on the impact of family involvement on student achievement, *The Evidence Grows.*
- **1981.** Joyce Epstein begins research on family involvement.
- **1983.** Harvard Family Research Project (HFRP) began its work to identify, conduct, and disseminate high-quality research and evaluation studies on family-school practices and programs.
- **1986.** *Beyond the Bake Sale: An Educator's Guide to Working with Families* published (Henderson, Marburger, & Ooms, 1986).

- **1987.** *The Evidence Continues to Grow* published by NCCE.
- **1989.** National Governors Association convened a bipartisan "Education Summit." At this summit, the groundwork was laid for the Goals 2000 Education Program, the major education reform framework in both the Bush and Clinton Administrations.
- **1992.** INTASC releases standards for teacher education. Standard 10 includes explicit focus on developing partnerships, collaboration, and communication with families and community members.
- **1994.** *A New Generation of Evidence: The Family is Critical to Student Achievement* by NCCE.
- **1994.** GOALS 2000–Educate America Act passed. The eighth goal was to increase family involvement in education. Also, in this year, NCCE became part of the Center for Law and Education.
- **1995.** First Parent Information Resource Centers (PIRCs) were created under Goals 2000 by the U.S. Department of Education. To this day, PIRCs provide families, schools, and organizations working with families with training, information, and technical assistance to understand better how children develop and what they need to succeed in school.
- **1995.** Joyce Epstein formed the National Network of Partnership Schools (NNPS) to which over 100 schools districts belong, pledging to implement six types of family involvement across their schools, through action teams for partnership.
- **2000.** Harvard Family Research Project launched the Family Involvement Network of Educators (FINE) to serve as a hub of resources for family engagement in children's education, and to enable colleagues in the field to connect and communicate. Monthly bulletins to over 5,000 members bring them up-to-date on the latest research and other developments.
- **2001.** Passage of No Child Left Behind (NCLB) – portion of legislation provides explicit rights and assurances to families.
- **2002.** *A New Wave of Evidence* published to complete series of "evidence" publication by Southwest Educational Development Laboratory.

## THE PROMISE AND POTENTIAL OF FAMILY ENGAGEMENT

In a series of reports over the past twenty-five years, Henderson and her colleagues have reviewed the growing research evidence that demonstrates the power of family engagement to advance children's academic achievement. Although critics have pointed out that many of these studies are correlational (albeit with rigorous statistical controls), the consistent convergence of data does document the validity of a significant relationship between engaged families and successful children.

To further support the conclusions gathered over the past four decades supporting the positive benefits that accompany family engagement, recent controlled research studies have systematically demonstrated the impact of family engagement on children's learning and school environments. These experimental and quasi-experimental studies have connected family engagement to academic achievement (i.e., standardized tests, grade point average, course completion), motivation toward school (i.e., attendance, courses attempted), and attitudes toward education (see Henderson & Mapp, 2002, for review). These positive effects are insensitive to demographic variables; that is, regardless of culture, race, or income, engaged families afford their children positive academic gains.

### Cultural Considerations

Despite the universal positive impact of engaged families, there is evidence for higher rates of engagement for White, middle-class families in the United States (Lareau & Horvat, 1999). Explanations for this disparity along cultural lines provide meaningful guidance to educators in attempting to bridge this gap in family-school partnerships.

First, many schools hold limited views of family engagement (e.g., room parent, tutor), precluding a segment of their stakeholders from becoming valued resources, especially those experiencing barriers of language and access. Second, an established body of literature documents the difficulty many families from minority cultures experience in trying to become fully assimilated members of the school community. Families of color and those with less income and education often feel excluded and "outside" the majority culture of the school, often dominated by White, middle-class employees and family leaders

(Ogbu, 2003). Third, traditional school structures and settings often do not provide venues or opportunities that allow families to have free and comfortable access to school staff or activities.

On the other hand, when schools and communities become deliberate in their attempts to make schools more "family friendly" and access the many talents or potential contributions that varied families can offer, cultural variations can be overcome. These gains are achieved when school leaders and staff re-examine the school culture and families' perceptions of the school climate. Through this process, the school can identify strategies that can overcome existing barriers to promoting positive involvement for all families (Henderson & Mapp, 2002).

## Models of Family Engagement

It is widely accepted in the field of family engagement that multidimensional views of family engagement are appropriate when attempting to examine the ways in which schools and families become active partners in the education of children. An early conceptualization focused on the locus of the impact for promoting engagement, contrasting among family, school, and community as the primary driving forces behind family involvement efforts (Gordon, 1977). New conceptualizations push for a broader range of true partnering that is drawing all three entities into the planning and implementation of family involvement. While a broad-based approach to promoting family engagement is the key to success, the greatest attention has been provided to classifying family profiles in an effort to support broader methods of supporting families who generally range from being active and "in charge" or passive and "reactive to schools" (Marcon, 1999). For instance, Williams and Chavkin (1989) focused on the roles families typically adopt (i.e., audience, home tutor, program supporter, co-learner, advocate, and decision maker), acknowledging that all families have the potential to serve in multiple ways. Shifting focus to the activities that families are likely to engage in, Ho Sui-Chu and Willms (1996) described four types (i.e., discussing school activities, monitoring out-of-school activities, contacting school staff, and volunteering or attending school events).

Like families, schools can range from passive to active in their efforts to promote family engagement. Cervone and O'Leary (1982) forwarded five broad strategies schools engage in to support family involvement (i.e., reporting progress, providing special events, family education, families teaching in school, families as decision makers). Among the different models available, the most widely recognized is Epstein's Six Types of Parent Involvement (2001), which has the flexibility to be used to identify strategies that can be applied by families, schools, or communities to promote multiple forms of family involvement. The following six types of family involvement and strategies that schools can adopt to support each type illustrate this model:

- *Parenting*–help all families establish a home environment that is supportive to students by ensuring the families have access to information on child-rearing, development, and education
- *Communicating*–develop open lines of communication between school and home that involves contact for positive as well as negative events
- *Volunteering*–improve recruitment, training, and flexibility for volunteer opportunities (be clear in the requests for support)
- *Learning at home*–involve families in school learning activities at home
- *Decision making*–include families in decision making, policy setting, and organizations affiliated with the school mission
- *Collaborating with community*–coordinate community resources that can be helpful to the school and families

Ideally, all families would be active in all six types of involvement. However, the model is sensitive to the reality that different families have special strengths, availability, and interests related to school. In this way, Epstein's model is intended to provide schools and families with a framework to use as a starting point to identify strategies or activities that can promote family engagement. The goal of this model is to provide committed families with at least one avenue through which they can provide active support to their children's educational activities.

## Successfully Implementing Family Engagement Programs in Schools

To maximize the probability of having a notable and sustained change in family engagement, the following general strategies have proven successful (Henderson, Mapp, Johnson, & Davies, 2007). First, schools should adopt multidimensional orientations to family engagement (e.g., Epstein's model). Second, identification of cultural differences among the school's families allows the school to be proactive in providing a setting that is more comfortable to families from diverse backgrounds. Third, when developing family-based activities, it is ideal to link the special events to what children are learning in the classroom to support families' use of complementary educational activities in the home. Fourth, the school needs to promote a culture of partnership that recognizes the dual needs to provide a "family friendly" school and a school that places decision-making power with families as well as school leaders. Finally, schools need to continually focus on their "outreach" efforts, adopting both school-based and family-based methods for reaching families in the school community.

Hoover-Dempsey and Sandler (1997) revealed key factors influencing the probability that families would decide to participate in school-driven family involvement efforts. Families were most likely to participate when they (a) perceived themselves as capable of providing useful help, (b) believed families should be a part of the schooling process, (c) felt wanted or needed by either their child or the school, (d) viewed themselves as available to support school efforts, and (e) felt the school provided concrete and valued suggestions for ways to become involved.

School programs therefore tend to be successful when they promote engagement through a multifaceted approach that centers on clear communication and flexible avenues for family involvement. One successful model for promoting school-level family engagement was developed by the Indiana Partnerships Center, a U.S. Department of Education Parent Information Resource Center. Their model rests on three primary factors necessary to promote success: education, physical presence, and collaboration (see Cassady et al., 2004).

### *Stakeholder Education*

The education component involves educating school staff, families, and administrators alike on how to implement family engagement models that are flexible and respect individual differences. Through collaborative training academies, all stakeholders construct broad conceptualizations of family involvement. In addition, the school partners engage in an initial needs assessment in which families and school staff work together to identify the true needs of the school. Once these needs are identified collaboratively, investment and dedication from all sides increase. A clear action statement or mission statement that has been identified by both families and school staff as essential can be articulated.

### Conspicuous Presence

The second factor for success was a physical presence for families in the school. The most successful approach is establishing highly visible family centers in the school that are staffed by families. Finding space in schools has never been easy, but re-allocating an underused staff workroom or conference room or even converting a large utility closet have all proven successful in helping families feel welcome and incorporated in the school setting. Another way to promote the physical presence and recognition of families in schools has been to merely provide a noticeable "uniform" (e.g., t-shirt or hat) for volunteers.

In the highly successful Security Dads program (and other iterations following their lead), volunteering fathers (broadly defined) wear clear identifiers such as bright t-shirts, jackets, or hats that are typically donated by community partners. A case study examining this nationally recognized program demonstrated this physical presence was directly connected to a revival of discontinued after-school activities (Cassady, Wallace, & Wallace, 2005). The inner-city school where Security Dads is housed had closed down all after-school groups and athletics due to several violent events occurring at school functions. This loss of a safe school culture was the impetus that sparked the Security Dads program, which has been in operation for over ten years. In the 2004-2005 academic year, thirty-eight volunteering fathers logged 4,320 hours of volunteer time *during school* for that year, in addition to attending all major school events *after school*, providing security and safety merely through their presence (Cassady et al., 2005).

### Deliberate Collaboration

The third factor found effective in promoting family engagement was collaboration (Cassady et al., 2004). Training practices that involve families and teachers working together provide an initial avenue for overcoming negative stereotypes, where both families and teachers view the other as disinterested or incapable of working toward active family involvement. When teachers and families identify core goals in a collaborative process, they have immediate access to a larger pool of resources (i.e., school, family, community) for making the engagement efforts a reality.

Evaluation of programs promoting family engagement in schools demonstrated that least successful schools were those without active participation from one of three stakeholder groups: family, administrator, or teacher (Cassady, 2006). That is, bilateral discussions between teachers and families fell short of full success because there was often a broader picture missed across the school. Commitment to family engagement at the school level without explicit connection to family members also led to failure, primarily because families were alienated or did not have investment in the program. And when families and administrators worked to develop family centers without actively informing or involving teachers, there was limited success because teachers were unaware of the resources available through the family center (e.g., greater communication, recruitment of volunteers).

## IMPLICATIONS FOR TEACHER EDUCATION

Most teacher education programs provide a cursory coverage of family involvement or family engagement in one or more classes (Shirley et al., 2006). Chavkin and Williams (1988) provided one of the most comprehensive reviews of teacher education programs' attention to family engagement. In their regional analysis of the southern and southeastern segment of the United States, the results indicated that the most common treatment of family involvement was in a single-class presentation, which only 37 percent of the teacher educators claimed to devote to the topic. Contrasting the paucity of coverage at the undergraduate level with the simultaneous agreement among families, teachers, school administrators, and teacher educators that family engagement instruction should be required in preservice teaching programs suggests that teacher education programs are failing their constituents (Chavkin & Williams, 1988).

Tichenor (1998) supported these findings, revealing that preservice teachers at the end of their programs repeatedly called for more explicit training and exposure to family involvement practices that would be successful in their future classroom placements. In addition to the preservice teachers' awareness that they needed more information, Tichenor documented belief patterns among preservice teachers at the beginning and end of their programs that demonstrated stereotypic views of family involvement tendencies based on race and gender were not shifted over the course of their learning. That is, naïve misconceptions that there are racial or gender differences in family involvement interest and willingness were not overcome during their teacher education training. If nothing else was addressed, the most basic finding reported by family involvement experts (e.g., Henderson et al., 2007) resound that *all* families are committed to their children. The differences in family engagement levels are almost universally driven by situational factors that discourage involvement through cultural alienation or logistic barriers.

For those programs that do provide explicit instruction on family engagement or family-related topics, the bulk of information transmission comes from a student teaching or practicum experience (Tichenor, 1998). Outside of this hit-and-miss treatment of family engagement training, there are documented programs that provide promise to developing and delivering quality instruction for including families in schools effectively. Unfortunately, strategies that have been shown to be effective often exist in programs that are transient or provided to a limited enrollment population. However, the availability of burgeoning evidence of successful instructional strategies arising at the same time that the INTASC standards provide external pressure to document attention to promoting family involvement strategies provides some promise for extending these program efforts.

## Professional Development Schools Model

One model that has been productive in promoting teacher education programs' delivery of instruction that impacts skills and dispositions of their preservice teachers has been to partner with local schools through symbiotic relationships such as a professional development school. These programs may involve practicum experiences for preservice teachers, formal instruction within the school setting, or other methods that merely place the preservice teachers in the school during instructional times. Seeing schools in action is a positive step for teacher education, but these programs seldom place preservice teachers in contact with families, simply because there are few families around during school hours.

One school-university partnership program that explicitly focused on family engagement used preservice teachers and faculty skills in gathering materials and preparing documents on family engagement strategies and resources to provide the school staff with information and materials to promote family involvement (Rogers, Danielson, & Russell, 2000). This experience was judged to be a success for the preservice teachers, who gained theoretical knowledge on family involvement. However, the experience also revealed that the local schools were not enacting those strategies consistently (Rogers et al., 2000). As such, the disconnect between the university focus and the reality observed in their school interactions was striking and likely invalidated much of what they were learning.

## Immersive Learning Model

Shirley and colleagues (2006) demonstrated that greater levels of immersion in the school and community culture were necessary to truly interact with school families. To enable the students to become familiar with the needs and interests of families in the urban schools, the students were required to interact with families from the community, provide information to families at open house night in the school, and create and implement a family engagement strategy in the urban high school. The outcomes of Shirley and colleagues' work revealed that the university students did acquire a broader recognition of the family needs in the school setting, were more sensitive to the interests of the families, and gained an appreciation for strategies that were useful in connecting the families to the school in a positive fashion. However, these effects are unlikely to be replicated in programs that do not provide for consistent interaction with school families.

The findings identified several challenges that provide barriers to widespread implementation in teacher education programs. These barriers included finding space in local schools to house the program, perceived inequity over course requirements and grading by the university students, and preservice teachers' reservations with entering into the socioculturally diverse setting characteristic of this urban school experience, which was dramatically different than their relatively homogeneous university experience (Shirley et al., 2006). To promote success in such immersive learning settings, the authors proposed that full disclosure or program transparency was essential. For instance, prior to enrollment, preservice teachers should be given a list of locations for all activities and a description of course requirements to avoid immediate resistance when the course begins.

## WHERE DO WE GO FROM HERE?

Naturally, it is our contention that quality teacher education programs need to provide explicit training in family engagement practices. However, the process through which that may occur varies widely dependent upon the programmatic features and existing structures. In our experience, this is generally handled by individuals within the teacher education program who are familiar with standards-alignment activities. That is, the core members who oversee alignment with licensing or accreditation standards (e.g., the National Council for Accreditation of Teacher Education, state licensing boards) or with meeting the guidelines for some other group of nationally derived standards (e.g., INTASC) are in the best position to help identify the programmatic location that is best equipped to include family engagement training.

Positive approaches that are likely to be successful include adding the content to a capstone or final professional experience course delivered by a university-based instructor (not left to a supervising teacher in the schools), use of a seminar-based crediting program in which experts in family involvement deliver workshops on the topic and each student has a variety of opportunities to attend a series of trainings on the topic (perhaps supported through distance education initiatives), infusion in existing courses that are "catch-alls," or make it an ever-present initiative that is included in all courses at some level (where reasonable). While each of these strategies is popular for meeting the seemingly unending parade of topics that need to be included in a degree program that is already overloaded with credit hours, they each have pitfalls that institutions need to navigate.

Capstone courses that provide coverage of information at the end of the training cycle often experience overload in addressing important topics or serve as post-student teaching group therapy sessions. Important content in these courses is often glossed over. Furthermore, these courses are generally a last class for the education majors and can experience a degree of "burn-out" for the participants. At the least, it seems to be late in the preparation program to throw in a final comment about family engagement as the future teacher is going off to the "real world." Without earlier presentation of these topics, preservice teachers are unlikely to make useful observations in their practicum experiences or infuse family engagement content with their other professional learning information.

Seminar-based programs or independent study approaches to picking up content that seems to be missing in a program is a "duct-tape" solution to teacher education. While it mimics true professional development, there tends to be a perception that these topics are less important. Why else are they relegated to the noncourse route? There is great promise in programs that have a well-organized noncourse method for requiring content coverage. However, it is our belief that this content warrants some level of face-to-face interaction, even when supported through a technology learning module process.

Adding the content to a catch-all course is dangerous, particularly in larger programs. One of the authors has taught such a course for years and has been asked within that one course to cover various topics in addition to the regular content, simply because "they won't get it anywhere else." These topics included special education identification and treatment, diversity awareness, communicating with families (!!!), technology in the classroom, meeting state content standards with lesson plans, and behavior management strategies. Each of these topics is a course to itself, in an ideal program. Adding one more important topic is likely to lead to failure in many ways, including the application of "academic freedom" by instructors in a multi-section program. Variability in presenting family engagement models is likely, and when the content is not a necessary component of a particular course and defined clearly, there are likely going to be gaps in presentation.

Finally, making family engagement a topic of primary importance in a teacher education program by making all courses responsible for the content is another solution that will likely have short-term success but fade into mediocrity in short order. These institutional approaches to instruction have been attempted with technology, diversity, special needs, and other key issues in teacher training. However, over time there is a gradual fading in individual course's attention to the core topic for several reasons. One of the most seductive reasons an instructor in this type of program cuts that content is that "everyone else is teaching it anyway, and I am already behind." That is, diffusion of responsibility allows everyone to be excused from being accountable for presenting the content.

So, where to go? Individual programs should identify specific classes where the content can be covered consistently, ideally with some aspect of immersion involved to provide realistic contextual exposure to families in school settings. These may include courses focusing on diversity, classroom management, or professional practices. The content should also be infused in all courses at some level, as a supportive process. That is, in special education courses, attention to how to communicate with families of children with special needs should be taken on. When presented within a larger framework of a broad view of family engagement, this can be covered in short order focusing on the technical aspects of rights and protections with privileged communication rather than going into depth on how one might effectively open lines of communication with families.

## QUESTIONS TO PROMPT DISCUSSION

To guide programs toward meeting the needs on these issues, some guiding questions are appropriate. For instance:

1. How early is presentation of the core information (types of family engagement) necessary within the teacher education program?
2. What access do preservice teachers have to working with family volunteers in local schools?
3. What existing university-school partnerships can be enhanced through involvement of preservice teachers with family volunteers on school activities?
4. How can the logistical barriers of immersive learning experiences that engage preservice teachers with families be overcome?
5. What community leaders are available to discuss the importance of family-school-community partnerships on a regular basis?
6. Which unit or department will be the host to family engagement content?

7. How will we measure students' mastery for the knowledge, skills, and dispositions of effective family engagement?

## REFERENCES

Cassady, J. C. (2006). Indiana Partnerships Center final program evaluation: Parent Information Resource Center Program Years 2002–2006. Unpublished technical report filed with the U.S. Department of Education, August 1, 2006.

Cassady, J. C., Wallace, L., & Wallace, A. (2005). *Security Dads case study.* Technical evaluation report submitted to U.S. Dept of Education as part of Parent Information Resource Center evaluation report.

Cassady, J. C., Speirs Neumeister, K. L., Ballard, K. D., Garvey, J., Wallace, L., & Wallace, A. (2004). *Promoting parental leadership in the schools: Fathers programs and parent centers.* Paper discussion session at the American Educational Research Association 2004 Annual Meeting, San Diego, CA.

Cervone, B. T., & O'Leary, K. (1982). A conceptual framework for parent involvement. *Educational Leadership, 40,* 48–49.

Chavkin, N. F., & Williams, D. L. (1988). Critical issues in teacher training for parent involvement. *Educational Horizons, 66,* 87–89.

Epstein, J. L. (2001). *School, family, and community partnerships: Preparing educators and improving schools.* Boulder, CO: Westview Press.

Gordon, I. J. (1977). Parent education and parent involvement: Retrospect and prospect. *Childhood Education, 54,* 71–77.

Henderson, A. T. (1987). *The evidence continues to grow: Parent involvement improves student achievement.* Columbia, MD: National Committee for Citizens in Education.

Henderson, A. T. (1986). *Beyond the bake sale: An educator's guide to working with parents.* Columbia, MD: National Committee for Citizens in Education.

Henderson, A. T., & Mapp, K. L. (2002). A new wave of evidence: The impact of school, family, and community connections on student achievement. SEDL.

Henderson A. T., & Mapp, K. L. (2002). *A new wave of evidence: The impact of school, family, and community connections on student achievement.* Austin, TX: Southwest Educational Development Laboratory.

Henderson, A. T., Mapp, K. L., Johnson, V. R., & Davies, D. (2007). *Beyond the bake sale: The essential guide to family-school partnerships.* New York: The New Press.

Henderson, A. T., Marburger, C., & Ooms, T. (1986). *Beyond the bake sale: An educator's guide to working with parents,* Columbia, MD: National Committee for Citizens in Education.

Ho Sui-Chu, E., & Willms, J. D. (1996). Effects of parental involvement on eighth-grade achievement. *Sociology of Education, 69,* 126–141.

Hoover-Dempsey, K. V., & Sandler, H. M. (1997). Why do parents become involved in their children's education? *Review of Educational Research, 67,* 3–42.

Lareau, A., & Horvat, E. M. (1999). Moments of social inclusion and exclusion: Race, class, and cultural capital in family-school relationships. *Sociology of Education, 72*(1), 37–53.

Marcon, R. A. (1999). Positive relationships between parent school involvement and public school inner-city preschoolers' development and academic performance. *School Psychology Review, 28*(3), 395–412.

Ogbu, J. U. (2003). *Black American students in an affluent suburb: A study of academic disengagement.* New York: Lawrence Erlbaum Associates.

Rogers, S., Danielson, K., & Russell, J. F. (2000). Collaborating to promote effective elementary practices across seven school districts. *Peabody Journal of Education, 75*, 133–144.

Shirley, D., Hersi, A., MacDonald, E., Sanchez, M. T., Scandone, C., Skidmore, C., & Tutwiler, P. (2006). Bringing the community back in: Change, accommodation, and contestation in a school and university partnership. *Equity and Excellence in Education, 39*, 27–36.

Tichenor, M. (1998). Preservice teacher attitudes toward parent involvement: Implications for teacher education. *The Teacher Educator, 33*, 248–259.

Williams, D. L., & Chavkin, N. F. (1989). Essential elements of strong parent involvement programs. *Educational Leadership, 47*, 18-20.

# Chapter 10

# MULTICULTURAL EDUCATION IN TEACHER EDUCATION

H. Richard Milner, IV, Judson Laughter, and F. Blake Tenore

*In order to educate teachers so that they will convey images, perspectives, and points of view in the curriculum that will demystify social realities and promote cultural freedom and empowerment, we must radically change the ways in which they acquire knowledge.*

(Banks, 2006, p. 218)

## INTRODUCTION

In this chapter, we discuss multicultural education in teacher education. In particular, we focus on the goals and importance of multicultural education in teacher education, the benefits of multicultural education, the contexts of multicultural education, who can and should teach about multicultural education, and approaches to multicultural education. We offer implications for teacher education and suggestions for future directions. We begin with a timeline of multicultural education in teacher education.

## TIMELINE

Below is a timeline capturing the history of multicultural and teacher education. It is interesting to look back and see how we have progressed and regressed over time. While the timeline begins in the nineteenth century, it is important to note that the ancient Greek notion of multicultural education is similar to that toward which many strive today. In the fifth century BCE, Herodotus examined the customs of distinct countries in order to understand their way of life and to attain a critical perspective on his own. He compared the nature of things (*phusis*) to convention (*nomos*). In 44 BCE, Cicero wrote *De Officiis*, proclaiming a duty to treat humanity with respect and aliens with hospitality. The Stoics learned to converse with local differences in order to discern and respect the humanity in all, a goal toward which some work today (for more, see Nussbaum, 1997).

As topics have progressed and regressed in the field of multicultural education, it is interesting to note how many of the same debates surrounding teacher education recycle over time. Since the late nineteenth century, battles have been fought concerning the roles and responsibilities of the teacher, how and where teachers were prepared, what the role of liberal arts should be in teacher preparation, and what research paradigms and questions were most capable of bringing about "right" changes in teacher education. At present the majority of U.S. teachers are prepared in four-year colleges and universities, but scholars have considered ways to educate teachers in different contexts. Again, educators and researchers find themselves grappling with centuries-old questions about what should be taught in schools, by whom, where, and with what level of professional development.

- **1839.** The first public normal school is established in Lexington, Massachusetts (Borrowman, 1965).
- **1888.** Charles Kendall Adams argues for teaching pedagogy in colleges and universities (Borrowman, 1965).
- **1890.** National Education Association Committee of Twelve on Rural Schools calls for professionally trained teachers, wider establishment of Normal Schools, and the introduction of pedagogy study in lab schools (Schwartz, 1996). Around 39 percent of school-aged Blacks are enrolled in high schools, mostly private (Anderson, 1988).
- **1895 through 1915.** Booker T. Washington establishes centers for industrial education, including the Tuskegee Institute, seeking to create independently sustainable communities.
- **1899.** The Supreme Court opinion in *Cumming v. School Board of*

*Richmond County, GA* effectively upends the 1896 decision in *Plessy v. Ferguson* and establishes the de jure separation of races in education.

- **1903.** WEB DuBois publishes *The Souls of Black Folk* and offers a counter argument to Washington, today known as the Talented Tenth.
- **1914.** Large numbers of immigrants in the teaching force make uniformity in teacher preparation difficult (Schwartz, 1996).
- **1916.** Thomas Jesse Jones studies Black secondary education and finds most black high schools are academic with a large focus on languages (Anderson, 1988).
- **1928.** The Meriam Report claims Native American education should be tied more closely to their communities (Anderson, 1988).
- **1946.** Commission on Teacher Education finds that optimal teacher preparation integrates strong general education with professional training. Programs expand to look more like traditional Arts and Sciences degrees including general education, subject-matter specialty, methods and pedagogy courses, and field experiences (Schwartz, 1996).
- **1950.** American Council on Education sponsors College Study in Intergroup Relations to improve multicultural component of teacher education (Nussbaum, 1997).
- **1960s.** Institutions respond to the Civil Rights Movement and establish mono-ethnic courses taught by ethnic members with a focus on White racism (Banks, 2006).
- **1970s.** Most lab schools are closed (Schwartz, 1996). Mono-ethnic courses evolve into multiethnic studies courses that are less politically oriented (Banks, 2006).
- **1977**: National Council for Accreditation of Teacher Education (NCATE) first publishes multicultural education requirements and standards.
- **1980s.** Education research focuses on, "What do students know and how do they know it?" Progressive tradition develops and beginning teachers have some input in the direction of their preparation (Carter, 1990, cited in Wideen, Mayer-Smith, & Moon, 1998).
- **1990s.** Education research is characterized by a concern for multiculturalism, gender, and systemic reform. Preparing

teachers for diverse classrooms becomes a major concern as traditional forms of learning to teach appear problematic (Artiles, Trent, & Kuan, 1996; Grant, 1994).

- **2000 to present.** Multicultural teacher education generally is conceived as a singular addition or elective and is often not centralized in the preparation of teachers (Vavrus, 2002).

## GOALS AND IMPORTANCE OF MULTICULTURAL EDUCATION

As the United States becomes increasingly diverse and multicultural, researchers and theoreticians agree that multicultural education is a necessity. Public schools and teacher-education programs work to prepare students to live and function in society (Banks, 1998; Ford, 1996). Students from various ethnic backgrounds need to encounter and experience curricula highlighting, showcasing, and speaking from the point of view of people of color, women, and other marginalized groups. Multicultural education recognizes that perspectives vary with lived experience; it is important for students in public and higher education to understand themselves and others as cultural, racial, gendered, and ethnic beings in order to live and thrive in a global society. Indeed, multicultural education has great importance in the preparation of students (from P-16 through graduate and professional education) as people from various walks of life work to live together.

This is not to say, however, that multiculturalism or multicultural education can be entered into lightly, the product of emotional hearts without the support of active minds, critiquing current systems. Without a critical stance–toward society, its schools, and those emblazoning "multicultural" on their curriculum guides and textbooks– multicultural education becomes only a bolt-on addition to whatever curriculum is already in place (Banks, 2006), leaving in place the mono-cultural system with just a few decorative lessons. Multicultural education should hearken to its critical ancestors and head the call toward social activism.

It is insufficient merely to adopt the word *multicultural* as a descriptor of adding a couple heroes and holidays of non-White society. It is insufficient to use the word *multicultural* as a euphemism for non-White, whether in relation to students, teachers, or curricula. The

critical–meaning both *needed* and *social-activist*–stance toward multicultural education requires looking past the binaries of "us" and
"them," past "Black" and "White," to a place where we begin to question those continua and what they hide by drawing our eyes only to
the extremes. "Multi" means many: many to be studied, many to be
understood, many to be lifted up, many to be celebrated, many to be
brought into communion with one another as equals. Thus, critical
multicultural education is important to understand and implement in
teacher education and ultimately for its adaptation into P-12 contexts.

The goals of multicultural education can be essential for student
learning in both public schools and in teacher education. For instance,
Banks (1998) maintained that a goal of multicultural education was to
"increase educational equality for both gender groups, for students
from diverse ethnic and cultural groups, and for exceptional students"
(p. 22). Jenks, Lee, and Kanpol (2001) suggested that additional goals
of multicultural education involved "knowledge of cultural and racial
differences and issues; the critical examination of one's own beliefs
and values regarding culture, race, and social class; and an understanding of how knowledge, beliefs, and values determine one's behavior. . ." (p. 88). However, critics suggest that multicultural education can divide society. They maintain that the ever-presence of our
differences somehow divides the country and that schools should work
to create a melting pot–where students are educated to become American. Further, critics reject the idea that various ethnic groups living in
America should maintain their cultural and racial awareness, heritage,
identity, and ways of knowing. Ladson-Billings (1992a) responded to
these pervasive critiques by stressing that multicultural education
"advocate[s] unity *and* diversity" (p. 310). She goes on to suggest that
"cultural differences do not [and should not] necessarily result in lack
of unity" (p. 308). Rather, multicultural education may help build
bridges and unite diverse groups.

Pervasive questions on the goals and importance of multicultural
education include the following: Should those of us concerned about
the preparation of teachers for public school classrooms, educate and
prepare prospective teachers and, in turn, their P-12 students to embrace and celebrate other cultures? If so, how can we prepare students
to live and function in society and help them maintain their multidimensional identities? If not, how do we ensure that students are able
to live and function in society without the necessary cultural knowl-

edge and understanding of themselves and others? Can multicultural education ensure that all students have a better chance at experiencing learning? Who benefits from and should be exposed to multicultural education?

## Who Benefits from Multicultural Education?

A recurring question emerging in the literature is for whom multicultural education is intended and needed. In other words, who may benefit from multicultural education? That is, in what types of schools, with what population of students, and by what means ought multicultural education be present in the curriculum—if present at all? Understandably, multicultural education may be advantageous for students of color and other marginalized students because the approach incorporates these students' cultures and experiences in addition to others. Some students are at a disadvantage because their cultures are inconsistent with their teachers' cultures (Banks, 1998). These cultural inconsistencies can result in mismatches in the classrooms (Ladson-Billings, 1994). Thus, it is conceivable that multicultural education is important for ethnically diverse groups of students. But is multicultural education beneficial for White students as well?

Research suggests that multicultural education is also important and beneficial for White students (Banks, 1998; Lewis, 2001). Exposure to and experience in thinking about the world from diverse perspectives may help all students develop critical thinking skills and a broader base of knowledge for living and functioning in a highly diverse society. Banks (1998) explained that multicultural education "is to help *all* students, including White mainstream students, to develop the knowledge, skills, and attitudes they will need to survive and function effectively in a future U.S. society in which one out of every three people will be a person of color" (p. 23). In this line of thinking, multicultural education is not only concerned with and beneficial for students of color, but it is also advantageous for White students. However, as Jenks, Lee, and Kanpol (2001) put it, "In suburban schools in which the population is basically white and middle-class, multicultural education is often viewed as unnecessary" (p. 87), and teachers, community members, and parents often adopt color-blind and culture-blind ideologies and philosophies (Johnson, 2002; Lewis, 2001; Milner, 2003, 2005; Milner & Smithey, 2003), refusing to acknowledge the centrality and importance of race and culture in education and society.

When teachers do not "see color" or at least acknowledge that race matters, there may be "ignored discriminatory institutional practices toward students of color such as higher suspension rates for African-American males" (Johnson, 2002, p. 154) in conjunction with students of color being referred to special education and lower tracked courses in general. When teachers pretend they do not see color and culture, they do not consider cultural and racial experiences in the teaching and learning process and, ultimately, students may suffer. Banks (2001) explained that "a statement such as 'I don't see color' reveals a privileged position that refuses to legitimize racial identifications that are very important to people of color and that are often used to justify inaction and perpetuation of the status quo" (p. 12).

The idea that racial discrimination and cultural misunderstandings do not exist in predominantly White settings is a fallacy. Students in these settings do not live in a vacuum; they will experience diversity, and they must learn to live with other people in the world. In Banks' (1995) words, "multicultural education, . . . if implemented in thoughtful, creative, and effective ways, has the potential to transform schools and other educational institutions in ways that will enable them to prepare students to live and function effectively in the coming century" (p. 391). Thus, the context in which multicultural education is implemented is very important to its effectiveness.

## How Do Contexts Matter in Multicultural Education?

Because individual philosophical positions about the relevance and importance of multicultural education differ, the contexts where multicultural education is implemented matter significantly. School setting can either enable or stifle success in the classroom; the belief systems, goals, missions, and discourses of the school can circumvent teachers' desires to transform the curriculum into multicultural. In Buendia, Gitlin, and Doumbia's (2003) words, "The present-day contexts of schools may push critically minded teachers . . . in ways that undermine their desires" (p. 317). Teachers (of any ethnic background) may struggle to incorporate multicultural education in settings where colleagues or institutions are unsupportive of such a focus. As Banks and Banks (1995) explained, "The school culture and social structure are powerful determinants of how students [and teachers] learn to perceive themselves. These factors influence the social interactions that take place between students and teachers . . . both inside and outside the classroom" (p. 153). The milieu and persistent discourses characterizing a teacher's workplace are essential to both what a teacher practices and how. Many White teachers, particularly preservice teachers just beginning their teacher-education programs, wonder just who can and should teach multicultural education. In other words, is it appropriate for White teachers to teach multicultural education in any context?

## Who Can and Should Teach Multicultural Education?

Who teachers are (their roles and identities), their experiences, and stories often appear in their work with students. Thus, teaching is a personal and political endeavor and preparing teachers to understand themselves (their beliefs, values, and philosophies) can make them more productive multicultural educators. Teachers of any ethnic background can successfully teach culturally and racially diverse students. Ladson-Billings (1994) described the successful pedagogical practices of teachers from various ethnic backgrounds with African-American students. Milner (2005a) described a Black teacher who was successful in developing and implementing a multicultural curriculum with her predominantly White students. The idea is that teachers from various racial and ethnic backgrounds can be successful with students in a range of contexts from urban to suburban.

Thus, the goal of successfully implementing multicultural content in a particular setting has more to do with what teachers possess in terms of their knowledge, then who the teachers are. Gay (2000) wrote, "members of one ethnic group [can be] successful teachers of students from other ethnic and racial groups" (p. 205), even when the teacher is White and is teaching predominantly Black or Latino/a students about multicultural education.

Because the number of culturally, racially, and linguistically diverse students in the United States is increasing at a high rate, and because teachers remain largely White, middle class, and female, studies have consistently explored the success of White teachers teaching in predominantly African American or other ethnically diverse settings (Cooper, 2003; Johnson, 2002; Ladson-Billings, 1994; Rushton, 2004). This important line of research, commonly known as the demographic focus helps us think about and conceptualize some of the complexities inherent in the cultural and racial disconnections, connections, and mismatches that often emerge in classrooms between teachers and students. As Foster (1995) and Smith (2000) explained, teachers' backgrounds (cultural, racial, linguistic, and ethnic) play important roles in the education of students, particularly students of color. At the same time, teachers should act as learners in their classroom and approach, develop, and implement multicultural education with a great deal of care and sensitivity to all the students in the classroom.

## How Do Teachers Approach Multicultural Education?

During classroom discussions and in readings, Gay (2000) asserted that students often felt "insulted, embarrassed, ashamed, and angered when reading and hearing negative portrayals of their ethnic groups or not hearing anything at all" (p. 116). Thus, it is not enough to incorporate the historical, political, and social experiences, events, and challenges of various ethnic groups into the curriculum. Rather, the nature of that curriculum content (what is actually included, how, and why) is very important as students in public schools and in teacher education come to understand themselves and others in a pluralistic society. Moreover, it is important for P-16 students to be given the opportunity to critique and analyze information they read, hear, and are taught. To be clear, teachers' approach to multicultural education should go beyond mere exposure to a wide range of content by individuals from various walks of life. A central goal and approach to multicultural education should be for P-16 students to have the opportunity to critically and analytically engage the materials to which they are being exposed (Ladson-Billings & Tate, 1995).

In short, when approaching multicultural education, teachers should: (1) exhibit care and sensitivity in the development and implementation of multicultural content; (2) act as learners in the classroom and negotiate the knowledge and expertise in the classroom; (3) provide spaces for students to critically and analytically engage the multicultural content; and (4) work to understand themselves in relation to others.

## IMPLICATIONS FOR TEACHER EDUCATION

What are some implications for teacher education? First, teacher-education programs should consider developing critical multicultural educational experiences for their preservice teachers. Such multicultural educational experiences include, but are not limited to: (1) coursework on multicultural education (particularly courses that allow students to critically examine various texts and experiences); (2) research experiences on and about multicultural education; (3) fieldwork, including student teaching and practicum experiences in highly diverse, urban, and multicultural settings; and (4) opportunities to bridge their practical experiences with theory.

The content of their educational experiences has a strong influence on whether teachers embrace multicultural education or reject it in the P-12 classroom (Milner, 2003). If teachers leave teacher-education programs and enter their P-12 classrooms without any knowledge and skills for teaching culturally and racially diverse students, teachers and schools may continue to fail their students, particularly their students of color. Unfortunately, teacher-education programs resemble, in some ways, the curriculum of public schools; the curriculum does not take into consideration issues of race, culture, or gender in the construction or implementation of the curriculum. Consequently, ethnically and racially diverse students suffer from poor instruction and underdeveloped curriculum. Research and theory are clear that teachers in public schools and at the college level should rethink, renegotiate, and transform the nature of their curriculum from more traditional models where many ethnic groups are either misrepresented or not represented at all to curricula that are more inclusive of various racial, linguistic, and cultural groups (Arias & Poynor, 2001; Banks, Cookson, & Gay, 2001; Dillard, 1996; Troutman, Pankratius, & Gallvan, 1999). Ideally, there should be programmatic synergy in the teacher-education programs so that students experience more than a stand-alone course about multicultural education.

In addition, teacher education should consider working to recruit and retain teachers who have a desire to teach in highly diverse and urban school settings. Such recruitment and retention can be helpful when teacher educators work to provide the highest levels of multicultural instruction. They can move beyond superficial discussions and experiences because preservice teachers (1) have a desire to learn about multicultural education and (2) are willing to work hard to increase what they know.

Third, teacher educators themselves may need to become more educated about multicultural education and its usefulness. For instance, do teacher educators know and understand the major strands of the discussion in previous sections of this chapter? Do teacher educators understand the goals and importance of multicultural education, who benefits from multicultural education, how contexts matter in multicultural education, who can and should teach multicultural education, and how teachers can approach multicultural education?

## WHERE DO WE GO FROM HERE?

It is very important to note that race-conscious scholars often criticize multicultural education as a liberal response to issues of power, hegemony, and oppression. Moreover, they argue that race is not centralized, is often trivialized, and is only marginal in the grand scheme of multicultural education. These issues have validity, but it is far beyond the scope of this chapter to tackle them. More attention needs to be placed on this issue in research and practice in teacher education.

Perhaps more than anything, teacher-education researchers should continue studying their multicultural practices in teacher education. We need to know how teachers develop multicultural competence: what do teacher educators do to assist preservice and in-service teachers in their multicultural development? Models and typologies exist in teacher-education literature, serving as heuristics to help researchers and theoreticians think about the stages of development among teachers in the process of creating multicultural content and instruction to enhance student learning. These models can also prompt movement in the creation of content and instruction from the lesser *heroes and holidays* approach to a deeper understanding of context and curricula (Grillo, 1998; McAllister & Irvine, 2000). Developing the skills to create and to deliver effective multicultural content is a process that must be studied in order to draw conclusions about its procedural effectiveness. Perhaps the most widely recognized models to help gauge teachers' (both preservice and inservice) stages of development in the process of multicultural curricula were developed by Sleeter and Grant

(1994) and Banks (1998), although other models exist (Grillo, 1998; McAllister & Irvine, 2000). In the future, additional models need to be developed to allow researchers and teacher educators opportunities to expand what they know about multicultural education, teaching, and teachers.

Banks' (1998) model is centered on the importance of helping students come "to know, to care, and to act" (p. 32). He maintained that students must:

> question the assumptions of institutionalized knowledge and...use knowledge to *take action* that will make the world a just place in which to live and work. . . . When we teach students how to critique the injustice in the world, we should help them to formulate possibilities *for action* to change the world to make it more democratic and just [our emphases added]. (p. 18)

Helping all students reach a level of consciousness and awareness can enable their success as they interact with their peers in school as well as others outside of school.

However, helping preservice teachers in teacher education programs and in public schools get to this ultimate stage of action seems to be a difficult feat (Milner, 2005a). Even teachers highly conscious of race, culture, gender, and ethnicity, for example, may find it difficult to reach the highest level of the models, those that focus on social action. Clearly, it is difficult to guide students' actions once they have left the classroom. Teachers can encourage students to engage in action-related activities while in their classrooms but cannot control students' behaviors or actions once they have left the classroom. Teachers have the potential to influence and guide students' thinking but cannot necessarily influence or guide their actions.

Ultimately, it is left up to students once they have acquired new and expanded knowledge about social injustice issues to change or modify their actions once they have graduated. By helping students reach a level of cognitive transformation through exposure to such a curriculum will help ensure that they become actors and facilitators of change in society, speak out against injustice, and accept, as well as embrace, different ethnic, cultural, linguistic, and racial groups. The idea is that once students *know* better, they are more likely to *do* better. Teacher education must be a place where the Wizard's curtain is pulled back, where future teachers investigate the ideological definitions they hold as second nature. To *know* better means that future teachers must understand how race and racism work in schools and in our society to prevent the adoption of authentic multicultural education. Future attention needs to be placed on these and related issues to determine what types of coursework and field experience can best prepare a teaching force that is more and more mono-cultural to teach successfully in schools that are more and more multicultural.

## QUESTIONS TO PROMPT DISCUSSION

A first step toward any monumental change is to get people talking. Here we offer a few questions that could be used in several locations, from teacher-education courses to planning for the P-12 classroom. While these may seem general fact-finding questions, when asked in a specific context of specific people, the answers can provoke critical discussion.

1. What are the goals and essential components of multicultural education and why?
2. What makes multicultural education critical in teacher education and P-12 schools?
3. How can we determine the importance of multicultural education in every type of P-12 school?

## REFERENCES

Anderson, J. (1988). *The education of Blacks in the South, 1860-1935.* Chapel Hill, NC: University of North Carolina Press.

Arias, M. B., & Poynor, L. (2001). A good start: A progressive, transactional approach to diversity in preservice teacher education. *Bilingual Research Journal, 25*(4), 417–434.

Artiles, A. J., Trent, S. C., & Kuan, L. I. (1996, April). *The preservice education of teacher for student diversity: An analysis of the special education empirical literature.* Paper presented at the Annual Meeting of the American Educational Research Association, Chicago.

Banks, J. A. (1995). Multicultural education and curriculum transformation. *Journal of Negro Education, 64*(4), 390–400.

Banks, J. A. (1998). Curriculum transformation. In J. A. Banks' *An introduction to multicultural education.* (2nd edition.). pp. 21–34. Boston, MA: Allyn and Bacon.

Banks, J. A. (2001). Citizenship education and diversity: Implications for teacher education. *Journal of Teacher Education, 52*(1), 5–16.

Banks, J. A. (2003). Teaching literacy for social justice and global citizenship. *Language Arts, 81*(1),18–19.

Banks, J. A. (2006). *Cultural diversity and education: Foundations, curriculum, and teaching* (5th edition). New York: Pearson.

Banks, C. A., & Banks, J. A. (1995). Equity pedagogy: An essential component of multicultural education. *Theory into Practice, 34*, 152–158.

Banks, J. A., Cookson, P., & Gay, G. (2001). Diversity within unity: Essential principles for teaching and learning in a multicultural society. *Phi Delta Kappan, 83*(3), 196–203

Borrowman, M. L., (Ed.). (1965). *Teacher eEducation in America: A documentary history. Classics in Education.* New York: Teachers College Press.

Buendia, E., Gitlin, A., & Doumbia, F. (2003). Working the pedagogical borderlands: An African critical pedagogue teaching within an ESL context. *Curriculum Inquiry 33*(3), 291–320.

Carter, C. (1990). Teachers' knowledge and learning to teach. In W.R. Houston (Ed.) *Handbook of research on teacher education.* (pp. 291–310. New York: Macmillan.

Cooper, P. M. (2003). Effective white teachers of black children: Teaching within a community. *Journal of Teacher Education, 54*(5), 413–427.

Dillard, C. B. (1996). Engaging pedagogy: Writing and reflection in multicultural teacher education. *Teacher Education, 8*(1), 13–21.

Ford, D. Y. (1996). *Reversing underachievement among gifted Black students: Promising practices and programs.* New York: Teachers College Press.

Foster, M. (1995). African-American teachers and culturally relevant pedagogy. In J. Banks (ed.), *Handbook of research on multicultural education* (pp. 570–587). New York: Simon & Schuster.

Freire, P. (1998). *Pedagogy of the oppressed.* New York: Continuum.

Gay, G. (2000). *Culturally, responsive teaching: Theory, research, and & practice.* New York: Teachers College Press.

Grant, C. A. (1994). Best practices in teacher preparation for urban schools: Lessons from the multicultural teacher education literature. *Action in Teacher Education, 14*(3), 1–18.

Grillo, B. A. (1998). Multicultural education: A developmental process. *Montessori Life, 10*(2),19–21. (Retrieved January 5, 2005, from Education Full Text.)

Jenks, C., Lee, J. O., & Kanpol, B. (2001). Approaches to multicultural education in preservice teacher education: Philosophical frameworks and models for teaching. *The Urban Review, 33*(2), 87–105.

Johnson, L. (2002). My eyes have been opened: White teachers and racial awareness. *Journal of Teacher Education, 53*(2), p. 153–167.

Ladson-Billings, G. (1992). The multicultural mission: Unity and diversity. *Social Education, 56*(5), 308–311.

Ladson-Billings, G. (1994). *The dreamkeepers: Successful teachers of African-American children.* San Francisco: Jossey-Bass.

Ladson-Billings, G. (1995). Multicultural teacher education: Research, practice and policy. In J. A. Banks & C.A. McGee Banks (Eds.), *Handbook of research on multi-*

*cultural education* (pp. 747–759). New York: Macmillan.

Ladson-Billings, G., & Tate, B. (1995). Toward a critical race theory of education. *Teachers College Record, 97*(1), 47–67.

Lewis, A. E. (2001). There is no "race" in the schoolyard: Colorblind ideology in an almost) all White school. *American Educational Research Journal, 38*(4), 781–811.

McAllister, G., & Irvine, J. J. (2000). Cross-cultural competency and multicultural teacher education. *Review of Education Research, 70*(1), 3–24.

Milner, H. R. (2005a). Developing a multicultural curriculum in a predominantly White teaching context: Lessons from an African American teacher in a suburban English classroom. *Curriculum Inquiry, 35*(4), 391–427.

Milner, H. R. (2005b). Stability and change in prospective teachers' beliefs and decisions about diversity and learning to teach. *Teaching and Teacher Education, 21*(7), 767–786.

Milner, H. R. (2003). Teacher reflection and race in cultural contexts: History, meaning, and methods in teaching. *Theory into Practice, 42*(3), 173–180.

Milner, H. R., & Smithey, M. (2003). How teacher educators created a course curriculum to challenge and enhane preservice teachers' thinking and experience with diversity. *Teaching Education, 14*(3), 293–305.

Nussbaum, M. (1997). *Cultivating humanity.* Cambridge, MA: Harvard University Press.

Rushton, S. P. (2004). Using narrative inquiry to understand a student-teacher's practical knokwledge while teaching in an inner-city school. *The Urban Review,* 36(1), 61–79.

Schwartz, H. (1996). The Changing Nature of Teacher Education. *Handbook of Research on Teacher Education.* J. Sikula, T. J. Buttery and E. Guyton. New York, Simon & Schuster Macmillan, 3–13.

Sleeter, C., & Grant, C. E. (1994). *Making choices for multicultural education* (2nd ed). New York: Merrill.

Smith, R. W. (2000). The influence of teacher background on the inclusion of multicultural education: A Case study of two contrasts. *The Urban Review, 32*(2), 155–176.

Troutman, P. L., Jr., Pankratius, W. J., & Gallavan, N. P. (1999). Preservice teachers construct a view on multicultural education: using Banks' levels of integration of ethnic content to measure change. *Action in Teacher Education, 20*(1), 1–14.

Vavrus, M. (2002). *Transforming the multicultural education of teachers: Theory, research, and practice.* New York, Teachers College Press.

Wideen, M., Mayer-Smith, J., & Moon, B. (1998). A critical analysis of the research on learning to teach: Making the case for an ecological perspective on inquiry. *Review of Educational Research, 68*(2), 130–178.

Wink, J. (2000). *Critical pedagogy: Notes from the real world.* (2nd eEd.ition). New York: Longman.

# Chapter 11

# TEACHING WITH DIGITAL TECHNOLOGY

Karen Swan, Lin Lin, and Mark van't Hooft

*Digital technologies are for education as iron and steel girders, reinforced concrete, plate glass, elevators, central heating and air conditioning were for architecture. Digital technologies set in abeyance significant, long-lasting limits on educational activity.*
(McClintock, 1999, paragraph 10)

## INTRODUCTION

Technology has always been a part of schooling; in fact, it was the invention and rapid spread of printed texts that made schooling possible. However, many technologies have failed to find a significant place in classrooms even though they were enthusiastically embraced by educators (Cuban, 1986). In the twentieth century, technologies such as radio, movies, and television have suffered that fate. We do not have room to discuss this long history of technological innovations and schooling, so we confine ourselves to discussing digital technologies. We use this term instead of the more common term *computer* to encompass the wide range of new tools that are introduced in classrooms on a daily basis, including digital video, mobile devices, podcasting, student response systems, computer-mediated communications, and social networking applications. Specifically, we will focus on three interrelated issues that are driving debates around digital technologies and education in general.

The first issue is centered on digital technologies' effect on teaching and learning. Some educators contend that technologies are just delivery systems (e.g., Clark, 1994); others argue that technologies are tools that significantly affect thinking and learning for good or ill (e.g., Kozma, 1991). Somewhere in the middle is a large group of scholars who argue that digital technologies have the potential to meaningfully affect classroom learning but will do so only to the extent that teaching practices change to make use of their unique capabilities (e.g., Kozma, 1991).

The second issue focuses on how to make the most effective use of digital technologies in teaching and learning. This issue is intimately related to the previous one, and even those who argue that digital technologies have minor or ill effects on learning can argue that students should at least learn about them. Other focal points of study in this area have included concepts teaching, drill, and practice of academic skills, tools for thinking and learning, collaborative learning, and knowledge construction. A growing movement among educational technologists favors a ubiquitous computing approach, in which digital tools are available to support teaching and learning anywhere and anytime, and in a variety of ways (van't Hooft & Swan, 2007).

The third issue in educational technology focuses on teacher professional development, and how best to prepare teachers to teach with digital technologies. In most cases (with the possible exception of online learning), learning to use digital technologies in education seems strangely divorced from advocated and actual uses in classrooms. Rapidly changing technologies also force teachers and teacher educators to constantly examine how they learn and how they help others learn to teach with technologies.

To put these issues in context, the following timeline highlights major milestones in the short history of digital technologies and education. Even limiting these to digital technologies, however, still leaves far too many for the scope of this book; thus we present only those events with significant implications for professional development.

## TIMELINE

- **1960s:** Programmed Logic for Automated Teaching Operations (PLATO), one of the first generalized Computer Assisted Instruction (CAI) systems was developed at the University of Illinois. PLATO not only popularized the basic CAI drill-and-practice approach, it pioneered such key educational computing concepts as online forums, email, chat rooms, instant messaging, remote screen sharing, and online games. Later taken over by Control Data Corporation, PLATO systems were produced until 2006.

- **1973:** Minnesota Educational Computing Consortium (MECC) created by the state legislature to study and coordinate computer use in Minnesota schools. As the use of microcomputers in schools increased, MECC became a national advocate for computers in schools and corresponding professional development. MECC also was one of the first organizations developing educational software for personal computers, creating such early classics as *Oregon Trail, Number Munchers,* and *Lemonade Stand.*

- **1980:** Seymour Papert published *Mindstorms: Children, Computers, and Powerful Ideas*; at the same time Apple computers started making their way into schools. This triggered a grassroots movement among elementary school teachers in particular for integrating Logo programming and constructionist methods across the curriculum. Learning Logo, however, required extensive training and ongoing support, prompting a call for professional development around technology and technology issues.

- **1985:** The Apple Classrooms of Tomorrow (ACOT) project began. ACOT was a decade-long research and development collaborative that brought together public schools, universities, research agencies, and Apple Computer to create computer-saturated classrooms and research the potential of technology for teaching and learning. The project showed that the use of technology in the classroom required a change of a teacher's instructional role. This resulted in new models of professional development situated within contexts of practice, and emphasizing mentoring and reflection.

- **1989:** Tim Berners-Lee invented the World Wide Web, a system of interlinked hypertext documents that can be accessed via the Internet. This was followed in the early 1990s by a series of Internet browsers such as Mosaic, Internet Explorer, and

Netscape that made it easy for the general public (including students and teachers) to access the World Wide Web. Besides resulting in the development of a substantial amount of professional development about the Internet and its potential for teaching and learning, more teacher professional development has moved online.

- **1998-2003:** The International Society for Technology in Education released its technology standards for students (NETS-S; 1998), teachers (NETS-T, 2000), and administrators (NETS-A, 2003). The NETS are a set of national standards for appropriate, effective, and meaningful uses of technology for teaching and learning. The NETS have been adopted by virtually every state and are often consulted for professional development purposes.

- **1997:** The *Report to the President on the Use of Technology to Strengthen K-12 Education* was made public by the panel on educational technology. Prominent among its major recommendations was that special attention be given to professional development. The panel recommended that at least thirty percent of all educational technology funding be spent on professional development, and that teachers be provided with mentoring and time to develop ways of integrating technology into classroom teaching and learning.

- **2000:** *Computers as Mindtools in Schools* by David Jonassen was published. The book's publication marked widespread acceptance in the educational technology community of the cognitive tools approach to technology integration and a change in the way technology was introduced to teachers at both the pre-service and in-service levels.

- **2000 and beyond:** Mobile technology was introduced into classrooms. Devices such as handheld computers and mobile phones began to provide opportunities for learners to connect classrooms and the world, physical and digital environments, and formal and informal learning. Professional development related to mobile devices began to focus on one-to-one models of teaching and learning with digital technology.

## THE MEDIA AFFECTS DEBATE

Much of what we take for granted in today's digital culture was invented by Douglas Engelbart (1963), who believed the most important aspect of his work was designing tools for augmenting human intelligence. Was he right? Was he even on the right track? Can technology make a difference in education or life, and if so, what kind of difference? Educators have been debating these types of issues for decades.

### McLuhan and the Medium Theorists

At one end of this debate are Marshall McLuhan (1964) and the medium theorists (e.g., Bolter, 1991; Meyrowitz, 1996; Stephens, 1998) who believe that media and technologies impact individuals and society apart from whatever content is transmitted. Like Engelbart (1963), McLuhan (1964) saw media and technology as extensions of our senses and minds. He maintained that the medium is the message, that there are dominant forms of communications in cultures that evolve and change, and the dominant form will shape people's behavior and thinking in a particular era. McLuhan (1964) argued that the habits of mind shaped by constant familiarity with the unique ways in which different media structure information had a more significant impact on human thought than the messages they carried. He maintained, for example, that the invention of printed text led to analytic, linear, progressive habits of mind, which in turn enabled the Enlightenment. He further contended that our society is passing from a print-based era to an electronic era, and that such a passage would change our thinking. For example, in the 1960s, McLuhan argued that because of instantaneous video communications, the world was becoming a global village in which we are more likely to see ourselves as part of an international community. Today, we see how prescient he was.

Scholars who accept McLuhan's (1964) argument are known as medium theorists. Some think that our move from a print-based to a digital culture is destroying our ability to think critically and logically (Postman, 1985), a position echoed by teachers who bemoan their students' lack of reading and writing skills. Others are more optimistic and argue that digital technologies support nonlinear thinking (Bolter, 1991), shared experiences (Meyrowitz, 1996), new forms of thought

(Stephens, 1998), and student-centered learning (Papert, 1993). A third group, McLuhan among them, thinks that the move from print to digital culture is happening and will continue to affect our thinking, regardless how we feel about it (Tyner, 1998). This point of view has been most recently expressed in calls for changing education to respond to the needs of the Net Generation (Oblinger & Oblinger, 2005).

## Method Over Medium

At the other end of the media effects debate are those who think technology will never influence learning, a perspective that has been championed by Clark (1994). Clark differentiates between instructional media and instructional methods. He contends that media are just delivery mechanisms for methods, like trucks that deliver food. He argues that, just as different trucks cannot influence the nutritional value of food, different technologies cannot influence the quality of learning. He further contends that simply because a particular technology is not commonly used to deliver a particular instructional method, this does not automatically mean it cannot be used in that manner, and notes that "a number of very different media attributes serve the same or similar cognitive functions" (1994, p. 22).

While Clark's (1994) arguments have engendered a good deal of criticism because his truck analogy evokes a behaviorist, delivery model of learning that has fallen out of favor, they seem to premise a significant portion of thinking about technology in education today. For example, a great deal of research in online education has been focused on demonstrating no significant differences in learning between traditional and online environments (Russell, 1999). Similarly, the No Child Left Behind legislation mainly funds initiatives designed to deliver content instruction using digital technologies.

## The Potential of Technology

In the middle of the media effects debate are educators who maintain that digital technologies have the potential to meaningfully affect learning, but they will only do so to the extent that we make use of their unique capabilities. Kozma (1991), for example, responded to Clark (1994) by arguing that specific media attributes make particular methods possible. He contended that differing media can be analyzed in terms of cognitively relevant attributes and described in terms of capability to present particular representations and perform certain operations in interaction with learners, and that this has important implications for educators. We must, he argued, specify the mechanisms through which cognitive processes are influenced by media attributes, and identify appropriate uses for these attributes to support learning. Mayer (2001), for example, has specified both cognitive processes and appropriate uses of multimedia to support learning. That Mayer's work is supported by decades of experimental research bodes well for the middle position in the media effects debate (e.g., Mayer & Moreno, 2002; Moreno & Mayer, 2002).

Of course, this middle position has important implications for appropriate uses of technology in schools. If the integration of digital technologies into classroom teaching and learning is most useful when they are used to their best effect, then it is very important to determine what that best effect is.

## APPROPRIATE USES OF TECHNOLOGY IN SCHOOLS

The second hotly debated issue in educational technology is concerned with how to make the best use of technology in schools. Educators experimented with computer-supported learning in schools even before the invention of the personal computer. The early work was characterized as focused on three distinct educational uses of computers: as tutors or teaching machines, as cognitive tools to scaffold thinking and learning, and as tutees, or universal machines to be programmed by students to support their learning (Taylor, 1980). The distinction between using computers as tutors and using them as tutees parallels the media effects debate and has similarly stimulated heated debate within technology education that continues today. However, using technology applications as tools to support thinking and learning is the most commonly accepted position today.

### Computer-Based Instruction

The use of digital technologies to instruct has its roots in Skinner's (1958) work on teaching machines. In the 1970s, instructional technologists began experimenting with moving Skinner's vision to its obvious instantiation on computer systems (Suppes, 1988). What have come to be called Interactive Learning Systems (ILS) are capable of managing the delivery of individualized instruction to large numbers of students at a variety of achievement levels, providing students with instantaneous feedback on their performance, and providing teachers with extremely fine-grained diagnoses of student abilities. Moreover, several meta-analyses of research comparing learning from such systems with traditional classroom learning have found that students learn more and faster using ILSs than they do in traditional classrooms (Niemiec & Walberg, 1987; Swan, Guerrero, Mitrani, & Schoener, 1990).

The major objection to ILSs and the technology-as-tutor approach in general is epistemological. Many educators argue that such an approach is teacher-centered and does not reflect what we currently know about how people learn. On the other hand, the technology-as-tutor approach appeals to many teachers because it is closest to traditional practices and accepted teaching roles. Indeed, many schools and school districts employ ILSs today; they have strong appeal in our No Child Left Behind era for their proven effects and their ability to directly incorporate learning standards and provide data for decision making. It should be noted, however, that significant teacher professional development is needed as optimal use of ILSs requires teacher use of system diagnostics. Even so, the technology-as-tutor approach has a long history in educational technology innovations down to the present day. Innovations including artificial intelligence tutors (Sleeman & Brown, 1982), hypertext applications (Bolter, 1991), many multimedia programs (Mayer, 2001), and student response systems (Penuel et al., 2005) essentially adopt a teacher-centered approach, as do a good deal of online learning programs, especially in the areas of corporate training and P-16 education.

## Constructivism

On the other end of the continuum in the appropriate-uses debate are Seymour Papert (1993) and the constructionists. Papert is best known for his creation of the Logo programming language, a powerful computer language designed to be used by children. His vision for computers in education was focused on learner-centered environments in which children programmed computers rather than being programmed by them. Papert called his technology-as-tutee approach to learning "constructionism," viewing it as a variant of constructivism, which "attaches special importance to the role of constructions in the world as a support for those in the head" (Papert, 1993, p. 142). He argued that by constructing and manipulating "quasi-concrete" representations of knowledge on computers, children would form more robust internal knowledge structures. As in ILS research, a number of studies have reported significantly enhanced learning of mathematical concepts (Clements & Gullo, 1984), physics (diSessa, 1986), geometry (Noss, 1987), and problem solving (Swan, 1989) through Logo-based interventions. Special versions of Logo have successfully been developed for teaching complex systems (Resnick, 1994), geometry (Lehrer & Chazan, 1998), and computational thinking (diSessa, 2000).

However, teaching with Logo not only requires a fundamental rethinking of teaching roles, it also requires intense and ongoing teacher professional development. In addition, learning with Logo takes up a large amount of class time as students need to learn to program in it before significant learning gains can be realized. Thus, after widespread adoption in the late 1980s and early 1990s, particularly in elementary classrooms, Logo programming has faded from classroom use. However, Papert's (1993) notions of constructionism, computer objects to think with, and microworlds, immersive digital environments designed for student exploration of particular concepts, still have many enthusiastic adherents. A wide range of technology-supported educational innovations ranging from classroom commonplaces like interactive storybooks (Labbo & Kuhn, 2000), simulations (Reed & Jazo, 2002), and exploratory environments (Stevenson, 2002), to emergent approaches such as serious games (Gee, 2003) and augmented reality (Rogers & Price, 2007) are rooted in constructionist epistemology.

## Cognitive Tools

The middle ground in the appropriate-uses debate, the technologies-as-cognitive tools approach, is the most widely accepted in schools today, most likely because it not only straddles the instructionist/constructivist debate, but also can be implemented in very small steps. The cognitive-tools approach views digital technologies as tools that support teaching and learning in much the same way that

traditional media do. On one end of the digital tools continuum are
tools such as multimedia presentations and student response systems
that support teacher-centered instruction. At the other end are tools
that support collaboration and knowledge construction. In the middle
are a range of digital tools that can be employed in either instruction-
ist or constructivist ways—tools such as graphics packages, databases,
and communication tools. Moreover, it is widely argued that students
be introduced to digital tools simply because they are commonly
employed in society today (Partnership for 21st Century Skills, 2003).
Most educators who adopt a technologies-as-cognitive tools approach
also argue for constructivist implementations, contending that such
uses lead to higher-order thinking and learning (Reeves, 1996). Many
also conceive of thinking and learning as distributed, viewing digital
technologies as extensions of human cognition in much the same way
as Engelbart (1963) and McLuhan (1964) did. This is the position
taken by Jonassen (2000), who refers to digital technologies as "mind
tools." He identifies six categories of digital tools that, when used by
learners to represent what they know, necessarily engage them in critical thinking about the content they are studying. These include:

- semantic organizing tools, which help learners analyze and organize what they know or are learning;
- dynamic modeling tools, which help learners describe dynamic relationships among ideas;
- information interpretation tools, which help learners access and
  process information;
- visualization tools, which help learners represent and convey
  mental images and reason visually;
- conversation tools, which support interpersonal exchanges and
  collaborations among students; and
- knowledge construction tools, which support learners as
  designers.

## TEACHER LEARNING AND PROFESSIONAL DEVELOPMENT

The third issue in ongoing educational technology debates is concerned with how to best prepare teachers to teach with digital technologies. No matter what the approach to technology use, teachers are
critical elements in the technology integration equation.

## Challenges

The effects of digital technologies on teaching and learning depend for a large part on the complex process of professional development: when, what, where, and why teachers learn to teach with new technologies. There is an often-repeated expression in education that people tend to teach the way they were taught. If preservice teachers follow the practices of their professors, their use of technology in education will be largely based on the examples set for them in their university teacher education programs. To apply technologies effectively in their teaching, preservice teachers must see technology incorporated throughout their teacher education programs, emergent in their university learning and activities, and modeled by their professors and peers in classes and field placements (Doering, Hughes, & Huffman, 2003). Quantity makes a difference. Unfortunately, research has also found that preservice teacher education does not adequately prepare future teachers to teach with technology (Pope, Hare, & Howard, 2002).

To incorporate technology effectively, teachers need to feel comfortable about quickly acquiring the required skills and knowledge. Research indicates that there is a relationship between teacher confidence in technology abilities and the likelihood of technology integration (Nisan-Nelson, 2001). Also, besides the level of computer use, teacher interest in technology for learning is the most important factor that determines technology integration (Keiper, Harwood, & Larson, 2000). As a result, the quality of preservice teachers' experiences with computer technology is an important factor.

In sum, teacher education programs are challenged to prepare teachers capable of and committed to using technology for teaching and learning. Teachers must be able to use technologies in their curricula to promote learning, improve achievement, and provide students with the skills they need in their future education and workplace careers.

## Responses

The Preparing Tomorrow's Teachers to Use Technology Program (PT3) has been one of the national initiatives to respond to the challenge of teacher learning with technologies. Starting in 2000, the PT3 program has provided grants to consortia that help future teachers become proficient in the use of technologies. More than 400 institutions of higher education have received funding to restructure their teacher education programs so that they can prepare prospective teachers to effectively use technology in their P-12 classrooms. Research shows that PT3 grants have helped teacher educators and teachers to become confident technology users and supported innovative projects integrating technology into teaching and learning (Ludwig & Taymans, 2005).

Among various teacher professional development programs aimed at technology integration, two models are prominent: the traditional training or workshop model and the situated learning perspective. A workshop usually occurs in one or two-day sessions and focuses on technical skill development, incorporating demonstrations and explanations for specific problems, strategies, and solutions. Workshops are efficient and important ways to help professionals acquire technical skills within their time constraints (Berry, 2005).

However, this model has received criticism for not leading to long-term changes in actual practice. Ball and Cohen (1999), for example, noted that decontextualized workshops are "often intellectually superficial, disconnected from deep issues of curriculum and learning . . . and noncumulative" (pp. 3–4). Moreover, due to their focus on isolated technical skills, teachers walk away from a workshop without seeing the connections between technical skills and their own teaching (Ludwig & Taymans, 2005).

As an alternative, researchers and teacher educators have increasingly argued that effective professional development must be situated in classroom practice in such a way that teachers are active learners who construct their own understandings (Putnam & Borko, 2000). The situated learning perspective recognizes that, especially in a field like educational technology, teacher learning should be situated within the ambiguity and chaos that is the lived reality of their classroom experiences (Britzman, 2003). Teachers should exert control over the type and content of their experiences and receive follow-up support for what they have learned (Wilson & Berne, 1998).

In the situative model, teacher educators work with teachers in their classrooms and other school settings. Teacher learning is intertwined with their authentic and ongoing practice and what they learn will indeed influence their teaching practice in meaningful ways. This approach values the critical importance of the context in which teachers work and also recognizes that learning happens over time. It recognizes teachers as agents of change and creators of their craft and moves beyond the passive transmission of information more characteristic of the workshop model.

However, there are issues with this approach too, one of which is scalability. Having teacher educators spend considerable amounts of time working alongside teachers is not practical on a widespread basis. In addition, learning that takes place outside of chaotic classrooms affords teachers with opportunities to reflect and think in new ways without being constrained by existing classroom situations. Multiple contexts, therefore, are often recommended for facilitating knowledge transfer from workshops to classroom teaching.

Reflective practice and collaborative inquiry are two of the most important elements for innovative and sustainable teacher learning and professional development with technology (King, 2003). Findings from research about teacher inquiry also reveal that collaborative inquiry groups, team learning, and communities of practice are effective teacher learning models that enable participants to sustain educational reform, improve practice, and improve teachers' instruction and students' learning (Ludwig & Taymans, 2005).

Learning to teach with technology is a substantial endeavor, requiring personal and continuous commitment, and lifelong learning (King, 2003). Rather than just learning how to use the latest software, lifelong learning focuses on a process of ongoing discovery and learning that inspires teachers and teacher educators to become confident technology-using teachers. It should be cultivated in teacher education programs, beginning at the preservice level.

Lifelong learning also means self-directed learning. Self-directed teacher learners actively and continuously seek and find new things to learn on their own, determine how they learn best, and seek out information, resources, and professional development opportunities (Knowles, 1975). Therefore, it is critical for teacher educators to cultivate and support teachers' interests in self-directed learning. Self-directed learning with technology can be greatly facilitated through professional networks and relationships. In-service and preservice teachers need consistent opportunities to learn to use information technology over time in multiple and authentic contexts (Reeves, 1996).

In that vein, technologies themselves can provide tools to facilitate teacher learning about technology. For example, online learning communities allow teachers to share resources and discuss strategies and approaches even though separated in space and time. At the preservice level, electronic portfolios enhance traditional teaching portfolios by allowing the use of multiple representations to display teaching development with technology (Wiedmer, 1998).

## IMPLICATIONS FOR TEACHER EDUCATION

No matter whether or how you believe technologies affect thinking and learning, what you think their most appropriate uses in schools are, or what methods you believe will best prepare teachers to use technologies in their classrooms, digital technologies can no longer be viewed as optional, available to only a small segment of the world's teachers and students. They are essential instruments in a teacher's twenty-first century toolkit. Digital technologies are not only becoming commonplace in schools, their integration into classroom teaching is recognized as a vital part of educational planning at all levels.

Indeed, McClintock (1999) argues that recent innovations in digital technology have the potential to dramatically change teaching and learning in three ways. First, the growth of the Internet and broadband, wireless communications can change schools and classrooms from isolated places with relatively scarce access to information to ones with rich connections to the world and all its ideas. He argues that basic pedagogical approaches must accordingly change from disbursing scarce knowledge to enabling students "to use with purpose and effect their unlimited access to the resources of our cultures" (McClintock, 1999, paragraph 12). Secondly, easy access to multimedia allows knowledge construction to assume many forms, and basic educational strategies must be broadened correspondingly to include the intellectual recognition of skills in such areas. Thirdly, McClintock points to digital tools designed to automate lower-level intellectual skills, allowing their users to concentrate on higher-level thinking. He argues that the basic curricular question, What knowledge is of most worth? (1999, paragraph 15), must accordingly be rethought.

## WHERE DO WE GO FROM HERE?

McClintock (1999) maintains that his observations are not normative, but rather factual. Innovations in digital technologies have already changed what is educationally possible. To realize that promise, teaching, and teacher professional development must significantly change. Digital technologies will remain "oversold and underused" (Cuban, 2001) unless and until teacher professional development changes dramatically to address technology integration as an integral part of classroom practice.

## QUESTIONS TO PROMPT DISCUSSION

These questions may help you reflect on the issues presented in this chapter.

1. Where do you stand in the Great Media Effects Debate? Are you a medium theorist? Do you agree with those who say technology will never make a difference? Why?
2. How should technology tools be used in schools? Should they be used as tutors, tutees, or cognitive tools? Why?
3. Should preservice teacher education adapt to reflect pedagogical changes inherent in changes in digital technology, or is good pedagogy a constant?

## REFERENCES

Ball, D. L., & Cohen, D. K. (1999). Developing practice, developing practitioners: Toward a practice based theory of professional education. In G. Sykes and L. Darling-Hammond (Eds.), *Teaching as the learning profession: Handbook of policy and practice* (pp. 3–32). San Francisco: Jossey Bass.

Berry, B. (2005). The future of teacher education. *Journal of Teacher Education, 56*(3), 272–278.

Bolter, J. D. (1991). *Writing space: The computer, hypertext, and the history of writing.* Hillsdale, NJ: Lawrence Erlbaum Associates.

Britzman, D. P. (2003). *Practice makes practice: A critical study of learning to teach.* Albany, NY: State University of New York Press.

Clark, R. (1994). Media will never influence learning. *Educational Technology Research and Development, 42*(2), 21–29.

Clements, D. H., & Gullo, D. F. (1984). Effects of computer programming on young children's cognition. *Journal of Educational Psychology, 76*, 1051–1058.

Cuban, L. (2001). *Oversold and underused: Computers in the classroom.* Cambridge, MA: Harvard University Press.

Cuban, L. (1986). *Teachers and machines: The use of classroom technology since 1920.* New York: Teachers College Press.

diSessa, A. A. (2000). *Changing minds: Computers, learning, and literacy.* Cambridge, MA: MIT Press.

diSessa, A. A. (1986). Artificial worlds and real experience. *Instructional Science, 14*, 207–227.

Doering, A., Hughes, J., & Huffman, D. (2003). Preservice teachers: Are we thinking with technology? *Journal of Research on Technology in Education, 35*, 342–361.

Engelbart, D. C. (1963). A conceptual framework for the augumentation of man's intellect. In Howerrton, P.W. & Weeks, D. C. (Eds.) *Vistas in Information Handling, Vol. 1.* Washington, DC: Spartan Books, 1-29.

Gee, J. P. (2003). *What video games have to teach us about learning and literacy.* New York: Palgrave/St. Martin's.

Jonassen, D. H. (2000). *Computers as mindtools in schools: Engaging critical thinking.* Upper Saddle River, NJ: Prentice-Hall.

Keiper, T., Harwood, A., & Larson, B. E. (2000). Preservice teachers' perceptions of infusing computer technology into social studies education. *Theory and Research in Social Education, 28*, 566–579.

King, P. K. (2003). *Keeping pace with technology: Educational technology that transforms.* Cresskill, NJ: Hampton Press, Inc.

Knowles, M. S. (1975). *Self-directed learning: A guide for learners and teachers.* Englewood Cliffs, NJ: Prentice Hall/Cambridge.

Kozma, R. (1991). Learning with media. *Review of Educational Research, 61*(2), 179–211.

Labbo, L. D., & Kuhn, M. R. (2000). Weaving chains of affect and cognition: A young child's understanding of CD-ROM talking books. *Journal of Literacy Research, 32*(2), 187–210.

Lehrer, R., & Chazan, D. (1998). *Designing learning environments for developing understanding of geometry and space.* Mahwah, NJ: Lawrence Erlbaum Associates.

Ludwig, M., & Taymans, J. (2005). Teaming: Constructing high-quality faculty development in a PT3 project. *Journal of Technology and Teacher Education, 13*(3), 357–372.

Mayer, R. (2001). *Multimedia learning.* Cambridge: Cambridge University Press.

Mayer, R. E. & Moreno, R. (2002). Aids to computer-based multimedia learning. *Learning and Instruction, 12*, 107–119.

McClintock, R. (1999). *The educator's manifesto: Renewing the progressive bond with posterity through the social construction of digital learning communities.* New York: Institute for Learning Technologies, Teachers College, Columbia University. Retrieved June 7, 2007, from http://www.ilt.columbia.edu/publications/manifesto/contents.html

McLuhan, M. (1964). *Understanding media: The extensions of man.* New York: The New American Library.

Meyrowitz, J. (1996). Taking McLuhan and "medium theory" seriously: Technological change and the evolution of education. In S. Kerr (Ed.), *Technology and the future of schooling* (pp. 73–110). Chicago: The University of Chicago Press.

Moreno, R. & Mayer, R. E. (2002). Verbal redundancy in multimedia learning: When reading helps listening. *Journal of Educational Psychology, 94*, 156–163.

Nisan-Nelson, P. (2001). Technology integration: A case of professional development. *Journal of Technology and Teacher Education, 9*(1), 83–103.

Niemiec, R., & Walberg, H. J. (1987). Comparative effects of computer-assisted instruction: A synthesis of reviews. Journal of Educational Computing Research, 3(1), 19-37.

Noss, R. (1987). Children's learning of geometrical concepts through Logo. *Journal for Research in Mathematics Education, 18*, 343–362.

Oblinger, D., & Oblinger, J. T. (2005). Educating the net generation. Boulder, CO: Educause. Retrieved October 14, 2006 from: http://www.educause.edu/content.asp?PAGE_ID=5989&bhcp=1

Panel on Educational Technology. (1997). *Report to the President on the use of technology to strengthen K-12 education.* Washington, DC: Executive Office of the President of the United States; President's Committee of Advisors on Science and Technology.

Papert, S. (1980). *Mindstorms: Children, computers, and powerful ideas.* New York: Basic Books.

Papert, S. (1993). *The children's machine.* New York: Basic Books.

Partnership for 21st Century Skills (2003). *Learning for the 21st Century.* Retrieved June 28, 2005 from http://www.21stcenturyskills.org/

Penuel, W. R., Crawford, V., Boscardin, C. K., Masyn, K., Debarger, A. H., & Urdan, T. C. (2005). *Teaching with student response system technology: A survey of K-12 teachers.* Menlo Park, CA: SRI International. Retrieved March 29, 2006 from http://ctl.sri.com/publications/displayPublication.jsp?ID=381

Pope, M., Hare, D., & Howard, E. (2002). Technology integration: Closing the gap between what preservice teachers are taught to do and what they can do. *Journal of Technology and Teacher Education, 10*(2), 191–203.

Postman, N. (1985). *Amusing ourselves to death.* New York: Penguin Books.

Putnam R., & Borko, H. (2000). What do new views of knowledge and thinking have to say about research on teacher learning? *Educational Research, 29*(1), 4–15.

Reed, S. K., & Jazo, L. (2002). Using multiple representations to improve conceptions of average speed. *Journal of Educational Computing Research, 27*(1&2), 147–166.

Reeves, T. C. (1996). Technology in teacher education: From electronic tutor to cognitive tool. *Action in Teacher Education, 17*, 74–78.

Resnick, M. (1994). *Turtles, termites, and traffic jams: Explorations in massively parallel microworlds.* Cambridge, MA: MIT Press.

Rogers, Y., & Price, S. (2007). Using ubiquitous computing to enhance and extend and enhance learning experiences. In M. van't Hooft & K. Swan (Eds.), *Ubiquitous computing in education: Invisible technology, visible impact* (pp. 424–459). Mahwah, NJ: Lawrence Erlbaum Associates.

Russell, T. L. (1999). *The no significant difference phenomenon.* Montgomery, AL: IDEC. Retrieved September 19, 2003 from http://teleeducation.nb.ca/nosignificantdifference/

Skinner, B. F. (1958). Teaching machines. *Science, 128*(3330), 969–977.

Sleeman, D., & Brown, J. S. (1982). *Intelligent tutoring systems.* New York: Academic.

Stephens, M. (1998). *The rise of the image and the fall of the word.* Oxford: Oxford University Press.

Stevenson, I. (2002). Microworlds and direct manipulation environments: The case of Newtonian mechanics. *Journal of Educational Computing Research, 27*(1&2), 167–183.

Suppes, P. (1988). Computer-assisted instruction. In D. Unwin & R. McAleese (Eds.), *The encyclopaedia of educational media communications and technology* (2nd Edition; pp. 107–116), New York: Greenwood Press.

Swan, K. (1989). Logo programming and the teaching and learning of problem solving. *Journal of Artificial Intelligence in Education, 1*(1), 73–92.

Swan, K., Guerrero, F., Mitrani, M., & Schoener, J. (1990). Honing in on the target: Who among the educationally disadvantaged benefits most from what CBI? *Journal of Research on Computing in Education, 22*(4), 381–403.

Taylor, R. P. (1980). *The computer in the school: Tutor, tool, tutee.* New York: Teachers College Press.

Tyner, K. (1998). *Literacy in a digital world: Teaching and learning in the age of information.* Mahwah, NJ: Lawrence Erlbaum Associates.

van't Hooft, M., & Swan, K. (Eds.; 2007). *Ubiquitous computing in education: Invisible technology, visible impact.* Mahwah, NJ: Lawrence Erlbaum Associates.

Wiedmer, T. L. (1998). Digital portfolios: Capturing and demonstrating skills and levels of performance. *Phi Delta Kappan, 79*(8), 586–589.

Wilson, S., & Berne, J. (1998). Teacher learning and the acquisition of professional knowledge: An examination of research on contemporary professional development. *Review of Research in Education, 24*, 173–206.

# Chapter 12

# BEYOND GOOD VERSUS EVIL: WHAT PRESERVICE TEACHERS NEED TO UNDERSTAND ABOUT ASSESSMENT

Heidi Andrade

*Given their own personal histories, our students are able to hate standardized testing and at the same time reproduce it faithfully in their own pre-post testing routines, if they are not given the opportunity to develop and try out other meaningful forms of assessment situated in practice. So we must teach them how to do assessment well.*

(Shepard, 2000, p. 7)

## INTRODUCTION

A common lament from school administrators is that new teachers do not really know how to assess. No one blames the teachers, of course. The implied or real finger is pointed at teacher educators: "Why," administrators ask, "aren't teacher education programs teaching teachers how to assess?" Well, some are. It is true, however, that assessment-related experiences and coursework are generally too few and far between (Kornhaber, 2007). Those that do exist generally do not prepare preservice teachers for the Age of Accountability in which they will work. They should. New teachers need to understand the purposes, features, and relations of at least two types of assessments: Those they will be required to administer for the purposes of accountability—summative assessments—and those they will be expected to create and use for the purposes of teaching and learning—formative assessments.

## TESTING AS ASSESSMENT'S HISTORICAL TAPROOT

Our implicit and explicit theories about teaching and learning drive our instruction. We now teach our education students about social constructivism, among other things, and use interactive, collaborative, experiential pedagogies that reflect modern theories of educational psychology. Many of our current theories of assessment, however, reflect outdated theories of teaching and learning rooted in the psychological theories of intelligence measurement (Gipps & Stobart, 2003). Standardized testing dominates in such a paradigm, to the chagrin of many educators. For example, referring to objective tests as the "single most striking feature of achievement testing in the United States from the beginning of the [20th] century to the present day," Shepard (2000, p. 5) critiques their petrifying effect on curriculum and instruction. Similarly, in an article entitled "The mismeasurement of educational quality," Popham (2000) argues that our national obsession with standardized tests does harm to students who, he claims, are the victims of "educators' sometimes mindless pursuit of higher test scores" (p. 12).

Shepard, Popham, and others (Black, Harrison, Lee, Marshall, & Wiliam, 2004; Gardner, 2006) call for new conceptions of and approaches to assessment that reflect modern theories of teaching and learning. The need is clear. The seminal review of classroom assessment practices conducted by Black and Wiliam (1998) revealed what they called "a poverty of practice" in terms of formative assessment in most classrooms: "There is a wealth of evidence that the everyday practice of assessment in classrooms is beset with problems and shortcomings," including but not limited to tests that encourage rote, superficial learning, assignments that emphasize quantity over quality, comparative assessments that leave low-achieving students believing they are unable to learn or work to high standards, and grading practices that are "conscientious but often fail to offer guidance on how work can be improved" and sometimes even "reinforce underachievement and underexpectation by being too generous or unfocused" (p. 141). Further, the assessments used by many teachers were found to serve managerial roles at the expense of learning. As a result, teachers knew little about their individual students' learning needs and either could not or did not use their assessments to adjust instruction and increase learning.

Black and Wiliam's (1998) review issued something of a clarion call for reform in classroom assessment practices and in teacher preparation regarding assessment. Nearly a decade later, policymakers and researchers are still debating the best ways to assess students and schools. The debate often pits summative and formative assessments against each other.

## TIMELINE

Understanding the contest between summative and formative assessment requires knowing a bit about the history of evaluation in the United States. As demonstrated by the following summary, excerpted in part from a review of high-stakes testing written by The Gale Group (2002), today's assessment theories and practices have been shaped by a partnership of high-stakes testing and federal legislation.

- **1965:** *The Elementary and Secondary Education Act.* Accountability testing in the United States started as part of the same legislation (Title I of the Elementary and Secondary Education Act [ESEA]) that first allocated federal funds to improve the academic achievement of children from low-income families. Federal dollars came with a mandate that programs be evaluated to show their effectiveness.
- **Early 1970s:** The infamous decline in *Scholastic Aptitude Test (SAT)* scores. The public's generally positive view of America's schools changed with the SAT test score decline, despite the fact that a panel commissioned by the College Board in 1977 found that two-thirds to three-fourths of the score decline was attributable to an increase in the number of poor and minority students gaining access to college (undeniably a good thing), not to a decline in the quality of education.
- **Mid to late 1970s:** Minimum competency tests. The minimum competency testing movement was the first in a series of educational reforms where tests were used not just as measures of

the effectiveness of reforms but also as the primary drivers of reform. By 1980, thirty-seven states had taken action to mandate minimum competency standards for grade-to-grade promotion or high school graduation.

- **1983:** The *A Nation at Risk* report (National Commission on Excellence in Education, 1983). The authors of *A Nation at Risk* concluded that minimum competency examinations were a problem because the "'minimum' tends to become the 'maximum,' thus lowering educational standards for all" (p. 20). Reactions to this report included course-based graduation requirements, extended time in the school day and school year, and more homework and testing.

- **1987:** John Cannell's study, dubbed the "Lake Wobegon Report." Despite the rhetoric of rigorous academic curricula, the new tests adopted in the mid-1980s were predominantly multiple-choice, basic-skills tests. By the end of the 1980s, there were signs that impressive score gains on these tests were not due to real learning gains. For example, Cannell's study showed that all fifty states claimed their test scores were above the national average.

- **1990s:** Standards-based reforms. Disenchantment with traditional tests led to calls for more challenging curricula focused on reasoning, understanding, and the ability to apply knowledge. Reformers called for a change in the content and format of assessments to forestall the negative effects of "teaching to the test." Various terms, such as *authentic*, *direct*, and *performance-based assessment*, were used to convey the idea that assessments had to reflect important learning goals.

- **2002:** The No Child Left Behind Act of 2001 (Public Law 107-110), commonly known as NCLB, was signed into federal law on January 8 (see http://www.ed.gov/nclb). The NCLB Act aimed to improve the performance of schools by increasing standards of accountability, as well as providing parents with more flexibility in choosing the schools their children attend. The effectiveness and desirability of NCLB's measures—including and especially the increased requirement for testing in grades 3 through 12—were a matter of vigorous controversy.

At the time this chapter was written, the reauthorization of the *NCLB Act* was being debated in the U.S. Congress. Likely revisions included provisions for greater state freedom from NCLB's controls and punishments, but the impact of the Act and its requirements for frequent, high-stakes testing is unlikely to wane in the near future. Preservice teachers must be prepared to balance the demands of externally imposed evaluations and useful classroom-based assessments.

## SUMMATIVE VERSUS FORMATIVE: COMPETING VIEWS

Perhaps the most important concept in modern classroom assessment is the distinction and relationship between summative and formative assessment, yet the two are often confused. Most people think of assessment simply as the test at the end of a unit that tells teachers whether or not students "got it." That is a summative view of assessment and tells only part of the story. A significant element of effective classroom assessment is formative—the kind of ongoing, regular feedback on student work that leads to adjustment and revision by both the teacher and the students (CERI, 2005). Starkman (2006) explains the differences between summative and formative assessment in terms of their respective uses:

> The goal of summative assessment is typically to provide an overall measure of student performance for someone outside the classroom—a report card for parents, an SAT score for college admissions officials. The consequences of this measure can be critical—being promoted or not, getting into college or not. By contrast, the goal of formative assessment is to provide feedback for someone inside the classroom—an indication of how well a student is doing in a given subject at a given level. The consequences are more immediate, such as individualized instruction. Broadly speaking, summative assessment answers the question "How did I do?"; formative assessment answers the question "How am I doing?" (p. 1)

## Summative Assessment: How Did I Do?

Summative assessment is the evaluation *of* learning and is done primarily for the benefit of external monitors and decision makers, such as school districts and state and federal agencies (Resnick, 2004; Scriven, 2003). The standardized test is perhaps the best known example of a summative assessment. According to Cizek (2005), high-stakes standardized tests are tests to which positive or negative consequences are attached, including tests used to make decisions regarding promotion or retention of students, salaries or bonuses for teachers, and state recognition of high-performing schools or take-over of low-performing schools. Cizek's definition of such tests emphasizes the need to make decisions. In fact, he claims that the "only way to avoid many of the issues associated with high-stakes testing would be simply to avoid making any decisions at all" (p. 31).

Cizek and other advocates defend tests in terms of their ability to discriminate between students who have and have not mastered a prescribed set of knowledge and skills. Crocker (2003), for example, acknowledges the important gate-keeping function of tests and warns educators of the value of preparing students to take and pass tests:

> As school accountability becomes reality, effective teachers will need to know how to prepare their students for assessments. They also will recognize that anyone who wants to become a fire fighter, a cosmetologist, realtor, electrician, nurse, landscape architect, accountant, physician, or a worker who sprays crops for insects on a farm must know how to take and pass examinations. . . . They will ill-serve their students if they are dismissive, disdainful, or antagonistic about the significant role that tests will play in their students' lives beyond that classroom. (p. 10)

Advocates also note the validity and reliability of tests. The testing profession has made improvements in the format, accuracy, dependability, and utility of tests and, as a result, "never before has obtaining such an abundance of accurate and useful information about student learning been possible" (Phelps, 2005, p. xii). It is precisely the qualities emphasized by Phelps that attract decision makers and legislators: Modern tests tend to do a good job of sampling a wide range of content and of quickly producing reliable total scores and diagnostic subscores (Haladyna, Downing, & Rodriguez, 2002). As a result, tests help monitor the overall quality of educational systems.

That's the good news. The bad news is that the limitations of testing are well-known. Standardized tests have been soundly critiqued in terms of their lack of validity, or the failure to accurately measure meaningful knowledge and skills (Shepard, 2000). Although reliability is one of the strongest features of standardized tests, their validity is often questioned when students score highly on tests but cannot demonstrate competence with the supposed knowledge and skills.

Standardized tests also struggle with equity, or fairness to all test-takers, particularly in an increasingly diverse society, and they have been accused of having a corrupting influence on instruction, learning, and the teaching profession (Kornhaber, 2004). One example of such an influence can be found in Haney's (2000) study of "the Texas miracle," in which he revealed that scores on the Texas Assessment of Academic Skills (TAAS) had risen not because of progress in reducing dropouts or increasing achievement but rather because of a lack of rigor on the part of the tests, steady climbs in retention rates (especially for Black and Hispanic students), a doubling of the number of students who were classified as in special education and thereby exempt from taking the test, and a sharp upturn in the number of students taking the General Educational Development Test (the GED) to avoid the TAAS. Haney concluded that the gains on the TAAS reported by the State of Texas were "more illusory than real," and that the huge amount of time and effort devoted to getting students to pass the test was "hurting more than helping teaching and learning in Texas schools, particularly with at-risk students" (p. 2).

Cizek (2005), the testing expert cited earlier, undermines some of the most common critiques of testing by noting that they lack support in the scholarly testing journals. Perhaps more damaging is Cizek's assertion that many of the critics rely on little or no data or on evidence of questionable quality due to small sample sizes, methodological flaws, and interpretations rife with logical errors. He concedes, however, that "*the current generation of high-stakes tests is incapable of delivering on the promise of providing high-quality information that teachers can use for individualizing instruction for any particular student*" (p. 47, italics in original). Individualizing instruction is where formative assessment comes in.

## Formative Assessment: How Am I Doing?

Formative assessment is assessment *for* learning and is intended to directly and indirectly benefit the learner (Black & Wiliam, 2003; Boston, 2002; Sadler, 2005). Formative assessments happen before and while students work on assignments, rather than occurring only at the end of a unit. They provide teachers with information about students' learning needs, and students with feedback about the strengths and weaknesses of their work and learning, as well as opportunities to revise and improve upon both. A variety of formative assessments are currently in use by teachers all over the world, including teacher-student conferences, student self- and peer assessment, portfolios, and practice tests (CERI, 2005; Deakin-Crick et al., 2005). A formative conception of assessment honors the crucial role of feedback in the development of understanding and skill building. There is a body of research that clearly shows that feedback promotes learning and achievement (Black & Wiliam, 1998; Brinko, 1993; Butler & Winne, 1995), yet most students get little informative feedback on their work. Grades do not count as feedback: Feedback demands that students receive guidance on how to improve and opportunities for revision (Black & Wiliam, 1998).

Formative assessment provides feedback to students, but few teachers have the luxury of regularly responding to each student's work and learning. Fortunately, research shows that students themselves can be useful sources of feedback via self- and peer assessment (Andrade & Boulay, 2003; Andrade, Du, & Wang, 2007; O'Donnell & Topping, 1998). Self- and peer assessment are key elements in formative assessment because they involve students in thinking about the quality of their own and each others' work, rather than relying on their teacher as the sole source of evaluative judgments. As a result, students come to see assessment as a "source of insight and help instead of its being the occasion for meting out rewards and punishments" (Shepard, 2000, p. 10).

Formative assessments have tremendous potential to boost learning and academic achievement. However, they have turned out to be time-consuming, especially for the many teachers with limited experience with them. In addition, experiments with using formative assessments in a summative way has have revealed their lack of reliability in terms of scoring consistency—an unacceptable quality when they are used to make high-stakes decisions about consequences such as promotion and graduation (e.g., see Herman and Winters, 1994, regarding Vermont's experiment with statewide portfolios). Barriers to innovation in terms of assessment, including tensions between internal, classroom-based assessments and external, standardized evaluations, are also notoriously difficult to overcome (CERI, 2005).

## Formative Versus Summative: Good Versus Evil?

Many teachers sense a tension between formative and summative assessments, especially when pressures to teach to a test conflict with what they believe their students need to learn and grow (National Research Council, 2001). This tension is wherein lies the struggle between the two forms of assessment. A battle has been waged for years and rarely wanes in intensity. Shepard (2000), a staunch advocate of formative assessment, refers to the "contesting forces of good and evil assessment" (p. 7), with performance-based, formative assessment as good, and high-stakes testing as evil. On the other side of the battle field is former Secretary of Education Rod Paige, who calls any opponent of standardized testing (including, presumably, Dr. Shepard) "an apologist for a broken system of education," and who demands "an end to the excuses" (2001, p. B07).

An only slightly tamer version of the conflict reflected in the quotations above can be seen in the current debate about rubric-referenced assessment. A rubric lists the criteria for a piece of work, or what counts (e.g., purpose, organization, details, voice and mechanics are often what counts in a written essay), and articulates gradations or levels of quality for each criterion, from excellent to poor (e.g., from A to F) (Andrade, 2000). Advocates of rubric use point to research that shows that involving students in assessing their own work with a rubric can help them to think, learn, and produce high-quality work (Andrade & Du, 2005; Andrade, Du, & Wang, 2007).

Not all educators are in favor of rubric use, however. Mabry (1999) and Wilson (2006) argue that rubrics are in conflict with the assessment practices used by writing teachers and working writers. Most disturbing, according to Wilson, is the way in which rubrics threaten to undermine the responsive ways in which good teachers assess student progress by implying the need for inter-rater reliability. Warning that rubrics "enforce and perpetuate agreement in the field of writing assessment, making little room for the multiple perspectives, readings, and insights that would give us a better understanding of the complexities of the writing process" (p. 54), Wilson urges teachers to "pay attention to how the rubric mediates the teachers' thoughts, responses, and negotiation of conflict" (p. 56).

Wilson (2006) is right: Reliability should not replace responsiveness. The problem she identified, however, is rooted in what Harlen and James (1997) referred to as the confusion and fusion of summative and formative assessments. Even the most hard core measurement specialist is unlikely to demand that every classroom teacher abandon responsive assessment for scoring sessions with reliability estimates of 70

percent or more. That's not what teaching is about–that's what summative evaluation is about. Teachers risk throwing out the baby with
the bathwater when they reject rubrics because of a perceived emphasis on scoring over responding to student work.

## RECONCILING TWO TYPES OF ASSESSMENT

Noting that the tendency to blur the distinctions between summative and formative assessment has led to not only a scarcity of informative feedback for students but also a downgrading of teachers' professional judgment (Harlen, 2005a; Harlen & James, 1997) promotes a
more harmonious relationship between the two types of assessment.
Labeling as "simplistic" the assumption that formative assessment
must be standardized to be good, Harlen and James (1997) argue that
it is not necessary to be overly-concerned with reliability in teachers'
assessments since there is "always quick feedback for the teacher, who
usually has opportunities to use observations of the response to one
intervention as information in making the next one. . . . Through this
rapid loop of feedback and adjustment . . . , the information inevitably
acquires greater reliability" (p. 372).

Harlen and James' (1997) conception of reliability in formative assessment rests on its frequent, ongoing nature. Summative evaluation,
in contrast, tends to happen less frequently and must, therefore, be
subjected to more stringent measures of accuracy. One commonality,
though, is that both types of assessment rely on clear articulations of
goals and criteria. This is where a rubric can be a useful tool but not a
replacement for teachers' professional judgment: A rubric communi-
cates the goals and criteria for an assignment but still allows a teacher
to interpret and respond to a piece of student work. In another context, the same rubric could be used to assign a final score to a piece of
student work produced for an on-demand examination. Understanding and honoring the purposes of the assessment is key.

The foregoing discussion might suggest that there would be no contest between summative and formative assessment if we simply acknowledge their respective purposes by using summative assessments
solely for the purposes of accountability, and using formative assessments only to support learning and teaching in the classroom. Admit-
tedly, using each approach only according to its intended purposes

would go a long way toward resolving persistent and pernicious problems. Yet, frailties inherent to each approach are not easily resolved, and practitioners often find the distinctions to be somewhat artificial. Teachers point out that standardized tests have long fingers that reach into classrooms and put a stranglehold on curriculum, instruction and assessment (Popham, 2004). Preservice teachers must be armed with deep understandings of the purposes and limitations of each type of assessment to enter classrooms in which the contest lives on.

## IMPLICATIONS FOR TEACHER EDUCATION

The most self-evident implication for preservice teacher education is instruction in and experience with classroom assessment and high-stakes measurement. Stand-alone assessment courses in undergraduate and graduate programs are a good start but perhaps better is Shepard's (2000) recommendation to provide methods courses that embed assessment concerns within curriculum and instruction issues. Assessment courses must emphasize the value of using multiple measures when drawing inferences about student learning.

Teaching preservice teachers to keep the purposes of each type of assessment in mind is crucial in helping them learn to judge the appropriateness of one over the other. Harlen (2005b) recommends teaching teachers to judge the appropriateness of using an assessment for formative purposes by asking these questions: (1) Does it focus on how students learn? (2) Is it sensitive and constructive? (3) Does it foster motivation? (4) Does it promote understanding of goals and criteria? (5) Does it help learners to know how to improve? (6) Does it develop the capacity for self-assessment? and (7) Does it recognize all education achievements?

Harlen (2005a, 2005b) also notes that a skill in need of special emphasis in coursework and practicum is interpreting the results of formative assessments and deciding on next steps. Teachers must be prepared to adjust their instruction and to collaborate with students on determining what they need to do to improve their work and understanding. A discipline-based understanding of learning progressions, for example the Berkley Evaluation and Assessment Research (BEAR) System being developed by Wilson and his colleagues (2007), can be helpful in figuring out what students are likely to need next.

Perhaps most important, given our human tendency to do what was done to us, we must assess preservice teachers in ways that reflect what we know about good assessment. Alverno College, for example, sees assessment as an integral process to the learning experience of all students, including education majors. At Alverno, learning involves self, peer and faculty judgments of student performances based on public criteria (Bollag, 2006). Teacher education programs can similarly immerse their students in progressive assessment practices. By making our own assessments transparent, formative, collaborative, and constructive, we can give students firsthand experience with good assessment.

## WHERE DO WE GO FROM HERE?

Tweaking one component of a complicated system leads to little or no change: The whole system must be addressed. Here, in no particular order, is my wish list for change:

*Support pre- and in-service teachers in trying out and reflecting on new approaches to assessment.* Our teacher education programs do not exist in a vacuum: Preservice teachers work and learn in classrooms with practicing teachers who show and tell them how it really is. If practicums reinforce confusions about assessment, even the most progressive coursework will fail.

*Create a dialogue with teacher certification organizations* such as the Teacher Education Accreditation Council and the National Council for Accreditation of Teacher Education about raising the bar. Teacher educators are not immune to the pressures of external evaluation, so we should encourage all accrediting bodies to include specific, assessment-related requirements in their criteria for teacher education programs.

*Engage in dialogue with policymakers.* Shepard (2000) noted that researchers in the United States "have engaged policymakers and the public on the topic of testing but have focused almost exclusively on the features of state and district accountability testing programs" (p. 10). It is time to enlighten politicians about the other, formative side of the assessment coin.

## QUESTIONS TO PROMPT DISCUSSION

The questions that follow will help you reflect on the issues presented in this chapter.

1. Is there a fundamental rift between formative and summative assessment, or is there a possibility of harmony between the two? If the latter, what might it look like? If the former, should educators take sides?
2. How can we make teachers' voices heard in ongoing discussions and debates about assessment?

## REFERENCES

Andrade, H. (2000). Using rubrics to promote thinking and learning. *Educational Leadership, 57*(5), 13–18.

Andrade, H. & Boulay, B. (2003). The role of self-assessment in learning to write. *The Journal of Educational Research, 97*(1), 21–34.

Andrade, H., & Du, Y. (2005). Student perspectives on rubric-referenced assessment. *Practical Assessment Research & Evaluation, 10*(4). Available: http://PAREonline.net/getvn.asp?v=10&n=3.

Andrade, H., Du, Y., & Wang, X. (2007). *Putting rubrics to the test: The effect of models, criteria generation, and rubric-referenced self-assessment on writing.* Paper presented at meeting of the American Educational Research Association. Chicago, IL.

Black, P., & Wiliam, D. (1998). Inside the black box: Raising standards through classroom assessment. *Phi Delta Kappan, 80*(2), 139–148.

Black, P., & Wiliam, D. (2003). In praise of educational research: Formative assessment. *British Educational Research Journal, 29*(5), 623–37.

Black, P., Harrison, C., Lee, C., Marshall, B., & Wiliam, D. (2004). *Assessment for learning: Putting it into practice.* Berkshire, England: Open University Press.

Bollag, B. (2006). Making an art form of assessment: A small women's college has become a model for determining what students have learned. *The Chronicle of Higher Education, LIII*(10), A1–A4.

Boston, C. (2002). The concept of formative assessment. *Practical Assessment, Research & Evaluation, 8*(9). Available: http://pareonline.net/getvn.asp?v=8&n=9.

Brinko, L. T. (1993). The practice of giving feedback to improve teaching. *Journal of Higher Education, 64*(5), 574–593.

Butler, D., & Winne, P. (1995). Feedback and self-regulated learning: A theoretical synthesis. *Review of Educational Research, 65*(3), 245–281.

Cannell, J. J. (1987). *Nationally normed elementary achievement testing in America's public schools. How all fifty states are above the national average.* Daniels, WV: Friends for Education.

Centre for Educational Research and Innovation (2005). *Formative assessment: Improving learning in secondary classrooms.* Paris: Organization for Economic Co-operation and Development.

Cizek, G. J. (2005). Adapting testing technology to serve accountability aims: The case of vertically moderated standard setting. *Applied Measurement in Education, 18*(1), 1–9.

Crocker, L. (2003). Teaching for the test: Validity, fairness, and moral action. *Educational Measurement: Issues and Practice, 22*(3), 5–11.

Deakin-Crick, R., Sebba, J., Harlen, W., Guoxing, Y., & Lawson, H. (2005). Systematic review of research evidence of the impact on students of self- and peer-assessment. Protocol. In: *Research Evidence in Education Library.* London: EPPI-Centre, Social Science Research Unit, Institute of Education, University of London.

The Gale Group (2002). A short history of high-stakes testing. *Encyclopedia of Education.* Retrieved April 10, 2007 from http://www.answers.com/topic/testing-a-short-history-of-high-stakes-testing.

Gardner, J. (Ed.) (2006). *Assessment and learning.* London: SAGE Publications.

Gipps, C. & Stobart, G. (2003). Alternative assessment. In Kellaghan, T. & Stufflebeam, D. (Eds.), *International handbook of educational evaluation* (pp. 549–575). Dordrecht, The Netherlands: Kluwer Academic Publishers.

Haladyna, T., Downing, S., & Rodriguez, M. (2002). A review of multiple-choice item-writing guidelines for classroom assessment. *Applied Measurement in Education, 15*(3), 309–334.

Haney, W. (2000). The myth of the Texas miracle in education. *Education Policy Analysis Archives, 8*(41). Available: http://epaa.asu.edu/epaa/v8n41/.

Harlen, W. (2005a). Teachers' summative practice and assessment for learning: Tensions and synergies. *The Curriculum Journal, 16*(2), 207–223.

Harlen, W. (2005b). On the relationship between assessment for formative and summative purposes. In J. Gardner (Ed.), *Assessment and learning.* Thousand Oaks, CA: SAGE.

Harlen, W., & James, M. J. (1997). Assessment and learning: Differences and relationships between formative and summative assessment. *Assessment in Education 4*(3), 365–380.

Herman, J., & Winters, L. (1994). Portfolio research: A slim collection. *Educational Leadership, 52*(2), 48–56.

Kornhaber, M. (2004). Assessment, standards, and equity. In J. A. Banks & C. A. M. Banks (Eds.), *Handbook of multicultural education.* San Francisco: Jossey-Bass.

Kornhaber, M. (2007). Beyond standardization in school accountability. In G. L. Sunderman (Ed.). *The NCLB challenge: Achieving accountability, equity, and school reform.* Thousand Oaks, CA: Corwin Press.

Mabry, L. (1999). Writing to the rubric: Lingering effects of traditional standardized testing on direct writing assessment. *Phi Delta Kappan, 80*(9), 673–679.

The National Commission on Excellence in Education (1983). *A nation at risk: The imperative for educational reform.* Washington, DC: U.S. Departmet of Education.

National Research Council (2001). *Knowing what students know: The science and design of educational assessment.* Washington, DC: National Academy Press.

O'Donnell, A., & Topping, K. (1998). Peers assessing peers: Possibilities and prob-
    lems. In K. Topping & S. Ehly (Eds.), *Peer-assisted learning.* Mahwah, NJ: Lawrence
    Erlbaum Associates.
Organisation of Economic Co-operation and Development (2005). Formative assess-
    ment: Improving learning in classrooms. *Policy Briefs, November 2005.* Retrieved
    June 5, 2007 from http://www.oecd.org/dataoecd/19/31/35661078.pdf.
Phelps, R. (Ed.). (2005). *Defending standardized testing.* Mahwah, NJ: Lawrence Erl-
    baum.
Popham, J. W. (2000). The mismeasurement of educational quality. *The School
    Administrator, 11*(57), 12–15.
Popham, W. J. (2004). "Teaching to the Test": An expression to eliminate. *Educational
    Leadership, 62*(3), 82–83.
Resnick, M. (2004). *The educated student: Defining and advancing student achievement.*
    Alexandria, VA: National School Boards Association.
Sadler, D. R. (2005). Interpretations of criteria-based assessment and grading in
    higher education. *Assessment and Evaluation in Higher Education, 30*(2), 175–194.
Scriven, M. (2003). Evaluation theory and metatheory. In T. Kellaghan & D.
    Stufflebeam (Eds.), *International handbook of educational evaluation.* Boston: Kluwer.
Shepard, L. (2000). The role of assessment in a learning culture. *Educational
    Researcher, 29*(7), 4–14.
Shepard, L. (2000). The role of assessment in a learning culture. Educational
    Researcher, 29(7), 4-14.
Starkman, N. (2006). Formative assessment: Building a better student. *T.H.E. Journal.*
    Retrieved April 16, 2007 from http://www.thejournal.com/articles/19174_2.
Wilson, M. (2006). *Rethinking rubrics in writing assessment.* Portsmouth, NH: Heine-
    mann.
Wilson, M., & Black, P. (2007). *Assessing understanding through the use of learning pro-
    gressions.* Paper presented at the meeting of the American Educational Research
    Association, Chicago, IL.

# Chapter 13

# PREPARING SPECIAL EDUCATION TEACHERS FOR TOMORROW

Elizabeth Whitten, Lisa Dieker, Chris O'Brien, and Sarah Summy

*We can whenever and wherever we choose, successfully teach all children . . . we already know more than we need to know in order to do that.*

(Edmonds, 1979, p. 21)

## INTRODUCTION

In this chapter we will focus on the current state of preparing special education teachers to work with students with disabilities and the future direction and changes needed in the field. New research within the special education arena has led to a collaborative practice that has noticeably improved the lives of many students with disabilities. However, a gap continues to exist between empirically established practice and routine practice. Strategies for decreasing this gap include: partnership, collaboration, consultation, and professional development activities. The proposed chapter addresses all of these strategies as well as the preparation of teachers to deal effectively with the issues related to reducing the gap between research and practice.

## Major Developments in Special Education in American Public Schools and Related Impact on Special Education Teacher Preparation

- **1966.** ESEA provides for the Establishment of the Bureau of Education of the Handicapped (BEH) that provided federal foundation for local improvement of services for children with disabilities.
- **Pre-1970.** Special education teacher preparation programs housed within psychology program and not schools of education.
- **1973.** Section 504 of the Rehabilitation Act extended civil rights in public accommodations to include individuals with disabilities.
- **1975.** PL 94-142 Education for all Handicapped Children Act provided free appropriate public education for children with disabilities ages 3–21, ensured due process rights, established IEPs and LRE principle.
- **1975.** Extensive development of licensure/certification programs, and teacher preparation programs for special educators.
- **1980.** Only 15 states required general education teachers to complete coursework on educating students with disabilities.
- **1986.** PL 99-457, The Education of the Handicapped Act Amendments of 1986 extended services to preschool children and mandated early intervention services for infants with developmental disabilities.
- **Late 1980s.** Movement away from "disability of the week" to emphasizing curriculum modifications and adaptations within designated courses on mainstreaming.
- **1990.** Individuals with Disabilities Education Act of 1990 required transition services, added autism and TBI to eligibility for special education services.
- **1990s.** Development of collaboration models, conceptual work on co-teaching, and consultation approaches to service delivery.
- **1997.** The Individuals with Disabilities Education Act Amendments of 1997 emphasized general curriculum access.

- **1997.** Teacher preparation shifted gradually to collaborative service delivery models with substantial influence of inclusive education.
- **2001.** No Child Left Behind Act of 2001 (NCLB) emphasized "highly qualified" concept, the use of scientifically-validated instructional practices, and the addition of extensive accountability features to American public education.
- **2004.** Individuals with Disabilities Education Improvement Act of 2004 aligned special education services with NCLB requiring special education teachers to have expertise in core academic subjects.
- **2004.** Teacher preparation in special education emphasizes general curriculum access for children with disabilities, accountability for content knowledge based on high-stakes tests, positive behavior support strategies, response to intervention models, and use of ongoing formative assessments (CBM).
- **Twenty-first century.** Ninety-five percent of all teachers educate students with disabilites, schools of education create collaborative relationships across preservice faculty and general and special education, concept of universal design, 45 states and the District of Columbia require general education teachers to complete coursework on education students with disabilities.

### Preparing Special Education Teachers For Tomorrow

Teacher preparation programs of tomorrow must engage participants in a culture of collaboration and construction of knowledge through exemplary coursework and purposeful dialogue, state of the art content knowledge, focused field experiences, meaningful mentoring, peer-coaching, and transdisciplinary teamwork. Teacher preparation must provide students with advanced knowledge, skills, and experiences of the twenty-first century. Students need a solid foundation in the principles of research-based practices, subject matter content, data-based decision making, positive behavioral supports and interventions, collaboration and teamwork among educators, families, and community agencies, transition, diversity, mentorship, policy development and implementation, and research and evaluation (Carolan & Guinn, 2007).

## Research-Based Practices

Teachers in special education must have a thorough understanding of the teaching-learning process and skill in applying research-based instructional methods and strategies for individuals with disabilities. In addition to understanding instructional theories and practices appropriate for students with disabilities, teachers must demonstrate skill in developing educational curricula while considering the needs, competencies, cultures, and skills of all learners (Tomlinson, 2002). As we increase our knowledge base in alternative instructional formats, such as co-teaching, distance education, computer-based instruction, and various innovative technologies we must apply various theories of teaching and learning to develop effective educational interventions for *all* students (Boyer & Gillespie, 2000).

Additionally, teachers should be prepared in the teaching–learning process through in-depth preparation in research-based programs and strategies such as *Dynamic Indicators of Basic Early Literacy Skills (DIBELS*, Sixth Edition, Good & Kaminski, 2003), Teacher Work Samples (Renaissance Project, 2004), and Differentiated Instruction (Heacox, 2002; Marzano, Pickering, & Pollock, 2001; Tomlinson, 2001). As part of this state-of-the-art preparation, special educators need to be prepared to adapt curriculum and modify instruction to accommodate students with disabilities in general education settings (Byrnes, 2000; Greenwood, 2001; Wood, 2006); collaborate and team with other educators (Dieker & Murawski, 2003; Dettmer, Thurston, & Dyck, 2005); integrate cooperative learning and peer tutoring strategies (Maheady, Harper, & Mallette, 2001; Mastropieri et al., 2001); co-plan and co-teach with general education classroom teachers (Whitten & Dieker, 1995; Whitten & Dieker, 2004); effectively communicate and work with parents (Dettmer, Thurston, & Dyck, 2005); gather, evaluate, and report student academic and behavioral performance (Deno, 2003; Horner, Sugai, Lewis-Palmer, & Todd, 2001); identify community service and transition needs of students, and participate in transdisciplinary teaming necessary to develop and implement a sequential plan of action (Kohler, 2000).

During this time of high-stakes testing, teachers must learn core content supported by research-based practices for instruction in English (Atkinson et al., 2002), social studies (Carnine et al., 1994; Passe & Beattie, 1994), science (Mastropieri & Scruggs, 1992; Mastropieri et al., 2001), and mathematics (Allsopp et al., 2003; Baker et al., 2002), with a level of understanding to allow for practical suggestions for accommodations and modifications for students with disabilities served in the general education setting. Collaboration and co-teaching with must be a major emphasis throughout this process.

### Subject Matter Content

Historically, the Individuals with Disabilities Education Act (IDEA) has served as the foundational legislation for serving the educational needs of students with disabilities. In recent years, the field of special education has witnessed an ever-increasing emphasis on serving the needs of students with disabilities in the most inclusive environment (Dettmer, Thurston, & Dyck, 2005; Lerner, 2006). The most recent reauthorization of IDEA (2004) more closely aligns with the No Child Left Behind Act (NCLB), taking one more significant step toward the education of students with disabilities in the general curriculum and holding schools accountable for their education. Included in IDEA 2004 is the mandate for special educators to be "highly qualified" suggesting this language "has the same meaning given the term in . . . the Elementary and Secondary Education Act of 1965," more commonly known as No Child Left Behind. Essentially this indicates that preparation and certification in special education is not sufficient for teaching content to students receiving special education services—subject matter certification is required as well (CEC, 2004). Emphasis on serving students with disabilities in the general education classroom has significantly impacted teachers in core academic areas in secondary schools. Often, their preparation for a career in teaching is heavily focused on content knowledge with limited preparation in instructional strategies, which meet the needs of students with mild disabilities (Esposito & Lal, 2005). As a consequence, many core academic subject teachers (i.e., English, math, social studies, science) display a sense of frustration and resentment over their lack of preparation to work with the population of students for whom they are responsible. General education preservice teachers who provide instruction in secondary core academic areas typically have limited specific coursework related to instruction for students with disabilities. Rather, they may have, at the most, courses that describe characteristics of students with special needs. An unfortunate result of these feelings of inadequate preparation is a feeling of resentment toward students with disabilities and generally lowered expectations for performance (Griffin, Wohlstetter, & Bharadwaja, 2001).

Emphasis in NCLB on teacher competency in core academic subjects taught poses considerable challenges for special education teachers at the secondary level. Under NCLB (2001) a highly qualified teacher holds a minimum of a bachelor's degree, has obtained full state certification or licensure and has demonstrated subject area competence in each of the academic subjects in which they teach. The highly qualified special education teacher, teaching core academic subjects at the secondary level, must meet these standards in addition to holding full state certification/licensure in Special Education. Defining the highly qualified special educator was one of the major issues in the *Individuals with Disabilities Education Improvement Act of 2004*. In its final version, the bill passed by Congress on November 19, 2004, aligned IDEA with NCLB requirements. Now, as states rush to address the qualifications of special education teachers already employed, there is rising concern that increased federal regulations will exacerbate existing special education teacher shortages. The critical need to recruit and prepare highly qualified special education teachers has been ongoing in the field, however, the particular need for special educators prepared to teach students with disabilities who are working on state standards at all levels has now emerged. In addition, the need to diversify the teaching force requires that teacher recruitment and preparation be designed so as to enhance the number of special education teachers from traditionally underrepresented groups including those with disabilities and those with culturally and linguistically diverse backgrounds to reflect the diversity of students served in order to prepare a diverse teaching force that is highly qualified to truly meet the needs of society (Whitten & Rodriguez, 2003).

### Data-Based Decision Making

In order for learners with disabilities to demonstrate achievement, special education personnel must engage in data-based decision making (Deno, 2003). Teachers must be able to incorporate research findings and the procedures developed in model programs into daily practice. Teachers who function in this manner choose assessment tools that (a) assess the child in the classroom and in the curriculum, (b) evaluate the child's performance relative to his or her prior performance, (c) generate and evaluate intervention ideas based on collected data and (d) provide for ongoing progress monitoring. Specifically, strategies like Curriculum Based Measurement or CBM (Deno, 2003; Shin et al., 2000) can be used to monitor student performance in order to support a wide range of classroom decisions including the use of pre-referral intervention and conducting formative evaluation of academic progress. By continually assessing and analyzing and evaluating student performance, teachers can make decisions to adjust instruction based on data. This data provides the teacher with the information for differentiating instruction, grouping students, adapting materials, scaffolding instruction, and accommodating for individual students.

### Positive Behavioral Supports and Interventions

Perhaps no greater challenge facing educational professionals is present than understanding and addressing the variety of behavioral issues students are presenting. The issues of behavior management and intervention should not be in response to the presence of undesired behavior but should instead incorporate proactive intervention strategies (Horner, Sugai, Lewis-Palmer, & Todd, 2001). However, this process of incorporating proactive intervention strategies or positive supports is not completed in isolation and is the result of collaborative effort of all parties involved (Sugai & Tindal, 1993).

Establishing a learning community that consistently employs positive behavior supports is a process requiring many skills. The school-wide approach comprises a broad range of strategies with emphasis on three levels of data-based prevention strategies and long-term maintenance of target behavior including contextual use of positive reinforcement, direct teaching of behavioral expectations and social behaviors, and maximizing academic engagement and opportunities for success (Horner & Sugai, 2005). These skills should be integrated throughout student coursework and practica to support teachers in managing behaviors.

### Collaboration Among Educators, Families, and Community Agencies

Roles are changing in education for all stakeholders. Educators must strive to create a community of learners that foster collaboration across schools and communities. The focus on preparing educators in the area of collaboration enables teachers to more effectively meet the diverse needs of student populations at-risk for school failure (Bahr, Whitten, Dieker, Kocarek, & Manson, 1999; Dynak, Whitten, & Dynak, 1996; Whitten & Dieker, 2004).

Future special education teachers must be prepared as change agents for the field of education. They should develop skills in providing professional development or inservice workshops, consultation, co-teaching, collaborative problem solving, conflict resolution, and teaming along with the communicative skills necessary to serve as a collaborative consultant, team member, or facilitator.

The need for teachers to work collaboratively with parents is significant (Friend & Cook, 2007; Kroth & Edge, 1997) and made even more so by the issues often present for families in urban and rural settings (Gonzalez, Brusca-Vega, & Yawkey, 1997). The importance of communicating with families is intensified when there may be cultural differences between teachers and families (Hyun & Fowler, 1995; Taylor-Ritzler et al., 2001). Teachers should be responsive to the families; yet to accomplish this goal, teacher preparation programs must focus on the issues important to families (Friend & Cook, 2007; Kroth & Edge, 1997).

Collaboration between families and schools can lead to improved academic outcomes for students, decreased discipline issues and decreased absences (Corrigan & Bishop, 1997; National PTA, 1998; Rasmussen, 1998). In 1998, the National PTA developed *National Standards for Parent/Family Involvement* that emphasized the need for creating connections among schools, families and community resources. These standards were specifically developed for schools, but are equally important for universities preparing teachers to work with families (Gonzalez et al., 1997; Kroth & Edge, 1997).

### *Transition Practices*

Teachers must have a thorough understanding of a variety of issues facing students with disabilities. There are only two specifically mandated transition activities for students with disabilities. The first mandated transition experience involves children from the ages of birth to three and their families. An Individualized Family Service Plan is developed for each of these students to ensure a smooth transition to the appropriate setting.

The second mandated transition is for students who are reaching the age of 16. This coordinated set of activities is designed to support students moving from school to post-school activities. Educators must understand the need for effective secondary education and transition services (Kohler, 2000) specifically promoting attainment of transition related goals for low-income and ethnic minority students with disabilities (Taylor-Ritzler et al., 2001). Educators must be knowledgeable of these services and prepared to deliver them regardless of the large number of students with disabilities who are reported exiting school each year. Educators must improve the outcomes of these students through an understanding of the needs and skills of self-determination.

Teacher education will need to prepare students with expertise in research, policy, and best practice as they relate to the field of transition. Students should participate in coursework that will present educational concepts, history, legal issues and the current mandates under the Individuals with Disabilities Act of 2004 and the School-to-Work Opportunities Act. The focus of this curriculum is on the development of awareness, exploration, and preparation to deliver self-determined transition-focused education (Kohler, 2000).

### *Diversity*

Understanding the growing diversity of needs in our schools must be a priority for preparing tomorrow's teachers (Rogers-Adkinson & Griffith, 1999). Culturally diverse and responsive educators can impact attitudes and achievements of all students. They can transform the learning in all environments by creating a community that represents the diversity of the students they serve. Teachers with authentic knowledge about differences can better gauge their influence on student outcomes. Preparation programs must embrace diverse perspectives to develop a new cadre of teachers representing a broader segment of the population by fostering this climate throughout interdisciplinary coursework and field experiences.

There is an increasing gap between the number of minority students in special education and the number of minority teachers who teach them (Whitten & Rodriguez, 2003). This gap is compounded by projections that indicate the proportion of students of culturally and linguistically diverse backgrounds is expected to continue to increase in direct contrast to the proportion of teachers of culturally and linguistically diverse backgrounds (Voltz, Dooley, & Jeffries, 1999). At the secondary level, a significant proportion of students in special education are African American males, but only 2.3 percent of special education teachers are African American males. Nationwide, 40 percent of schools have no faculty of culturally and linguistically diverse backgrounds (Center on Personnel Studies in Special Education, 2004).

## *Mentorship*

Teacher preparation must be designed so that teachers are accountable and competent in the tasks that reflect the skills of the positions for which they are being prepared. Teacher preparation programs should provide mentoring experiences, which allow frequent opportunities for students to engage in teaching, research, and service activities in conjunction with faculty members and other professionals.

Increased awareness of the problems faced by inexperienced special education teachers as evidenced in the high rate of attrition from the field has focused attention on mentoring as a strategy of reform (Whitaker, 2000a). Effective mentoring requires that mentors possess expertise in teaching, knowledge of teacher development, beginning teacher problems, adult development, reflective practice, and the skills associated with recognizing effective teaching, as well as skills in cognitive coaching (Pipho, 2000). Qualities identified as important for special education mentors are matching knowledge and experience base to that of first year teachers' contexts, serving in nonevaluative roles, understanding of the mentor's role, providing emotional support, and demonstrating qualities such as being personable, open, caring, friendly, comfortable, nonthreatening, available, and flexible (Boyer, 1999; Whitaker, 2000b).

Mentor selection is key for successful experiences of teacher candidates. Concerns have been raised about the content of mentoring. Research has pointed to the focus and perceived value of mentoring as being emotional and technical support (e.g., Boyer, 1999; Whitaker, 2000b), but there seems to be less focus on supporting standards-based learning. The need for pushing new teachers to focus on learning and to support mentors in this area is critical, particularly for students with disabilities who all too often are taught by novice or uncertified teachers themselves.

## *Policy Development and Implications*

The American Education System is currently experiencing many new school initiatives/reforms (i.e., higher standards, response to intervention, site-based management, school choice and vouchers, accountability and testing, charter schools, private contracting etc.). The focus of preparing educators in the area of policy development and its subsequent implications allows for new teachers to address these initiatives in a confident and competent manner. Teachers also need to understand these initiatives from many different professional perspectives/cultures and a variety of localities (i.e., rural, suburban, and urban). With the passage of IDEA 2004, many policy and practice implications for all stakeholders remain unclear (Cernosia, 2007).

## Research and Evaluation

The field of special education needs teachers prepared to engage in a form of inquiry designed to improve their teaching. Teachers spend their school day involved in planning, action, reflection, and evaluation. Each of these modes are part of action research yet not often enough do teachers engage in building a collaborative community focused on improving their teaching practices and better serving their students. The major challenge for today's teachers is determining not only what a student should learn, but more importantly how a student learns (Holly, Arhar, & Kasten, 2005). Teachers must be prepared to create classroom environments where are all students can make annual yearly progress. To build this type of learning environment teachers must engage in inquiry based teaching using conversation and tools required by personnel who can engage in action research. Teachers must be able to incorporate research findings and the procedures developed in model programs into daily practice in field-based settings.

Teacher preparation is one of the most effective and important means of disseminating research and model program procedures to the field. Only the combination of a rich research environment and significant university investment in field-based service is likely to provide the background necessary to prepare the highest caliber of special education personnel and begin to bridge the gap between empirically established practice and routine practice (Greenwood & Abbott, 2001). Strategies for decreasing this gap include: partnership, collaboration, consultation, and professional development activities (Deno, 2000; Greenwood & Abbott, 2001). If teachers are to assume roles within an organization, then they must be prepared to conduct research in action-based service settings and to develop skills in the implementation and evaluation of existing program models.

## Implications

Although the need to better prepare teachers to bridge the gap between empirically established practice and routine practice has been clearly documented within the literature, model teacher preparation programs that have the capability to produce a highly effective teacher in every classroom are not readily accessible. The goal of a highly effective teacher in every classroom is attainable if teacher preparation programs use the strategies outlined within this chapter. Once again, strategies for decreasing this gap include: partnership, collaboration, consultation, and professional development activities.

Teacher preparation programs that do not embrace the active implementation of these strategies will continue to produce teachers that do not truly have the tools to close the achievement gap for all students; specifically the knowledge, skills, and dispositions to remain an active professional within the field. Programs designed using these strategies will produce a special education teacher who is a reflective practitioner, competent researcher, content expert, instructional and learning specialist, collaborator, knowledgable advocate and most importantly an active service provider to ensure the success of our ever-growing diverse population of students and youth with disabilities.

Faculty and administrators need to lobby for the necessary resources to implement these strategies that will meet the needs of the field. This includes but is not limited to: assessing community needs for personnel and subsequent program development to meet identified needs; securing financial resources to address the expense of higher education; hiring qualified faculty who are committed to preparing tomorrow's teacher; aligning faculty workload assignments that are conducive to the implementation of the aforementioned strategies; and future research reflecting the application of these strategies.

## WHERE DO WE GO FROM HERE?

The need for fully certified special education teachers employed full-time to provide special education and related services for school-age students nationally has reached record proportions. Special education is the greatest shortage area for teacher certification among the two hundred largest American cities (American Federation of Teachers, 1999). Teacher shortages in special education are especially of concern as the numbers of students with disabilities continues to rise. According to the U.S. Department of Education, Office of Special Education Programs, Data Analysis System's most current data of 2002–2003 school year, approximately 2,877,486 secondary students with disabilities, ages 12 through 17, were served in special education programs. In 2003, that number rose to 2,941,725, an increase of almost 65 thousand students, just in the 12 through 17 age category. About 42 percent of the students in this age range are served in the regular education class 79 percent of the time or more. These students would likely be working toward a standard diploma and may receive services from secondary special educators for part of their day (Whitten & Rodriguez-Campos, 2003).

Teacher education must develop a vision for change that addresses these critical shortages as well as the importance of transforming relationships between institutions of higher education, state departments, public schools, community agencies, and students with disabilities. The field must reflect on the past and focus on preparing tomorrow's special education teacher who is a reflective practitioner, competent researcher, content expert, instructional and learning specialist, collaborator, knowledgable advocate and most importantly an active service provider to ensure the success of our ever-growing diverse population of students and youth with disabilities.

If we are to reach the goal of a highly effective teacher in every classroom, then we must reach beyond the number of required courses and ensure that our teachers truly have the tools (i.e., knowledge, skills, and competencies) necessary to close the achievement gap for *all* students. Teachers must differentiate instruction to meet the needs of all their students. Classroom teachers are not prepared to effectively utilize research-based strategies in support of the content they teach, therefore, special education teachers will need to collaboratively support content teachers in the general education setting utilizing the many skills discussed in this chapter.

## QUESTIONS TO PROMPT DISCUSSION

Based on the content of this chapter, what components of teacher education do you currently practice in your program?

1. What practices will enhance your teacher education program?
2. How do you believe the fields of general and special education will continue to blend to improve practices for all students?
3. How do you think NCLB and IDEA will continue to complement one another?
4. What trends do you think will take place in the next ten years to better meet the needs of students in special education and teacher education?

## REFERENCES

Allsopp, D., Lovin, L., Green, G., & Savage-Davis, E. (2003). Why students with special needs have difficulty learning mathematics and what teachers can do to help. *Mathematics Teaching in the Middle School, 8*, 308.

American Federation of Teachers [AFT]. (1999). Survey & Analysis of Teacher Salary Trends. Retrieved August 24, 2001, fromhttp://www.aft.org/research/survey99/index.html

Atkinson, R. S., Wilhite, K. L., Frey, L. M., & Williams, S. C. (2002). Reading instruction for the struggling reader: Implications for teachers of students with learning disabilities or emotional/behavioral disorders. *Preventing School Failure, 46*, 158–162.

Bahr, M., Whitten, E., Dieker, L., Kocarek, C., & Manson, D. (1999). A comparison of school-based intervention teams: Implications for educational and legal reform. *Exceptional Children, 66*, 67–84.

Baker, S., Gersten, R., & Lee, D. S. (2002). A synthesis of empirical research on teaching mathematics to low-achieving students. *Elementary School Journal, 103*, 51.

Boyer, L., & Gillespie, P. (2000). Keeping the committed: The importance of induction and support programs for new special educators. *Teaching Exceptional Children, 33*, 10–15.

Byrnes, M. (2000). Accommodations for Students with Disabilities: Removing Barriers to Learning. *NASSP Bulletin, 84*, 21–27.

Carnine, D., Miller, S., Bean, R., & Zigmond, N. (1994). Social studies: Educational tools for diverse learners. *School Psychology Review, 23*, 428–441.

Carolan, J., & Guinn, A. (2007). Differentation: Lessons from Master Teachers. *Educational Leadership, 64*, 44–47.

Cernosia, A. (2007). The new state of special education: Key policy and practice implications of the IDEA 2004 and 2006 regulation. 28th National Institute on Legal Issues of Education Individuals with Disabilities, San Diego, CA.

Corrigan, D., & Bishop, K. K. (1997). Creating family-centered integrated service systems and interprofessional educational programs to implement them. *Social Work in Education, 19*, 149–163.

Council for Exceptional Children (2004). Analysis for IDEA conference: CEC recommendation H. R. 1350 and S. 48. Retrieved April 24, 2005. from http://www.

cec.sped.org/pp/August2004AnalysisforIDEAConferenceCECRecommendations.pdf

Deno, S. L. (2003). Developments in curriculum-based measurement. *Journal of Special Education, 37*, 184–192.

Dettmer, P., Thurston, L., & Dyck, N. (2005). *Consultation, collaboration and teamwork for students with special needs.* Needham Heights, MA: Allyn & Bacon.

Dieker, L. A., & Murawski, W. W. (2003). Co-teaching at the secondary level: Unique issues, current trends, and suggestions for success. *High School Journal, 86*, 1.

Diversifying the special education workforce: District recruitment and retention strategies. (2004). Special Education Workforce Watch: Insights from Research (Vol. PB-10.): Center on Personnel Studies in Special Education.

Dynak, J., Whitten, E., & Dynak, D. (1996). Refining the general education student teaching experiences through the use of special education collaborative teaching models. *Action in Teacher Education, 19*, 64–74.

Edmonds, R. (1979). Effective schools for the urban poor. *Educational Leadership, 37*(1), 15–24.

Esposito, M. C. & Lal, S. (2005). Responding to special education teacher shortage in diverse urban settings: An accelerated alternative credential program. *Teacher Education and Special Education, 28*, 100–103.

Friend, M., & Cook, L. (2007). *Interactions: Collaboration skills for school professionals.* Pearson Publishing: Boston.

Gonzalez, V., Brusca-Vega, R., & Yawkey, T. (1997). *Assessment and instruction of culturally and linguistically diverse students with or at-risk of learning problems.* Needham Heights, MA: Allyn & Bacon.

Good, R. H. & Kaminskei R. A. (2003). Using dynamic indicators of basic early literacy skills (DIBELS). *OSSC Bulletin, 44*, 1–28

Greenwood, C. R. (2001). Introduction to the topical issue: Bridging the gap between research and practice in special education: Issues and implications for teacher preparation. *Teacher Education and Special Education, 24*, 273–275.

Greenwood, C. R., & Abbott, M. (2001). The Research to Practice Gap in Special Education. *Teacher Education and Special Education, 2*, 276–89.

Griffin, N. C., Wohlstetter, P., & Bharadwaja, L. C., (2001). Teacher coaching: A tool for retention. *School Administrator, 58*, 38–40. Denver, CO: Love Publishing.

Heacox, D. (2002). *Differentiating Instruction "in the Regular" Classroom: How to reach and teach all learners, grades 3–12.* Minneapolis: Free Spirit Publishing, Inc.

Holly, M. L., Arhar, J., & Kasten, W. (2005). *Action research for teachers.* Columbus, OH: Pearson.

Horner, R. H., & Sugai, G. (2005). School-wide positive behavior support: An alternative approach to discipline in schools. In L. Bambara & L. Kern (Eds.), *Positive behavior support* (pp. 359–390). New York: Guilford Press.

Horner, R.H., Sugai, G., Lewis-Palmer, T., & Todd, A.W., (2001). Teaching school-wide behavioral expectations. *Emotional & Behavioral Disorders in Youth, 1*, 77–83.

Hyun, J. K., & Fowler, S. A. (1995). Respect, cultural sensitivity and communication: Promoting participation of Asian families in the individualized family service plan. *Teaching Exceptional Children, 28*, 25–28.

Individuals with Disabilities Education Improvement Act of 2004. 20 U.S.C. § 1400 *et seq.* (2004) (reauthorization of the Individuals with Disabilities Act of 1990).

Kamps, D., Potucek, J., Dugan, E., Kravitz, T., Gonzalez-Lopez, A., Garcia, J., Carnazzo, K., Morrison, L., & Kane, L.G. (2002). Peer training to facilitate social interaction for elementary students with autism and their peers. *Exceptional Children, 68*, 173–87.

Kohler, P. (2000). *Taxonomy for transition planning: Linking research to practice.* Champaign, IL: University of IL.

Kroth, R. L., & Edge, D. (1997). *Strategies for community with parents and families of exceptional children* (3rd ed.). Denver, CO: Love.

Lerner, J. (2006). *Learning disabilities and related disorders.* Boston: Houghton Mifflin Publishing.

Maheady, L., Harper, G. F., & Mallette, B. (2001). Peer-Mediated Instruction and Interventions and Students with Mild Disabilities. *Remedial and Special Education, 22*, 4–14.

Marzano, R. J., Pickering, D. J., & Pollock, J. E. (2001). *Classroom instruction that works: Research-based strategies for increasing student achievement.* Association for Supervision and Curriculum Development: Alexendria, VA.

Mastropieri, M. A., & Scruggs, T. E. (1992). Science for students with disabilities. *Review of Educational Research, 62*, 377.

Mastropieri, M. A., Scruggs, T. E., Boon, R., & Butcher Carter, K. (2001). Correlates of inquiry learning in science. *Remedial & Special Education, 22*, 130–139.

National Center for Education Statistics [NCES]. (2005). *Digest of educational statistics.* Washington, DC: Author.

National PTA. (1998). *National standards for parent-family involvement programs.* Chicago: Author.

Passe, J., & Beattie, J. (1994). Social studies instruction for students with mild disabilities. *Remedial and Special Education, 15*(4), 227–233.

Pipho, C., (2000). A new reform model for teachers and teaching, *Phi Delta Kappan, 81*, 421–22.

Rasmussen, K. (1998). Making parent involvement meaningful. *Education Update, 40*, 1, 6, 7.

Renaissance Project. (2004). *Renaissance project for improving teacher quality: Student teacher work sample.* Retrieved July 11, 2004 from http://fp.uni.edu.itq.

Rogers-Adkinson, D. & Griffith, P. L. (1999). Comparing language disorders in two groups of students with severe behavior disorders, *Behavior Disorders, 22*, 160–166.

Scruggs, T. E., Mastropieri, M. A., & Boon, R. (1998). Science education for students with disabilities: A review of recent research. *Studies in Science Education, 32*, 21–44.

Shin, J., Deno, S. L., & Espin, C. (2000). Technical adequacy of the maze task for curriculum-based measurement of reading growth. *Journal of Special Education, 34*, 164.

Sugai, G. M., & Tindal, G. A. (1993). *Effective school consultation: An interactive approach.* Pacific Grove, CA: Brooks/Cole Publishing Co. (ERIC Document Reproduction Service No. ED 355 718).

Taylor-Ritzler, T., Balcazar, F. E., Keys, C. B., Hayes, E., Garate-Serafini, T., &

Espino, S. R., (2001). Promoting attainment of transition-related goals among low-income ethnic minority students with disabilities, *Career Development for Exceptional Individuals, 24*, 147–169.

Tomlinson, C. A. (2001). Grading for success. *Educational Leadership, 58*, 12–15.

Tomlinson, C. A. (2002). Invitations to learn. *Educational Leadership, 60*, 6–10

Voltz, D. L., Dooley, E., & Jeffries, P. (1999). Preparing special educators for cultural diversity: How far have we come? *Teacher Education and Special Education, 22*, 66–77.

Whitaker, S. D. (2000a). Mentoring beginning special education teachers and the relationship to attrition. *Exceptional Children, 6*, 546–566.

Whitaker, S. D. (2000b). What do first-year special education teachers need? *Teaching Exceptional Children, 33*, 28–36.

Whitten, E., & Dieker, L. (Winter, 1995). Intervention assistance teams: A broader vision. *Preventing School Failure, 40*, 41–45.

Whitten, E., & Dieker, L. (2004). Blurring the boundaries through collaborative teaching. In M. Leng Han Hui & D. R. Christopher (Eds.), *Inclusive Education in the New Millennium.*

Whitten, E., & Rodriquez-Campos, L (2003). Trends in the special education teaching force: Do they reflect legislative mandates and legal requirements? *Educational Horizons.*

Wood, J. (2006). *Teaching students in inclusive settings: Adapting and accommodating instruction.* Upper Saddle River, NJ: Merril/Prentice Hall

Zebehazy, K., & Whitten, E. (1998). Collaboration between schools for the blind and public schools during the transition of students with visual impairments. *Journal of Visual Impairment & Blindness, 97*, 73–84.

# PART IV
# THE FUTURE OF TEACHER EDUCATION

# Chapter 14

# PERSISTENT TENSIONS IN AMERICAN TEACHER EDUCATION: THE FUTURE OF TEACHER EDUCATION

ALLEN D. GLENN, DAVID IMIG, AND DALE G. ANDERSEN

*There is always a well-known solution to every human problem— neat, plausible, and wrong.*

(Mencken, 1920, p. x)

## INTRODUCTION

The previous chapters in this text point to a series of abiding tensions in teacher education in the United States and abroad. Of particular note are the challenges of increased accountability and the demand for teachers more skilled in managing and teaching in extraordinarily diverse classrooms. As one reads these chapters, it is possible to come away with a sense that "if only" Americans could step back from the accountability demands placed on teacher education and instead embrace the intentions of teacher educators, teacher preparation programs would flourish, alternative providers would disappear, and policymakers and families would see the efficacy of higher education-based teacher education. The chapters reflect a confidence that we, teacher educators, know and can deliver high-quality schooling for all children. This belief is not surprising, because the vast majority of teacher educators is committed to improving teaching and take great pride in their work. What is clear to us, however, is that these commitments are not enough to address the challenges confronting teacher education. During the coming decade, we believe public and policy demands will become more strident and pervasive. As a consequence, many teacher education programs will be reshaped, new providers will emerge, and some long-established programs will close. Why do we make such a claim?

We believe that while arguments for higher education-based programs are both worthy and based on a growing knowledge base, there are many who do not believe or support the arguments put forth by teacher educators. In fact, we assert that many of the arguments for higher education-based programs have little credence with policymakers who enact school laws and fashion policies regarding teaching and teacher education. They have reached the conclusion that there is little, if any, difference between beginning teachers prepared by colleges and universities and those who come to teaching through alternative routes (Gordon, Kane, & Stanger, 2006). Using gain scores of students on standardized tests, they have concluded that alternative-route and traditional-route teachers have about the same effect on student performance. These policymakers and other critics of public schools and teacher education see the world quite differently than those who currently prepare teachers including some of the authors in this text.

In this concluding chapter, we examine the tensions between higher education-based teacher educators and those who suggest that established teacher education programs are insufficient or inadequate to prepare teachers for tomorrow's learners. Drawing upon the work of the authors in the preceding chapters and our own research, we propose a set of critical issues facing teacher education and predict how these issues will play out over the next decade. We do so knowing that it is always risky to predict the future; however, we believe the issues and trends identified will be major determinants of tomorrow's teacher education programs.

## TENSIONS AND CHALLENGES IN TEACHER EDUCATION

Critics and reformers of teacher education would lead one to believe that the field is reluctant to renew its programs and hesitant to respond to the changing needs of today's classrooms (Ballou & Podgursky, 2000; Finn, 1999; Goodlad, 2007; Hess, 2001; Walsh, 2001).

While there is undoubtedly some validity in such criticisms, the field, as described in the chapters of this text, has and continues to attempt to respond to emerging needs and the changing demographics of American society. For example, preparation programs now focus less on teacher performance and more on student learning, have become more data based, more closely tied to P-12 classrooms, more sensitive to the humanitarian aspects of teaching and learning, and more aware that today's students live in a highly technological, global world. Most teacher educators would claim that programs are markedly different than five years ago. Critics, on the other hand, would say, "Not that different" and point to the fact that there remains a critical teacher shortage, student achievement is below standard, and new teachers appear to be ill-prepared to meet the challenges of today's classrooms. The simple reality is that both sides see the world differently. Both focus on the issue of student achievement, but come to markedly different conclusions as to the possible solutions. We predict that this tension between higher education-based teacher educators and policymakers and the public will continue and will shape the future of teacher education.

## The Demand for Teachers: A Double-Edged Sword

The United States has experienced teacher shortages multiple times over the past twenty-five years. This current shortage, however, is more serious because of changing public expectations for teachers and the demands to improve student learning. The shortage of teachers is fed by increased retirements, efforts to reduce class size, the attrition of beginning teachers especially in high needs schools, and an increased difficulty in attracting highly qualified female candidates. This shortage is exacerbated by public law that demands high-quality teachers in place in all classrooms. In addition, because of the growing diversity of today's classrooms, there is a critical shortage of teachers from different ethnic and racial groups. The overall shortage of teachers is complicated by the fact that demand varies significantly due to regional and state differences creating a surplus in some locations and a severe shortage in others. However, even in surplus locations, the demand for teachers in areas such as second language, special education, mathematics, and the sciences remain high. This demand may, in fact, exceed the number of teachers prepared to enter the field even though almost 240,000 new teachers are hired each year in the United States (Yasin, 1999). If traditional providers of teachers are not meeting the demand, what should be done?

As a consequence, educators, policymakers, and the public are taking a critical look at the way teachers are identified, recruited, selected, prepared, certified, placed, socialized, assessed, mentored, supported, compensated, and rewarded. In essence every aspect of teacher education is under critical review with a belief that all options should be explored.

To justify such rethinking, advocates point to headlines such as those of *The Washington Post's* front-page headline of "teacher shortage looms as law raises bar and boomer women retire" (p. 1) and the accompanying article that argued that "as hundreds of thousands of baby boomers retire and the No Child Left Behind Law raises standards for teachers, school systems across the country are facing a growing scarcity of qualified recruits" (Chandler, 2007, p. 1). What is occurring is a mismatch between the supply of beginning teachers from traditional higher education-based teacher education programs and the critical needs for high-quality teachers that are evident in more and more schools and school districts.

However, college and university teacher education programs, in most states, continue to have sufficient numbers of applicants, especially in elementary education and selected secondary majors to meet the capacity needs of the program, and additional resources are being used to both broaden the applicant pool and to attract a more diverse and high-quality pool of candidates. When applicants are sufficient and resources restricted, it sometimes is difficult to focus on emerging needs and to renew current practices in order to meet these needs. In such situations, teacher educators contend that they are doing all they can to provide the teachers needed.

The perceived inability of states to enlarge the capacity of current programs for whatever reasons has caused policymakers to seek alternative routes to teacher certification that would open the field to a wider group of individuals, prepare teachers to teach specific content or particular students, and achieve these goals more efficiently and cheaply. Some policymakers and critics argue for new forms of certification that would sidestep "approved" programs and suggest that alternatives should be supported and funded. In short, every aspect of teacher education should come under review, and this critical review, we believe, will continue for quite some time.

The challenge for teacher education is not to be lulled into believing that because the demand for teachers remains high that college and university programs have a monopoly on the preparation of tomorrow's teachers. While higher education-based programs, including the alternative programs they offer, continue to prepare the majority of beginning teachers, support and demand for alternative providers will continue to escalate.

## Program-Altering Issues for Teacher Education

Six major conditions are and will continue to shape the future of teacher education programs. Each is having a direct impact on programs, but taken together they may dramatically change the manner in which teachers are prepared in this country.

1. *Accountability demands continue to lead to dissatisfaction with public schools and teacher education.* As discussed in Chapters 1 and 2, a reality for all of education is the focus on accountability with the requirement that preparation programs demonstrate their effectiveness based on the learning of the P-12 students their graduates teach. We believe that No Child Left Behind (NCBL, 2001) legislation and its next generation of federal laws will make student academic learning more public with more testing and reporting, make schools accountable if students do not achieve minimum standards, and ensure that parents have *choices* in the schools their children attend. This legislative platform will be sustained as long as policymakers, businesspersons, and the public can point to the variance between the levels of literacy, numeracy, and intellectual skills needed for success in a competitive, global world and those skills being demonstrated by America's school-age population (Kirsch, Braun, Sum, & Yamamot, 2007).

In seeking answers to why so many United States students are not successful, critics point to teachers who appear to be unprepared to teach children from diverse backgrounds and those with special learning needs. They dismiss the significant differences in opportunities for learning among students and ask why these new teachers are not able to develop instructional strategies to meet more rigorous academic standards.

Critics and federal authorities also question why the current public school system should be the only model (U.S. Department of Education, 2007). Some contend that there should be a system of federal, state, and locally supported opportunities for learning provided by vouchers and tax credits. If so, charter public schools, private charter schools, religious and sectarian schools, and home schooling should be recognized options. As a result *choice* will continue to drive federal and state policy. The landscape for schooling and how students learn will continue to broaden with teaching and learning occurring in markedly different locations.

2. *There appears to be a mismatch between how teachers are currently being prepared and the type of teacher needed in today's classrooms.* The public concern about student success noted above has led to an examination of what is currently being taught in teacher education programs. A number of questions are being asked. For example, how well are current teachers being prepared to manage the dynamic population shift occurring in the United States as a result of an enormous influx of English Language Learners? (Merz-Frankel, Chapter 3). Or, how well are beginning teachers prepared to create appropriate assessments based on content standards or to adjust instruction to ensure that all students are able to meet the standards of common district assessments? Or, how can teachers be prepared for the realities of today's classrooms if they spend the majority of their time on-campus? Critics also suggest that the problems first-year teachers have in relating to, managing, and teaching today's students is further evidence that preparation programs are not graduating individuals ready for teaching.

At the P-12 school level similar concerns may be heard. With schools experiencing the demand for increased accountability, many are beginning to question whether or not having student teachers benefits the goal of having all students "proficient." This mismatch between preparation program and the demands of today's classrooms is prompting a reconsideration of fundamentals of teacher education.

3. *Teacher education is being asked to rethink its core content.* The co-editors of this text have provided an historical and analysis of the critical aspects of teacher preparation curriculum. As we examine the curriculum, we contend that all teacher education programs are a balance between what may be called "course work" and "field work" with "course work," the particular academic courses offered in the preparation program, receiving the greater attention by faculty. In the earlier chapters of this text, persuasive arguments were made for more courses focusing on children with special needs, literacy, diversity, assessment, multicultural education, ethical/moral rights, parent engagement, and digital technologies. Others interested in teacher education

would also argue for special attention to violence, drugs, HIV/AIDS, sex education, policy formation, and academic content learning. In almost each case, faculty would contend that academic study is essential if the prospective teacher is to understand and be able to use the knowledge in the classroom.

Over the years teacher educators, licensure and program approval agencies, accreditation associations, teacher organizations, and school leaders have struggled with what should be the minimum set of learning experiences for a beginning teacher. In response, teacher education programs have experimented with: (1) better integrated undergraduate programs, (2) extended programs, (3) requiring a subject matter major, (4) offering more theoretical or social foundations with a commitment to issues of social justice, (5) more time in schools or other settings that serve children and youth, (6) situating teacher education as a post-baccalaureate program, (7) giving more attention to the language and cultural diversity of students, and (8) seeking to build better capacity by using teaching and learning technologies. Study commissions have been convened, reports written, and articles have appeared in journals offering analysis of "the" problem of teacher education, and, in most cases, calling for the changes in the manner in which teachers are prepared. In many cases, philanthropic foundations and government agencies have responded with new resources. The most recent effort is the Carnegie Corporation's "Teachers for a New Era" that sought to build a partnership between the university and P-12 schools with a focus on student learning (Tucker, 1986).

What often receives less attention by faculty in teacher education programs is the area of "field work" – the experiences students have away from the campus in the community and in the school. It is the link between "course work" and "field work" where program coherence often falters. Preservice teachers note that student teaching is the most important learning experience in their preparation, not course work. Those advocating for renewal of teacher education then ask, "Why isn't course work better connected to the school experience?" Or, "Why are so many courses required if most of the critical learning takes place in the school setting?" Some suggest that there are too many courses in pedagogy, and teacher education would be better off eliminating most of them and focusing on school-based learning. Or, at a minimum advocates for change suggest that pedagogy courses should take place in schools where the realities of teaching may be clearly observed, modeled and practiced. And, finally some observers ask why programs of preparation should be so closely tied to the college/university calendar and credit system. These questions and others point to an unwieldy content accommodation problem for teacher education.

What is evident is that too much of content is "stuffed" into the early on-campus preservice program components with growing pressures to include even more. Re-examine the persuasive arguments made in earlier chapters for more attention to digital technologies, computer skills, and online delivery systems (Chapters 2 and 11), special needs children (Chapter 13), diversity (Chapters 4 and 5), collaborative research (Chapter 7), family/parent engagement (Chapter 9), better assessment techniques (Chapters 1 and 12), a stronger focus on multicultural education (Chapter 10), and the ethical and moral rights of teachers and their students (Chapters 5 and 6). One can be overwhelmed with the content demands.

These demands for more specialized content knowledge and skills bump up against policymakers' demands for fewer courses, lower financial costs, and reduced time needed to become a teacher. Teacher-education programs must once again examine the basic question of "What knowledge is of most worth?" For academics who focus on special areas of teaching and research this is a difficult challenge. It is also a difficult challenge for policymakers and accreditation agencies as they set the standards for teacher education.

4. *A growing tension between education faculty and teacher education programs.* On many campuses the tension between teacher education faculty who prize the academic study of teacher education as an area of inquiry and those who wish to do the field work preparation of candidates for teaching in diverse classrooms is a challenge. The former are often indifferent toward the practical problems in contemporary schooling while the latter view their colleagues' investigations as detached at a minimum and ethereal all too often (Davis, 2007).

A call for a closer partnership with the schools, for example, may likely turn the research component of the campus reward system toward efforts focusing on participatory design studies, action research and similar investigations on school sites employing collaboration with practicing teachers (Boyer, 1990; Glassick, Huber, & Maeroff, 1997). The daily, constant aspects of partnership work often does not appeal to the faculty who view "practical" issues as the work of others—

adjuncts, contract faculty, clinical faculty or supervisors—or even as anti-intellectual.

This division between the academic study of teaching and learning and teacher preparation is further complicated by the fact that institutional missions and state requirements vary across a spectrum from programs in research universities to programs in small private colleges and enrollment ranges from several hundred to fewer than a dozen. These factors influence and shape, to a significant extent, the unique characteristics of each program. Conversely, all must meet a common set of standards required by the individual states and seek to graduate individuals who must be "certifiable" in any state. Each individual teacher education program must find a balance between meeting state demands and the institutional mission as they search for internal coherence and external credibility.

5. *Curriculum, content, and delivery are being reshaped by emerging technologies.* In far too many public school classrooms the types of technology available to teachers and students is well beyond what is available in college and university teacher education programs. Many school districts have extensive web-based resources that allow teachers to access curriculum, lesson plans, assessment tools, and relevant student materials. Teachers commonly work together collaboratively via the Internet to discuss teaching and learning and to create new curriculum.

School districts seek beginning teachers who are adept at utilizing technology for instructional purposes and their own professional development. They expect teachers to be ready to learn how to use new technologies and to enable students to learn using these technologies. Critics wonder why interactive technologies are not being used in teacher education programs, are not used to observe and study teaching and learning in schools, and are not being used to provide alternative models to the typical course structure prevalent in most colleges and university programs.

As noted in the chapter by Laurie Mullen and Roy Weaver on "Preparing Future Teachers for Alternative Curriculum Delivery Models," traditional ways of instruction dominated by face-to-face interactions between a professor and a set of students are in need of serious rethinking. Alternative providers such as the University of Phoenix, Cappella, Regents On-line, and Western Governor's University understand this trend and are responding to market demands. While almost all colleges and universities have on-line courses, and technology courses for teachers and faculty who use technology, few teacher education programs have an integrated model where technology is commonplace in the delivery of the program.

6. *Changing nature of graduate and continuing education.* The emergence of new digital technologies, increased competition from for-profit providers and local districts professional development programs will shape graduate and professional education. For decades higher education-based advanced degree and professional education programs controlled the market. An advanced degree was the manner in which the teacher increased knowledge, gained new pedagogical skills, and moved-up on the salary schedule. Alternatives often were limited to which higher education institution one wanted to attend. In the 1990s, new technologies and alternative providers changed the environment. On-line programs and mixed model programs involving both on-line technology and face-to-face meetings offered convenience, flexibility, and choice. As the Internet has matured so has the ability to deliver programs that go beyond word-based on-line text (see Chapters 3 and 11). Teachers, principals, and other school personnel now have considerably more choice about how they pursue continuing professional development.

In addition to the increase in the number of ready-available providers, many school districts are providing more and more professional development as districts seek to bring more uniformity to the curriculum being taught and to instructional methods used in classrooms (Nagel, 2007). This movement and the concomitant debate about scientifically-based curriculum designs and appropriate instructional materials bring forth tensions between teacher education programs where teachers are prepared to use multiple instructional strategies and varied curriculum materials and districts that have chosen a specific curriculum, related materials, and an instructional strategy (Shaw, 2007).

These six broad-based issues, while not unique to just this point in teacher education history, we contend will have a profound impact on the future of teacher education. Based on these issues, we turn our attention to what we believe teacher educators must find as the hallmarks of teacher education.